OLD PEKING:

City of the Ruler of the World

OLD PEKING:
City of the Ruler of the World

AN ANTHOLOGY

SELECTED AND EDITED BY

Chris Elder

HONG KONG
OXFORD UNIVERSITY PRESS
OXFORD   NEW YORK
1997

Oxford University Press

Oxford New York
Athens Auckland Bangkok Bogota Bombay
Buenos Aires Calcutta Cape Town Dar es Salaam
Delhi Florence Hong Kong Istanbul Karachi
Kuala Lumpur Madras Madrid Melbourne
Mexico City Nairobi Paris Singapore
Taipei Tokyo Toronto Warsaw
and associated companies in
Berlin Ibadan

Oxford is a trade mark of Oxford University Press

First published 1997
This impression (lowest digit)
1 3 5 7 9 10 8 6 4 2

Published in the United States
by Oxford University Press, New York

© Oxford University Press 1997

British Library Cataloguing in Publication Data
available

Library of Congress Cataloging-in-Publication Data

Old Peking : city of the ruler of the world / an anthology
selected and edited by Chris Elder.
p.   cm.
Includes bibliographical references.
ISBN 0-19-590304-8
1. Peking (China)— Description and travel. 2. Peking (China)
– Social life and customs. I. Elder, Chris, date.
DS795.044   997
951'. 156 — dc21

97-18602
CIP

Printed in Hong Kong
Published by Oxford University Press (China) Ltd
18/F Warwick House, Taikoo Place, 979 King's Road,
Quarry Bay, Hong Kong

Peking—in this, as in several other ways, curiously resembling Oxford—can usually be relied upon to be characteristic.

Peter Fleming

News from Tartary, 1936

ACKNOWLEDGEMENTS

The publishers acknowledge with thanks permission to reproduce excerpts from copyright material as follows: *A Journey to China or Things Which Are Seen* by Arnold Toynbee, reprinted by permission of Constable Publishers; *Four-Part Setting, The Ginger Griffin,* and *Peking Picnic* by Ann Bridge, published by Chatto & Windus, reprinted by permission of the Peters Fraser and Dunlop Group; *Laughing Diplomat* and *The Last of the Empresses* by Daniele Varè, reprinted by permission of John Murray (Publishers) Ltd.; *The Gate of Happy Sparrows* by Daniele Varè published by Methuen & Co., reprinted by permission of Mrs Gianmarina Grose; *A Diplomat Looks Back* by Lewis Einstein, reprinted by permission of Yale University Press; *Escape With Me!* by Osbert Sitwell published by Macmillan & Co., reprinted by permission of David Higham Associates; *The Travels and Controversies of Friar Domingo Navarrete 1618–1686* edited by J. S. Cummins, reprinted by permission of the Hakluyt Society; *South China in the Sixteenth Century* edited by C. R. Boxer, reprinted by permission of the Hakluyt Society; *A Superficial Journey Through Tokyo and Peking* by Peter Quennell reprinted by permission of Faber & Faber Ltd.; *On A Chinese Screen* and *Collected Plays* by W. Somerset Maugham published by William Heinemann Ltd., reprinted by permission of Reed Consumer Books Ltd., and A. P. Watt Ltd. on behalf of the Royal Literary Fund; *British Diplomacy in China 1880–1885* by E. V. G. Kiernan, reprinted by permission of Cambridge University Press; *The Phantom Caravan* by Sir Owen O'Malley, reprinted by permission of John Murray (Publishers) Ltd.; *City of Lingering Splendour* by John Blofield © 1961, reprinted by arrangement with Shambhala Publications, Inc., 300 Massachusetts Avenue, Boston, MA 02115; *Twilight in the Forbidden City* by Reginald Johnston, reprinted by permission of Victor Gollancz Ltd.; *The Desert Road to Turkestan* by Owen Lattimore published by Methuen & Co., reprinted by permission of Routledge Publishers. *The Problem of China* by Bertrand Russell, reprinted by permission of the Bertrand Russell Peace Foundation Ltd.; *One's Company* by Peter Fleming, reprinted by permission of the estate of the author and Jonathan Cape Ltd.; *My Several Worlds* by Pearl S. Buck, reprinted by permission of Harold Ober Associates Incorporated, copyright © 1954 by Pearl S. Buck. *The*

PREFACE

If this collection does nothing else it will serve to illustrate how various and ingenious Western writers have been in their romanization of Chinese names. In my own introduction and notes, I have generally adopted the pinyin system, now standard in China. Occasional exceptions are words not Chinese in origin, or existing in a widely accepted Anglicized form: Genghis Khan, Jehol. Peking is, of course, Peking.

    The date assigned to the works from which quotations are drawn is in general that of first publication, occasionally first publication in English. Where there is a significant difference between the time of writing and the date of publication, both dates are given.

CONTENTS

INTRODUCTION

'It is the lot of few to go to Pekin', wrote John Barrow in the epigraph to his book of China travel in 1804, '*Non cuivis homini contingit adire Corinthum*'. The parallel implied in Barrow's adaptation of the Latin tag was an apt one. Peking at the threshold of Western familiarity was as much a byword for exoticism, luxury, and extravagance as Corinth had been two thousand years earlier. At the same time, it was a city still virtually closed to the scrutiny of those from beyond China's borders.

It was the lot of few to go to Peking, and it is accordingly less remarkable that those who did succeed in making their way to China's capital were so diligent in committing their impressions to paper. They recorded the architecture, the town structure, and the monuments; they wrote down their impressions of the streets, the shops, the climate, and the people. This book is a testament to their curiosity, their perspicuity, and their occasional impertinence.

Peking was not new in 1804. When Corinth was at its height as a centre of commerce and power, there already existed on the edge of the North China plain a city of considerable wealth. It was, in the records of the Han historians, 'rich in salt, fish, dates and maize'. Its name was Ji, but its role as capital of the state of Yan earned it also the title of Yanjing, 'the capital of Yan' or, from the literal meaning of *yan*, 'city of swallows'. 'Yanjing' remains a literary designation for Peking, 'Yan ren' for an inhabitant of the city.

The English historian Arnold Toynbee, happening upon Peking in 1929, thought its situation featureless. 'Peking is just something which human imagination and energy have done to so many square miles of the featureless, enormous North China plain: and if just this had not been done by men just here, those particular square miles would not have been distinguishable in any way from the thousands of others by which they are monotonously surrounded.'

If the city's situation lacks distinguishing features, however, it does not lack purpose. Peking is a frontier town. It stands at the

1

convergence of the three major passes controlling access to the fertile China plains from the uplands of Mongolia and Manchuria, and it is the starting point for the main roads south.

In Chinese classical thought, the capital of a state is protected by the enlightened and virtuous conduct of its ruler, rather than by being situated to strategic advantage. Those assuming power, however, while endorsing the principle, have generally chosen not to put it to the test. They have selected their capital with an eye to military advantage. So it was that when strength on the battlefield won political power for the people of a minority race in the north of China, they centred that power on Peking. In 1150, the Jin Dynasty, which had ousted the Song from North China, established its capital on the site of Yanjing and renamed it Zhongdu ('Middle Capital').

Within eighty years the Jin had themselves been overcome by a new and altogether more formidable force, the Mongol invaders of Genghis Khan. By 1279, the Mongols had established their supremacy not only over the Jin and the north, but over all China. The country was unified under the Yuan Dynasty, and Peking (now named Dadu—'Grand Capital') became for the first time the national capital of a united China. With brief interregnums, it has been so ever since.

Genghis Khan did not himself choose to establish his capital in China proper. He preferred to hold court on the steppes, at Karakorum, about 400 kilometres south-west of present-day Ulaanbaatar. It was his more sybaritic grandson, Khubilai, who initiated the shift south.

Khubilai Khan wanted to profit from Chinese knowledge. Perhaps mindful of the dictum quoted against the Mongols, 'It is possible to conquer from the saddle, but not to rule from the saddle', he set about building a wholly new city that would incorporate all the classical Chinese ideals. To facilitate his grand plan (and also, according to Marco Polo, to forestall the possibility of 'great disorders' among his new and not necessarily loyal subjects) Khubilai Khan established a new site for Dadu, just to the north-east of the old city.

Construction of an imperial capital was not a haphazard affair in traditional China. The city was intended to give physical expression to a Confucian world view. How it should be laid out to achieve this was set down quite precisely in the Confucian classics. Dadu followed the prescription to the letter. It was set four-

2

square on a north-south axis, facing the south, source of beneficent influences. At the centre, symbolic of the mandate of heaven, lay the palace city. Surrounding it was the imperial city, and beyond that again the outer city. Each was enclosed by its own wall. Set into the walls were the prescribed number of gates, and between the gates ran in a criss-cross fashion the prescribed number of roads. 'Thus the whole city is arranged in squares just like a chessboard', commented the admiring Polo, 'and disposed in a manner so perfect and masterly that it is impossible to give a description that should do it justice'.

Khubilai Khan made some concessions to his Mongol heritage. He filled the audience halls with carpets and drapes, he painted the walls white, rather than the Chinese red, and he planted desert grasses on the terraces. To the north, the outer boundary extended to enclose grasslands, so that China's new rulers could maintain their vocation as herdsmen, and retreat to their tents when the pressures of city life became too great.

The Yuan Dynasty was relatively short-lived. In 1368 the Mongols were in their turn toppled from power by a native dynasty, the Ming. The first Ming Emperor established his capital in the heart of China, at Nanjing ('Southern Capital') and Dadu became once more a garrison town, allocated the name Beiping—'Northern Peace'. The hope implied in the title proved illusory when the Beiping garrison commander unceremoniously dumped the second Ming Emperor, his nephew, and usurped the throne. After a brief hiatus intended to demonstrate fiscal responsibility (the first Ming Emperor had spent lavishly on Nanjing) Emperor Yong Le acceded to the petition of his courtiers to return the capital to his northern powerbase. Beiping became Beijing—the Northern Capital. In southern dialects, the pronunciation was closer to 'Peking', and so it was heard and recorded by foreigners.

Yong Le built to last. The new capital he constructed between 1406 and 1420 is in large part the Peking which survived to the twentieth century, and which still forms the heart of China's capital. It was built on the site of the Yuan capital Dadu, although it did not include the pastoral areas to the north, and it extended two *li* (Chinese miles) further to the south.

The possibility of malevolent influences from the former Yuan rulers was circumvented by burying the main throne hall of the

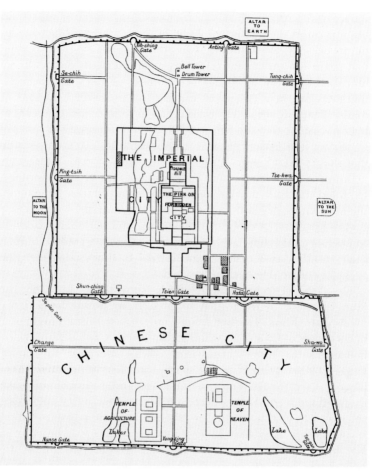

defeated dynasty under a 70-metre high mound of earth. The mound, Coal Hill, was created using spoil from a moat built around the palace complex, and from an extension to the lake system within the Imperial City. The highest point and the geographical centre of the new city, Coal Hill also performed another important role in the *feng shui* (geomancy) system by protecting the palace's inauspicious northern aspect.

The Ming city, more even than Dadu, embodied the key principles of the classic Chinese capital. The central axis was extended by the creation of Coal Hill, by the Bell and Drum Towers further north, and to the south by the Temples of Heaven and Agriculture. The

4

centrality of the Palace was underlined by setting its three main halls together in a core group, and elevating them above all others. The Forbidden City nestled inside the Imperial City inside the Inner City, three concentric sets of high walls. In 1553, one more wall was added, enclosing the outer city to the south.

After the Ming Dynasty came the Qing. In contrast with the mayhem and destruction of earlier changes of governance, that from the Ming to the Qing was almost without incident. 'When the Tartars entered the Imperial City, there were 7,000 pieces of Cannon mounted on the walls', Domingo Navarrete observed sardonically, 'but there being no body to play them, it was the same thing as if there had been none'. Faced with the inevitability of defeat, the last Ming Emperor slipped from his palace to hang himself on the slopes of Coal Hill, his greatest regret, in popular legend, that his reign had produced no actors of genuine talent.

The Manchu conquerors, finding the city intact, saw no reason for change or destruction. They took Peking as their capital. The Forbidden City became the home of the Manchu Emperors, the Imperial City the seat of the Manchu court.

Like the Mongols, the Manchus were racially distinct from the Han Chinese, and like the Mongols, they had no high trust for their newly acquired subjects. Accordingly, they instituted a policy of segregation within the capital. The Manchu occupation force, the army of the Eight Banners, was installed in the Inner City. With few exceptions, the Han Chinese were banished to the Outer City. The two districts acquired new names to reflect the division: the Tartar City and the Chinese City.

Peking's role as a physical symbol of the relationship between the Emperor and the elements of heaven and nature on the one hand, and the Emperor and his subjects on the other, came to an end when the Mandate of Heaven finally passed from the Qing Court in 1911. The new Republic had no need, and no right, to invoke heaven's authority (although Yuan Shikai made a brief personal foray in that direction in 1916). Deprived of its symbolic role, the city drifted. In 1928, it suffered a further reverse when the Nationalist government established its capital at Nanjing. The Northern Capital once more became 'Northern Peace'—Beiping. And once more the name was belied, this time through invasion and occupation by Japan. From 1937, the Japanese held and controlled the city until their final defeat in 1945.

Since 1949, Peking and Beiping have merged into Beijing, capital of the People's Republic of China. The outer walls have gone, the city has spilled out to accommodate a population much greater than ever before. There is an overlay of buildings suited to governance by a politburo rather than an emperor. But the traditions and the physical structures that have built up over the generations are in many cases preserved, by decree or by default. Within evolution, there is continuity.

*   *   *   *

Peking was not the first capital in China's 3,000-year history, nor is it perhaps the most noteworthy. It stands out in Western perceptions of China because its period of dominance roughly coincides with the period of significant contact with the West. For outsiders, Peking came to symbolize China's power, wealth, and magnificence, and at the same time its arrogance, secretiveness, and venality, because all these elements were viewed through the prism of the Chinese capital.

It was Marco Polo who first brought Peking to the attention of a wide audience in Europe. He travelled to China (or perhaps he did not) late in the thirteenth century. Whether his description is based on first-hand experience or on reports gathered from others, the *Book of Ser Marco Polo the Venetian* provides a lively and in many respects accurate account of the capital of Khubilai Khan. Like a number of other medieval travellers, Polo calls the city not Dadu but Cambaluc (Khanbaliq)—'city of the Khan'—from a Turkish usage then prevalent in Central Asia.

Marco Polo's account of a 'great and noble city' was backed up by the reports of a succession of Papal emissaries, despatched to convert, or at least to conciliate, the Mongol court. The Franciscan, John of Montecorvino, lived in the Mongol capital for more than thirty years. He built two churches there, supplementing his mission through the judicious purchase of young boys to be trained as choristers. 'And I ring the bells for all the hours and sing the divine office with a choir of "sucklings and infants."' The Emperor was, by Friar John's account, delighted, and so apparently was Pope Clement V, who created the Friar first Archbishop of Khanbaliq and Patriarch of the Orient.

John was joined for a time by Friar Odoric, of all the missionary reporters the most circumstantial in description, if not necessarily the most saintly in demeanour. In the course of extensive peregrinations through the East, he helped out in Peking for three years from about 1325. In 1330 he dictated a highly colourful account of his travels, including his experiences in the court of the Great Khan, a court 'truly magnificent, and the most perfectly ordered that there is in the world'. Odoric's book became hugely popular in Italy and beyond, and four hundred years later helped him to a beatification which, by common consent, he did not in the least deserve.

Peking under Mongol rule was described once more by Sir John Mandeville ('the Peregrinator') in his *Travels*, written in French around 1365. Mandeville's description of what he saw at the court of the Great Khan agrees closely with Odoric, which is not surprising since he stole it almost word for word from the earlier work. He profited also from Marco Polo and many others, to the point where there is considerable doubt whether Sir John in fact travelled anywhere in the East. 'If I had time and space to try to trace all the originals which Mandeville stole from', grumbled the nineteenth-century scholar, Sir Henry Yule, 'I suspect the knight would come out of the process almost in his buff.' Nevertheless, the imitator has outstripped the original. It is Mandeville, not Odoric, who has remained in print. Through the intervening centuries his *Travels* has been a constant point of reference for students of Western contact with the East.

The last Papal mission to establish contact with China before the collapse of the Yuan Dynasty was that of John of Marignolli, who was received by the Emperor Zhi Zheng in 1342. John travelled with an array of gifts representative of Western civilization, including, to the delight of the Mongols, a great horse 'eleven feet six inches in length and six feet eight inches high, black all over, except the hind feet, which were white'. John's account of the audience treats lyrically of the honour paid to his person and the humility with which the Emperor received the Christian message. The parallel narrative in the Chinese annals mentions only the horse.

Despite the Mongols' reputation for indiscriminate carnage, it was the order imposed by their conquests that made it possible for the early travellers from Europe to reach Peking, and it was the collapse of that order at the end of the Yuan dynasty that effectively closed the land route from Europe to Peking. The early years of the Ming dynasty are remarkable for the absence of first-hand Western accounts of the Chinese capital.

To some extent the gap is filled by Arab and Persian travellers. Ibn Batuta, born in Tangiers, was in Peking only a little after John of Marignolli (although the history of his travels was not known in Europe until the nineteeth century). The Embassy sent from Persia by Shah Rukh arrived in Peking in 1420, just at the time that the third Ming Emperor, Yong Le, was re-establishing his capital there. Although 'a hundred thousand scaffoldings' still concealed the outer walls, the present-day Forbidden City had just been completed after a construction period of nineteen years. The envoys attended a sort of housewarming, where they saw a retinue of tame elephants, and young girl attendants 'with faces like the moon'.

Direct Western knowledge of Peking resumed with the opening of the ocean routes to the East, initially by the navigators of Portugal. It was not always wholly planned, as in the case of Mendes Pinto, who, by his own account, was in 1542 shipwrecked off the South China coast, conducted in chains to Peking, and there cast into prison, 'where for our welcome we had at first dash thirty lashes apiece'. When he had got over his welcome, Mendes Pinto examined the city more closely, which he detailed as having 'three hundred and threescore gates . . . three thousand and three hundred pagodas and temples [and] a hundred and twenty canals'.

Mendez Pinto was (and by many still is) regarded as prone to exaggeration, if not outright falsehood. Soon after him, however, came a generation of sojourners whose veracity was hardly to be questioned: the Jesuit priesthood.

The Italian Matteo Ricci is rightly seen as the cornerstone of the Jesuit effort in China, although he succeeded in establishing himself in Peking only eight years before his death in 1610, and never in fact met the Wan Li Emperor with whom his name is associated. It was Ricci who decided that Western scientific knowledge offered the best hope of establishing credibility in the Ming court, and it was through Ricci's voluminous journals, first published in 1615, that the West was afforded a window into the physical and social realities of the Ming Dynasty capital.

The renewed drive to achieve missionary success in Peking made more ground than that during the Yuan Dynasty, but not a lot more. For one thing the Jesuits soon found that they had to share the field with other orders, resulting in schisms and rivalries that did credit to nobody. The caustic comments of the Spanish Dominican friar, Domingo Navarrete, who lived in China from 1658 to 1670, were a distinct set-back to Jesuit authority. While the order indignantly repudiated his *Travels and Controversies* ('It would be a rare page on which I did not discover at least one outrageous lie', expostulated one father), Navarrete's account circulated widely in Europe, and brought to an end the Jesuits' near-monopoly on information.

Moreover the invocation of Western learning turned out to be a two-edged sword. Scholars from the West found that the energy they would have liked to put into proselytising was diverted instead into stargazing, or cannon-founding, or the designing of rococo fountains and stately Italianate buildings to grace the pleasure gardens of the Qing court.

A hundred years after Ricci, Father Matteo Ripa, another inveterate recorder of events, found himself still obliged to present himself at the court of Emperor Kang Xi in the guise of a painter and engraver. By that time, however, the priests were installed in the court and frequently had contact directly with the Emperor himself. The better access did not noticeably improve the conversion rate, but in the case of Ripa did produce a unique description of the court and the city as they existed early in the eighteenth century.

Peking was by now no longer, to the West, the enigma it once had been. European states were beginning to seek closer contact, primarily to gain access to what was seen as the immensely wealthy China market. Diplomatic missions themselves increased knowledge. John Nieuhoff chronicled a Dutch embassy in 1656; 'Honest' John Bell, a Scotsman improbably attached as physician to the Russian envoy, published an account of the Ismailoff embassy in 1720. The tempo stepped up at the end of the century with the Macartney mission despatched by George III of Great Britain, which gave rise to a number of books (including that by John Barrow quoted at the beginning of this introduction) but no concrete results; the Titsingh mission from Holland two years later; and, redefining the boundaries of failure, the British Amherst embassy of 1816, which was turned round and on its way back home, empty handed, within twelve hours of arrival.

What the various foreign emissaries wanted from the Emperor, among other things, was the right to live and work in Peking. On this question the Chinese court had fixed views. It was enough to accept tributary missions from time to time. Permanent residence would be out of conformity with the supremacy of the Son of Heaven. What was more, it would be vexatious, and impractical, especially if everyone wanted to do it. As the Emperor Qian Long indulgently advised King George III:

> The territories ruled by the Celestial Empire are vast, and for all the envoys of vassal states coming to the capital there are definite regulations regarding the provision of quarters and supplies to them and regarding their movements. There never has been any precedent for allowing them to suit their own convenience. Now, if your country retains someone at the capital his speech will not be understood and his dress will be different in style, and we have nowhere to house him. . . . How can we go as far as to change the regulations of the Celestial Empire, which are over a hundred years old, because of the request of one man—of you, O King?

What diplomacy could not achieve, warfare must. China's first clash with the West, the Opium War of 1839 to 1842, did not touch Peking, for the Chinese signed a treaty at Nanking rather than risk an advance on the capital. The renewed hostilities launched by the British and French in 1856 were a different matter. The Anglo-French forces entered Peking, the Emperor departed incontinently for Jehol, and the magnificent pleasance of the Qing court, the Yuan Ming Yuan, was looted and put to the torch by the invading armies. Western civilization had at last won its way to China's capital.

With the establishment of the right of residence, Peking and the Pekinese were finally open to indiscriminate foreign survey. The trickle of first-hand reports—books, journals, articles—swelled to a stream, and in time to a flood. Diplomats contributed their impressions, correspondents and sinologists theirs. Superimposed on the views of residents were the ready assessments of travellers, visitors, and casual observers. 'Remembering all the tomes which burdened our shelves even before the days of travelling MPs,' J. O. P. Bland lamented in the early 1900s, 'one wonders, as the stream of books rolls on, what and where are the people who buy them?'

Peking never became a centre for foreign commerce. That role was assigned to Tientsin, seventy miles away, and to Shanghai. Because the capital was not designated a 'treaty port' in any of the successive agreements between China and the foreign powers, it was, at least in theory, illegal for foreigners to conduct business there. Foreign residents were most often occupied in the conduct of diplomacy, the provision of advice to the Chinese, the promulgation of religion or the pursuit of knowledge. More fleeting visitors might have aspirations in any of these areas, or simply wish to view that curious sight, the hitherto forbidden capital of a still reclusive society.

The diplomats did not feel constrained to confine themselves to their official reports. Early diplomatic life had a lively chronicler in A. B. Freeman-Mitford (later Lord Redesdale, and later still eclipsed by his grand-daughters, who achieved fame extending to notoriety as the 'Mitford gels'). Perhaps even more lively are the peppery comments of Sir Edmund Hornby, Judge of the (British) Supreme Court in China and a man much inclined to put his diplomatic colleagues to rights.

Within the Italian legation one of the interpreters, Guido Vitale, produced charming translations of Peking children's rhymes, while Daniele Varè recorded his two postings in a memoir never surpassed for its affectionate view of Peking life, *Laughing Diplomat*. Varè carried the same qualities of affection and humour to a series of fictional works. His rival in this field was Ann Bridge, wife of the British Counsellor Owen O'Malley, whose romantic fiction, set in the legation quarter of Peking, combines a high level of descriptive insight with an equally high order of snobbery.

Sir Robert Hart comes first among the advisers. Supreme head of the Chinese Maritime Customs Service for practically the whole of his working life, he at one time passed a period of sixteen years without once leaving Peking. Chinese historians have preserved four weighty volumes of his correspondence with the service's London office. Hart's many subordinates included Lennox Simpson, who under the pseudonym Putnam Weale wrote a very discreditable but not essentially inaccurate account of the Siege of the Legations, *Indiscreet Letters from Peking*. Simpson's indiscretion led him subsequently to enmesh himself in Chinese politics, and, in the end, fall victim to a political assassination in Tientsin.

J. O. P. Bland, whom we noted earlier complaining about the number of books on things Chinese, himself added quite considerably to the pile, including two in collaboration with the reclusive sinologist, Edmund Backhouse. Backhouse's purported translations of Qing Dynasty court documents are now considered in the main literary forgeries. Suspicions were first aroused by the unbelievably colourful account he left of his sexual exploits in the teahouses and brothels of the Chinese City. Ironically, according to those with experience of pre-war Peking, this account is on the whole closer to reality than most of his other writings.

Moving among the community that grew up, interacting with its members and recording the immediacy of their own impressions, were the visitors—the tourists, the seekers of beauty, and the fact-finders. Despite the greater commercial importance of the treaty ports, Peking was always central to travel: the seat of government, the determiner of culture, in Peter Quennell's definition, 'one of those focal points which we set ourselves as a future destination'.

It was still the lot of relatively few to go to Peking, and those who did were seldom backward in recounting what they found there. Some, like the American travel writer Eliza Scidmore, waited until they could claim a reasonable acquaintance (in her case seven visits over fifteen years) before committing thoughts to paper. Others did not.

Towards the end of the nineteenth century the city was host to a succession of political pundits who shaped outside views with thick volumes recording their experiences and the conclusions they drew from them: the journalist Henry Norman, the parliamentarian George Curzon, the naval officer turned financial adviser Admiral Lord Charles Beresford. Many justified the foreboding which US Minister Paul Reinsch gloomily committed to his diary about one such visitor: 'I fear he will suffer the usual disability of the passing visitor, that is, he will see the unfavourable aspects of Chinese life and will not stay long enough to appreciate the deeper virtues'.

Not all who wrote of Peking from slight acquaintance reflected an unfavourable perception. The British philosopher Bertrand Russell, lecturing at the National University of Peking for just one year, wrote appreciatively of the city and his sojourn. Arnold Toynbee, who paid a considerably briefer visit early in his distinguished career as an historian, thought the city the capital of the world, though a doomed one. Above all, Osbert Sitwell, stealing unashamedly and with acknowledgement from others who knew the city much better, created in *Escape With Me!* a lasting and enspiriting record of the city of Peking as it stood on the eve of the Japanese occupation.

*   *   *   *

You did not have to travel to Peking to write about it. Even those who, like Dr Johnson, only dreamed of going there, pictured clearly what they would find if they did. Chaucer, whose *Canterbury Tales* appeared less than a hundred years after Marco Polo, invoked the glories of the court at Khanbaliq, although he mistakenly placed Genghis Khan on the throne of his grandson Khubilai. Milton takes similar poetic licence in *Paradise Lost*, directing his gaze towards the splendours first of Khanbaliq and then of Pequin, apparently without realizing that they were the same city. Coleridge, who at least had his Khans sorted out, correctly named Khubilai as the instigator of the 'stately pleasure dome' established at Xanadu (Shangdu), the summer retreat of the later Mongol rulers.

Each of these literary inventions invoked Peking, or the court centred on Peking, as an embodiment of extravagance, splendour, and luxury. In this they did no more than follow the accounts, not always wholly objective, of those who had actually entered the walls of the city, and mixed with its inhabitants. 'Thus, then,' exclaimed Lord Macartney, bedazzled by the court of Qian Long, 'have I seen Solomon in all his glory'.

It was really only with the Anglo-French incursion of 1860 that a different tone began to enter the rapidly multiplying accounts of the Chinese capital. The tone was one of disappointment. 'The practical result [of the war] was not very great', recorded McCarthy's *History* in 1870. 'Perhaps the most important gain to Europe was the knowledge that Peking was by no means so large a city as we had imagined it to be.' It seems little enough to have fought a war for.

The West's military victory itself contributed to the change in attitude. The goal of the first Western envoys to Khanbaliq had been to persuade the Mongol rulers not to renew the attacks which had carried their armies as far west as Hungary, and had threatened to devastate Europe. Power asserted, and deference offered in response, had from that time fed into Western perceptions of the Great Khans, the Emperors who succeeded them, and the capital they inhabited.

Now, suddenly, China's leader proved a man of straw, his banners powerless to resist the onslaught of the technologically more advanced forces of Europe. True, as Bertrand Russell mused subsequently, military strength said nothing about wisdom or civilization. Nevertheless, the high ground had passed to the West, because 'it is easier for an Englishman to kill a Chinaman than for a Chinaman to kill an Englishman. Therefore . . . Chien Long is absurd.' And the same, Russell might have added but did not, goes for his capital.

It was not just military technology. Sojourners from post-industrial-revolution Europe were dismayed at Peking's lack of any of the amenities their society had come to take for granted. 'Peking is probably the only large city in the world', Mrs Archibald Little observed tartly, 'where no arrangements are made for sanitation or even for common decency.' Sanitation, and the smells arising from its lack, attracted a lot of adverse notice, but the condition of the streets, the inconvenience of the public transport, the absence of civic amenities, and the incidence of disease all came in for their share of criticism.

The undesirable aspects of Peking were the more apparent because the Western nations had, by force of arms, finally established the right of residence. There was therefore ample opportunity to observe, and to experience at first hand, the realities of life in what remained in most ways a medieval city. When it came to living in Peking, the realities did not always match up to the images built up over centuries of exclusion. The city was, Sir Harry Parkes was provoked into remarking in 1884, 'a damnable dungheap'.

Even if a carping note did creep into its notices, however, Peking never lacked for admirers even after 1860. The splendour of its monuments, the vitality of its people, the uniqueness of its way of life, were all the more apparent with increased freedom of access. Sights and society were analysed and categorized with great vigour. Tourists began to arrive, at first to stay with friends in the new legations, later to take part in package tours organized by Messrs Thomas Cook & Co from their office in the Hotel de Pekin. For every Harry Parkes there was a Lucian Kirtland, who regarded the city with affection extending to 'a sort of jealous intemperance'.

The truth is there has never been just one Peking. That is the reality that underlies all the reports, all the comments and accounts from personal experience that foreign acquaintance has produced. The descriptions and anecdotes reprinted in the succeeding chapters of this book reflect not just the city, but what those from outside have brought to it. In revealing Peking, the writers reveal themselves as well. As they were various, so are their perceptions various. Their idiosyncratic scrutiny has given rise to a literature that is many-sided, contradictory, sometimes mundane, often richly entertaining. In this it is a true mirror of the Peking it describes.

CHAPTER 1

PEKING FIRST

My capital is the hub and centre about which all quarters of the globe revolve.

EMPEROR QIAN LONG
An Edict to King George III of England, 1793

First impressions of Peking have always depended on what the
traveller expected to find. Even Marco Polo must have arrived
with some sort of vision, based on what he had heard from
his father and his uncle. His own breathless description set the
tone for many who followed, and was echoed in the literary
inventions of others who never visited Peking at all.

Between tradition and literature, Peking's notices led most
people to approach the city with their hopes high. The reality did
not always match the vision. For every traveller struck, like Polo,
by wonders 'past all possibility', there was another to agree with
the disgruntled nineteenth-century traveller who thought the
place a gigantic disappointment. 'It is worth coming to study,'
sniffed Henry Norman, 'but not to see.'

Physically, until their disappearance after 1949, the massive walls
of the outer city dominated the approach to Peking. They rose
straight out of the flat countryside, and only when their limits had
been breached did the city itself come into plain view. To a prosaic
observer like Carl Crow the walls added little to the prospect:
according to his *Handbook for China*, 'Peking from a distance looks
much like a giant box'. Yet travelling in by train, his fellow-
American Enid Saunders Candlin found herself reduced to tears
simply by the vision.

Within the walls lay a city that owed little to nature and
everything to art. To describe it in terms of other capitals was
scarcely possible—'I know not where to begin', lamented Mendez
Pinto.

What taxed Pinto's descriptive powers (though not for long)
was the 'excessive abundance of the city'. What others found
even more remarkable was the perfection of its artifice. Peking
was to be defined not in comparison with other capitals, but in its
own terms, as an architectural expression of the relationship
between the ruling forces of the universe, and their temporal
representative, the Son of Heaven. Thus envisaged, it was possible
to detect in the city's structure a reassuring symmetry, and even
domesticity, right down to Osbert Sitwell's pleasing vision of the
Imperial City wall as a 'red silk stomach protector'.

BEATING OF WINGS

Away back in the haze of the centuries preceding the Christian era there existed a Kingdom of Yen, whereof Peking was the capital. 'Yen' signifies swallow, so on the very threshold of its history there is a beating of bright summer wings and the glamour of royal palaces round this city, whereof it used to be truly held that it was built in harmony with all the beneficent influences radiating from heaven and emanating from earth.

A. E. Grantham
Pencil Speakings from Peking, 1918

PAST ALL POSSIBILITY

You must know that the city of Cambaluc hath such a multitude of houses, and such a vast population inside the walls and outside, that it seems quite past all possibility. There is a suburb outside each of the gates, which are twelve in number; and these suburbs are so great that they contain more people than the city itself. . . . In those suburbs lodge the foreign merchants and travellers, of whom there are always great numbers who have come to bring presents to the Emperor, or to sell articles at Court, or because the city affords so good a mart to attract traders. . . . And thus there are as many good houses outside of the city as inside, without counting those that belong to the great lords and barons, which are very numerous.

. . . To this city also are brought articles of greater cost and rarity, and in greater abundance of all kinds, than to any other city in the world. For people of every description, and from every region, bring things (including all the costly wares of India, as well as the fine and precious goods of Cathay itself with its provinces), some for the sovereign, some for the court, some for the city which is so great, some for the crowds of barons and knights, some for the great hosts of the Emperor which are quartered round about; and thus between court and city the quantity brought in is endless.

As a sample, I tell you, no day in the year passes that there do not enter the city 1000 cart-loads of silk alone, from which are made quantities of cloth of silk and gold, and of other goods.

Marco Polo
(trans. Col. Sir Henry Yule)
The Book of Ser Marco Polo the Venetian . . . , c.1300

MIGHTIEST EMPIRE

His eye might there command wherever stood
City of old or modern fame, the seat
Of mightiest empire, from the destined walls
Of Cambalu, seat of Cathaian Can
And Samarchand by Oxus, Temir's throne,
To Paquin of Sinaean kings, and thence
To Agra and Lahor. . . .

John Milton
Paradise Lost, 1667

PHYSICAL GEOGRAPHY

Yung Lo, of the ensuing dynasty, who is supposed to be the founder of the present Peking, is said to have consulted for his plan an eminent astrologer, Lu Po. The thaumaturge handed the Emperor a sealed envelope containing the plans of the new capital, based on the recognised principles of his magic. The city was to represent No-Cha, a mythical being with three heads and six arms, and a corresponding space or building was allotted to each part of his body. . . . Thus, to take a few instances, No-Cha's head—or heads— is the Ch'ien Men, the principal gate of the Tartar City (through which the Emperor used to be drawn by his elephants on his way to sacrifice at the Altar of Heaven, the supreme ceremony of the Chinese Year); an open gutter, now covered over, in the West City, represents his large intestine; a well in the Western Section of the

Forbidden City, his navel; two gates, facing the Yellow Temple and the Black Temple respectively, symbolise his feet, treading on 'Wind and Fire Wheels', while the red painted walls of the Imperial City constitute his red silk stomach protector.

Osbert Sitwell
Escape With Me!, 1939

KEY FEATURES

Peking has been described so often that it is unnecessary to do so once more. The only striking things about it are the size of its walls and its gateways, the filth of its streets, and the utter disregard for decency of its inhabitants.

Capt. Frank E. Younghusband
The Heart of a Continent, 1896

BEYOND COMPARE

This city of Pequin, whereof I have promised to speak more amply than yet I have done, is so prodigious, and the things therein remarkable, as I do almost repent me for undertaking to discourse of it, because, to speak the truth, I know not where to begin, that I may be as good as my word; for one must not imagine it to be either as the city of Rome, or Constantinople, or Venice, or Paris, or London, or Seville, or Lisbon, or that any of the cities of Europe are comparable unto it, how famous or populous soever they be: nay, I will say further, that one must not think it to be like to Grand Cairo in Egypt, Tauris in Persia, Amadabad in Cambaya, Bisnagar in Narsingua, Goura in Bengala, Ava in Chaleu, Timplan in Calaminhan, Martaban and Bagou in Pegu, Guimpel and Tinlau in Siammon, Odia in the kingdom of Sornau, Passarvan and Dema in the island of Jaoa, Pangor in the country of the Lequiens, Usingea in the Grand Cauchin, Lansame in Tartaria, and Meaco in Japan, all which cities are the capitals of many great kingdoms; for I dare well affirm, that all those same are not to be compared to the least part of the wonderful city of Pequin, much less to the greatness and magnificence of that which is most excellent in it, whereby I understand her stately buildings, her inward riches, her excessive abundance of all that is necessary for the entertaining of life, also the world of people, the infinite number of barques and vessels that are there—the commerce, the courts of justice, the government and the state of the *tutons, chaems, anchacys, aytaos, ponchalys,* and *bracalons,* who rule whole kingdoms and very spacious provinces, with great pensions, and are ordinarily resident in this city, or others for them, whenas by the king's command they are sent about affairs of consequence.

Fernand Mendez Pinto
(trans. Henry Cogan)
The Voyages and Adventures of Fernand Mendez Pinto . . . , 1614

FOUNT OF ALL KNOWLEDGE

Until Peking was opened to Europeans the southern Chinese used to stick at no lie about it. For instance, if they were told of some great scientific invention such as railways, the electric telegraph, or the like, they would say at once with the utmost coolness, 'Have seen! Have seen! Have got plenty Peking side!'

A. B. Freeman-Mitford
The Attaché at Peking, 1865 pub. 1900

A GIGANTIC DISAPPOINTMENT

You enter through a gate of no proportions or pretensions, you ride for a quarter of an hour among hovels and pigs, and then suddenly on climbing a bank a striking sight bursts upon you. A great tower of many storeys forms the corner of a mighty wall; from each of its storeys a score cannon-mouths yawn; for a mile or more the wall stretches in a perfectly straight line, pierced with a thousand embrasures, supported by a hundred buttresses.

Then you halt your pony and sit and try to realise that another of the desires of your life is gratified; that you are at last really and truly before the walls of the city that was old centuries before the wolf and the woodpecker found Romulus and Remus; in the wonderland of Marco Polo, father of travellers; on the eve of exploring the very capital and heart of the Celestial Empire . . .

When you ride on you discover that the cannon-mouths are just black and white rings painted on boards, and the swindle—fortunately you do not know it then—is your whole visit to Peking in a nutshell. The place is a gigantic disappointment.

Henry Norman
The Far East, 1895

WALLS WITHIN WALLS

This Metropolis has three Walls: The first which encompasses the other two, as the Fathers who liv'd there told us, and we our selves perceiv'd, is five Leagues in Circumference, a little more or less . . .

The Second Wall runs directly athwart from East to West; it is higher than the other, and so broad that two Coaches may go

abrest on it with ease. Within these two Walls, towards the South, the Chineses live at present, there are the Shops, Tradesmen, and Mechanicks: a Man may there find all he can wish or desire, at the same Rates as in any other Part of the Empire. On the North Side live the Tartars, the Soldiery and Counsellors, and there also are all the Courts of Justice. The third Wall is in the shape of a Half-Moon, and incloses the Imperial Palace, the Temples of their Ancestors, Gardens, Groves, Fish-ponds, and other places for Pleasure. This also is on the North side, and is almost a League in Circumference. The Chineses reckon nine Walls from the first Gate to the Emperor's Apartment, and so tell it as a piece of Ostentation, that their Emperor lies within nine Walls. They stood him [the last Ming Emperor] in little stead against the Robbers and Rebels!

Domingo Navarrete
*The Travels and Controversies of Friar
Domingo Navarrete*, 1676

RULER OF THE WORLD

The vast gate [Qian Men] . . . proclaims in a voice of thunder that here is the city of the Ruler of the world. Outside small men may build their houses like swallows' nests round an old manorial tower, but within alone is there a city of princes.

Revd Roland Allen
*The Siege of the Peking
Legations*, 1901

FANTASTIC ENTRY

In the old days before the Boxers, the Peking railway station was far beyond the walls of even the Chinese city—which has not a tithe of the lustre of the Tartar city, and is rather humble. Then you had to ride or drive from Machiapu, which is three miles beyond the Yung Ting Mên or Gate of Eternal Prosperity, and proceed two miles straight through the Chinese town, until you came on the mighty bastions and keeps of the *Ch'ien Men* or Main Entrance to the Tartar City, where the pleasure of your fantastic entry smote you full, and you hugged yourself even in the choking dust at an enchanted prospect which had no equal. For here would be great strings of camels halted in the wrong places, and calling streams of blasphemy from every other mother's son who trod or rode the roads; camels laden with merchandise and coal, and snarling shrilly after the manner of their kind at the indignities to which they were put. If it were winter there would be plenty of riding camels too, with Mongol men and women seated on top, kicking their beasts along in their coloured boots, and threading through the crush with marvellous skill. Sometimes there were two people mounted on a single animal, the woman on the pillion, clutching tightly to the man and laughing down at all who stared. Then there were strange palanquins slung between two mules, with sword-armed and dust-covered cavaliers ambling alongside, who had come all the way down through the great passes from distant Shansi and Shensi, and sometimes even from Mohammedan Kansu, which is very far. As you swung round the great keep, you would see to your left, out through a side entrance, the Tartar wall, mighty and massive, stretching away mile after mile, and capped and crowned at regular intervals with great *lou* or storied towers. Below the wall was a vast sand-stretch, furrowed by countless cart-wheels and often encumbered with thousands of camels coming or going, where you might gallop and gallop until you were fairly pumped and you reached a camel-back bridge—an almost perfect half-moon of stone, which, hoisting its back angrily in the air, advised immediate caution.

B. L. Putnam Weale
The Reshaping of the Far East, 1905

TEARS OF JOY

The train from Tientsin ran in under the Tatar wall, stopping near the Ch'ien Men, the huge gate which leads to the Forbidden City, at the heart of the town. I was once so overjoyed to see those walls

again as I came in from Peitaiho that I burst into tears, to my own
amazement. No other city ever did this to me, before or since.

Enid Saunders Candlin
The Breach in the Wall, 1973

TRIUMPHAL PROGRESS

Pagodas of Nang-yang, and Chou-chin-chou,
So lofty, to our trav'ling Britons bow;
   Bow, mountains sky-enwrapp'd of Chin-chung-chan;
Floods of Ming-ho, your thund'ring voices raise;
Cuckoos of Ming-fou-you, exalt their praise,
   With geese of Sou-chen-che, and Tang-ting-tan.

O monkeys of Tou-fou, pray line the road,
Hang by your tails, and all the branches load;
Then grin applause upon the gaudy throng,
And drop them honours as they pass along.

Frogs of Fou-si, O croak from pools of green;
Winnow, ye butterflies, around the scene;
   Sing O be joyful, ev'ry village pig;
Goats, sheep, and oxen, through your pastures prance;
Ye buffaloes and dromedaries, dance;
   And elephants, pray join th' unwieldy jig.

I mark, I mark, along the dusty road,
The glitt'ring coaches with their happy load,
   All proudly rolling to PE-KIN's fair town;
And lo, arriv'd, I see the Emp'ror stare,
Deep marv'ling at a sight so very rare;
   And now, ye Gods! I see the EMP'ROR *frown.*

And now I hear the lofty Emp'ror say,
'Good folks, what is it that you want, I pray?'
   And now I hear aloud MACARTNEY cry,
'EMP'ROR, my COURT, inform'd that you were rich,

Sublimely feeling a strong money-itch,
   Across the eastern ocean bade me fly;

With tin, and blankets, O great King, to barter,
And gimcracks rare for China-Man and Tartar.
But presents, presents are the things we mean:
Some pretty diamonds to *our gracious* QUEEN,
Big as one's fist or so, or somewhat bigger,
Would cut upon her petticoat a figure—
A petticoat of whom each poet sings,
That beams on birth-days for the Best of Kings.

Yes, presents are the things we chiefly wish—
   These give not half the toil we find in trade.'—
On which th' astonish'd Emp'ror cries, 'Odsfish!
   Presents!—present the rogues the Bastinade.'

Peter Pindar, Esq.
[John Wolcot]
*A Pair of Lyric Epistles to Lord Macartney
and his Ship*, 1792

FAILURE

When Wade was in England last year Lord Stanley said to him:
'Peking's a gigantic failure, isn't it? not a two-storied house in the
whole place, eh?'

A. B. Freeman-Mitford
The Attaché at Peking, 1865 pub. 1900

CONTINUOUS PERFORMANCE

Nowhere in China is the street life so busy, bright, and picturesque as
in Peking, with such unceasing variety of type and costume, incident
and spectacular display. The most noticeable and striking feature, the
peculiarity which gives most brilliancy and interest to all street scenes
and outdoor life, is the presence of women—tall, splendid Manchu

women, who walk with sturdy tread freely on their full-grown, natural feet, and balance their magnificent head-dresses with conscious pride. The Manchu women's coiffure is the most picturesque, and their long Manchu robe the most dignified of any costume in Asia. In my first breathless delight in each of these striking figures, these far north-eastern living pictures, I berated all my traveled acquaintances, who, harping on the dirt and the dilapidation, the offensive smells and sights, of Peking, had never told me of these Manchu women, with their broad gold pins, wings of blue-black hair, and great bouquets and coronals of flowers, the bewitching pictures in every thoroughfare. Nor any more had they given me an idea of the bewildering interest and richness of the street life, something of which at every moment catches and dazzles the eye and fixes one's attention—the real sights of Peking, not the walls and temples and monuments set down in the abbreviated and scholarly local guide-book, but the throngs of all classes of two races, who give continuous performances all over the twin cities.

E. R. Scidmore
China: The Long-Lived Empire, 1900

UNDESIRABLE RESIDENCE

Intersected by canals of stagnant green water, from which a fierce sun draws the most sickening odour, surrounded by frowning brown walls in a setting of sand, in spring swept by winds carrying clouds of fine dust, deluged in summer by rains which convert into quagmires the already impassable streets, inhabited by an infragrant population ignorant of the most elementary laws of sanitation, cleanliness or decency, Peking is enough to disgust at first sight the most hardened of travellers.

Lady Susan Townley
My Chinese Notebook, 1904

INORDINATE AFFECTION

My own affection for Peking is inordinate. Along with the tranquillity of positive friendship, it has a sort of jealous intemperance. It brooks no criticism of this city from the lips of others, not even if the criticisms may have some basis of fact.

Lucian S. Kirtland
Finding the Worthwhile in the Orient, 1926

ART NOT NATURE

The first and most awe-inspiring impression made by the panorama of Peking is that this city owes nothing to Nature. What a contrast to Constantinople, the imperial city with which I had been most familiar before! Why, if the act of God or of some Mongol conqueror were to remove every vestige of the works of Man from the shores of the Bosphorus and the Golden Horn, the grandeur of the scene would not be diminished, and it might even be enhanced. That line of domes and minarets along the crest of Stamboul, that white tower that crowns the slopes of Galata, those castles of Asia and Europe which beckon to one another across the narrowest reach of the Bosphorus—all these works of human hands merely set off the lines that have been laid down from time immemorial by Nature. Beautiful though they are, they are also superfluous. Why, even New York, with the vast amphitheatre of the harbour in the foreground, and behind it Manhattan Island standing up, one single rock, between the East River and the

Hudson, could dispense with the Statue of Liberty and the tall buildings. What triumphs of the perpendicular in architecture can ever hope to rival the Palisades? I thought of Rome; yet even in Rome Man's handiwork is not independent of the Seven Hills; and it was the Aventine and the Capitol—not the Pantheon or the Colosseum—that inspired Gibbon to write the *Decline and Fall*. And now here is Peking, a city no less imposing than Rome or New York or Constantinople; and everything that has gone to the making of Peking is artificial.

Peking is just something which human imagination and energy have done to so many square miles of the featureless, enormous North China Plain; and if just this had not been done by men just here, these particular square miles would not have been distinguishable in any way from the thousands of others by which they are monotonously surrounded. The very heights from which one surveys Peking—the Dagoba Hill and the 'Coal Hill' and the substructure of the Temple of Heaven—have been heaped up by human labour. It is true that Peking also has its natural hills—not in the centre but on the western horizon: those Western Hills that magically advance or retreat or disappear in accordance with the changes in the atmosphere. Here, however, it is the works of Nature that are superfluous, as at Constantinople it is the works of Man. On each of the days when I first looked at Peking from the Dagoba Hill and the 'Coal Hill' and the Temple of Heaven, the sky happened to be grey and the air murky, so that the farthest objects that stood out distinctly were the huge gabled towers that crown the gates in the city wall. Afterwards I saw the city from the same vantage-points again on days when the horizon extended to the Western Hills and when the sunshine was transmuting their hard, dry rocks into life-like lights and shadows. Yet I found that I had already received the complete impression of Peking on those first occasions. The beauty of the hills really added nothing to the beauty of the gates and the walls and the yellow tiles of the Forbidden City and the blue tiles of the Temple of Heaven and the white marble of the great Altar.

Arnold Toynbee
*A Journey to China or Things Which Are
Seen*, 1931

CHAPTER 2

THE FORBIDDEN CITY

*There is a certain quality of grandeur, an arrogance of power,
which could only have had its inspiration in the turbulent
imagination of the Mongols, not in the amiable cultural
traditions of the Chinese.*

LUCIAN S. KIRTLAND
Finding the Worthwhile in the Orient, 1926

The Forbidden City, the Purple City, the Great Within, has always been the heart of Peking as capital. In the traditional city view, it *was* Peking, the surrounding layers of the town having no purpose other than to serve the needs of the figure central to it, the Son of Heaven.

The Forbidden City that stands today is not the Palace City described by Marco Polo, although that was based on the same concept of an ideal capital, and occupied much the same position. It is the preserve created by the third Ming Emperor, Yong Le, at the beginning of the fifteenth century. In the intervening almost 600 years the halls and pavilions have been burnt down, rebuilt, restored, but the palace complex which Osbert Sitwell evoked so memorably in 1936 is in essence unchanged from that which Shah Rukh's ambassadors saw, still under scaffolding, in 1420.

Outsiders for a long time relied for their knowledge of the Imperial palaces on the accounts of the embassies occasionally admitted, together with what could be gleaned from court documents. The Forbidden City was, as its name implied, closed to the public gaze, Chinese and foreigner alike.

That seclusion ended with the Eight-nation Expeditionary Force of 1900, despatched to raise the Siege of the Legations. Their main purpose achieved, the troops turned their attention to the Imperial Palace, which had been hastily vacated by the court. When the great gates were opened to prevent further damage by the allies' artillery, the foreign conquerors were able to inspect at their leisure the halls and apartments of the Qing court. The Japanese made a photographic record, while the Westerners looted the apartments.

Although the Court did return from its 'tour of inspection', and the Forbidden City became once again, for a time, inviolate, it was only another eleven years before the Qing dynasty came to an end. The boy emperor, Pu Yi, was allowed to continue to occupy part of the Palace complex until 1924. But with the end of Imperial China, the Forbidden City lost its essential meaning. It became, and remains, a grand memorial, an evocation of a period of three dynasties and more than 700 years. Through all that time successive Sons of Heaven ruled their temporal dominions from within its walls, their throne the still centre about which the Chinese world revolved.

THE GREATEST PALACE

You must know that it is the greatest Palace that ever was . . . The building is altogether so vast, so rich, and so beautiful, that no man on earth could design anything superior to it. The outside of the roof also is all coloured with vermilion and yellow and green and blue and other hues, which are fixed with a varnish so fine and exquisite that they shine like crystal, and lend a resplendent lustre to the Palace as seen for a great way round. This roof is made too with such strength and solidity that it is fit to last for ever.

Marco Polo
(trans. Col. Sir Henry Yule)
The Book of Ser Marco Polo the Venetian . . . ,
c.1300

QUALIFIED RAPTURE

The splendour of the palace is equal to its extent; and though constructed according to the singular architecture of the Chinese, which resembles no other, except perhaps, in a slight degree, the Gothic, yet the whole is pleasing, and contains much that is excellent, and even wonderful.

Father Ripa
Memoirs of Father Ripa During Thirteen
Years' Residence at the Court of Peking . . . ,
c.1730, pub. 1846

THE GREAT KHAN AT HOME

But his own palace in which he dwells is of vast size and splendour. The basement thereof is raised about two paces from the ground, and within there be four-and-twenty columns of gold; and all the walls are hung with skins of red leather, said to be the finest in the world. In the midst of the palace is a certain great jar, more than two paces in height, entirely formed of a certain precious stone called *Merdacas* and so fine, that I was told its price exceeded the value of four great towns. It is all hooped round with gold, and in every corner thereof is a dragon represented as in act to strike most fiercely. And this jar hath also fringes of network of great pearls hanging therefrom, and these fringes are a span in breadth. Into this vessel drink is conveyed by certain conduits from the court of the palace; and beside it are many golden goblets from which those drink who list.

In the hall of the palace also are many peacocks of gold. And when any of the Tartars wish to amuse their lord then they go one after the other and clap their hands; upon which the peacocks flap their wings, and make as if they would dance. Now this must be done either by diabolic art, or by some engine underground.

Friar Odoric the Bohemian
The Travels of Friar Odoric of Pordonone,
c.1330

PHILOSOPHICAL EXERCISE

Every year that emperor keepeth four great feasts, to wit, the day of his birth, that of his circumcision, and so forth. To these festivals he summons all his barons and all his players, and all his kinsfolk ...And in one corner of a certain great place abide the philosophers, who keep watch for certain hours and conjunctions; and when the hour and conjunction waited for by the philosophers arrives, one of them calls out with a loud voice, saying: 'Prostrate yourselves before the emperor our mighty lord!' And immediately all the barons touch the ground three times with their heads. Then he will call out again: 'Rise all of you!' and immediately they get up again. And then they wait for another auspicious moment, and when it comes he will shout out again: 'Put your fingers in your ears!' and so they do. And then: 'Take them out': and they obey.

Friar Odoric the Bohemian
The Travels of Friar Odoric of Pordonone, c.1330

CAMBINSKAN

This Cambinskan, of which I have yow told,
In royal vestiment sit on his deys,
With diademe ful heighe in his paleys,
And halt his feste, so solempne and so riche,
That in this world ne was ther non it liche.

Geoffrey Chaucer
The Squieres Tale, c.1387

A MATTER OF TASTE

Within the northern enclosure is the palace, which is the most
splendid, as well as the most important part of Peking. According
to the Chinese, this is a very superb residence, with 'golden walls,
and pearly palaces,' fit for the abode of so great a monarch: to the
unprejudiced eyes of strangers, however, it presents a glittering
appearance, with its varnished tiles of brilliant yellow, which, under
the rays of the meridian sun, seem to constitute a roof of burnished
gold: the gay colours and profuse gilding applied to the interior,
give the halls a dazzling glory, while the suite of court yards and
apartments, vieing with each other in beauty and magnificence, all
contribute to exalt our apprehensions of the gorgeous fabric. We
must not expect to find much there that will gratify the taste, or
suit the convenience of those accustomed to admire European
architecture, and English comfort; but in the estimation of the
Chinese, their scolloped roofs, and projecting eaves, and dragon
encircling pillars; with their leaf-shaped windows, and circular
doors, and fantastic emblems, present more charms than the
Gothic and Corinthian buildings, or the curtained and carpeted
apartments of modern Europe.

W. H. Medhurst
China: Its State and Prospects, 1857

A CULMINATION

Across the first and greatest of the courts, runs down its marble channel in a wide and most delicate curve, the celebrated canal, Golden Water River, with three fine marble bridges crossing it. To me, for one, observing this prodigious enclosure, it always seemed that, in the fortress-like grandeur of the edifice behind, in the line of the canal and the poetry of its waters, flickering reflected sunlight under perfect spans, in the workmanship and design of the balustrades, in the vista of lofty, superb halls in front, with their scarlet and green eaves high in air, and still above, in the vista of roofs fitting, one into another, with supreme art, the Palace reached its culmination. The theme is one of ascent, flowing and progressive from flight of steps to flight of steps, from terrace to terrace, from lower deck to upper deck, from one building to another. The similarity and slight difference between court and court, roof and roof, outline and outline, invests it with the depth and immensity of a night sky when, gazing at it, you try to identify a single star. Yet each court constitutes a world of its own, remote in feeling as the moon; a world wherein nothing happens except the ceaseless, clock-like sweep of cold, golden light from east to west, across it, across the marble floors, across the broad and shallow flights of steps, across the canal, lying like a scimitar below, across the cracking, sagging terraces, their surface dry and powdery with age.

Osbert Sitwell
Escape With Me!, 1939

THE IMPERIAL WAY

The supreme wonder of Chinese architecture lies in its use of space. It is not only in the curved pillared roofs, built to imitate the pole-propped tents of their ancestors, that the architects of the Forbidden City betray their nomadic origin. By a strange skill in proportions, by isolating great pavilions in immense stretches of flagged paving, they have succeeded in bringing into their palace courts the endless spaces of the Gobi desert. The eye travels over the lower walls surrounding each mighty enclosure to distant roof-trees, and beyond these to others more distant still, with a sense of beholding mountain ranges hull-down on vast horizons; the gold of the roofs suggests the wonder of dawn and sunset on far-off snows. The world holds nothing to match this, knows nothing on such a scale. Not even Ang-Kor can approach those areas of granite pavement, those miles of scarlet wall.

Ann Bridge
The Ginger Griffin, 1934

NOTHING MUCH

The yellow-roofed buildings of the palace are closely walled in, and no foreign foot passes the threshold of the 'Forbidden City'; but I have looked at them through my glass from the top of the highest building in the neighbourhood, and they appear commonplace enough.

Henry Norman
The Far East, 1895

BAMBOO CURTAIN

Any one passing without proper authorization through any of the gates of the Forbidden City incurs a hundred blows of the bamboo. This law is invariably enforced, and quite lately the *Peking Gazette* announced the infliction of the penalty on a trespasser, and the degradation of the officer of the guard at the gate through which he had entered. Death by strangulation is the punishment due to any stranger found in any of the emperor's apartments; and with that curious introspection which Chinese laws profess, any one passing the palace gate with the intention of going in, although he does not do so, is to have a definite number of blows with the bamboo.

R. K. Douglas
Society in China, 1901

DESIRABLE PROPERTY

Nowhere is China greater and more manifest in beauty than in Peking. I felt the nobility of the wide streets, designed for a princely people, and the palaces and tombs remained as splendid monuments. Yet the monuments were falling into decay, and I remember my sadness one day when I visited the very palace where the Old Empress had liked best to live. It was under guard, for the new government, as we still called it, was conscious of its national treasures and the great imperial buildings of the past were all under military guard.

On this day I had lingered long in The Forbidden City, the idle soldiers staring at me curiously, and at last one of them beckoned me to follow him around the corner of a palace. Thinking that he wanted to show me something I had not yet seen, I followed. But when I reached the place where he stood, he put up his hand and pulled down a magnificent porcelain tile from the edge of a low roof, a tile of the old imperial yellow, stamped with a dragon.

'One silver dollar,' he said.

Pearl Buck
My Several Worlds, 1955

THE FIVE ALLUREMENTS

17th Day of the 6th Moon (13th July) [1900].—Jung Lu asked Her Majesty yesterday what she would do if the Boxers were defeated, and if Peking were captured by the foreigners. In reply, she quoted to him the words of Chia Yi, a sophist of the Han dynasty, in reference to the Court's diplomatic dealings with the Khan of the Hans:—

'If the Emperor wishes to gain the allegiance of other countries, he can only do so by convincing their rulers that he possesses the three cardinal virtues of government, and by displaying the five allurements.

These allurements are: (1) Presents of chariots and rich robes, to tempt the eye; (2) rich food and banquets, to tempt the palate; (3) musical maidens, to tempt the ear; (4) fine houses and beautiful women, to tempt the instinct of luxury; and (5) the presence of the Emperor at the table of the foreign ruler, to tempt his pride.

The three cardinal virtues of government are: (1) to simulate affection; (2) to express honeyed sentiments; and (3) to treat one's inferiors as equals.'

J. O. P. Bland and E. Backhouse
China Under the Empress Dowager, 1910

HONEYED SENTIMENTS

[At a reception for diplomatic ladies after the Boxer uprising] Tze-hi showed astonishing affability. She distributed rings, bracelets, and other gifts to adults and children alike, accompanied them to a luncheon, drank wine with some of them, lifted a tea-cup to Mrs. Conger's lips, and personally placed fragments of food in the mouths of the Minister's wives and on the plates of other guests. Finally she bade them farewell, saying: 'I hope that we shall meet oftener and become friends by knowing one another better.' It was noticed with astonishment that Her Majesty had picked up some English phrases, which a Peking correspondent gives as follows: '*Hao tu yiu; Ha-p'i niu yerh; Tè rin-kò t'i!*'

Philip W. Sergeant
The Great Empress Dowager of China, 1910

38

FUNNY HATS

It was a dismal morning when we went to see the Son of Heaven [in 1895]. A fine drizzle mixed with snow turned the earth, which had thawed a little, into black liquid mud. In my sedan chair I was carried to the German Legation to join the German Minister, whereupon our procession of chairs proceeded like a long serpent through the streets. Similar serpents emerged from all the different legations, some longer, some shorter. At a quick pace the chair-bearers, four for each chair, carried their burden along, carefully avoiding the most dangerous mud puddles, stones, and ditches. Each procession was accompanied by a Chinese escort on shaggy ponies, mostly amblers. Near the Tun An Gate a densely packed crowd with exceedingly dirty faces insolently pressed against the chairs to get a glimpse of the 'foreign devils' inside. The bearers had difficulty in progressing and had to push their way through the gateway. Inside the gate it was better, for unarmed soldiers, belonging to the yellow banner with red border, were lining the roadsides to keep the curious crowds at a little distance. We crossed the high arched bridge and arrived at the Tung Hua Gate where we had to alight from our chairs. Here only the heads of missions were provided with little open chairs carried by two bearers; the rest of the company had to go on foot between two rows of soldiers in blue jackets over their gowns and armed with enormous swords which hung horizontally at their left side. The place was swarming with mandarins in palace dress, of which the white fur lining neatly protruded along the edges. We walked over coconut matting which was soaked by the rain, to a primitive little waiting-house consisting of an entrance hall with a room on each side. An old red carpet lay on the ground, and walls and ceiling were papered with cheap Chinese wall-paper. A charcoal fire burned in a brazier, filling the room with fumes, and here we waited till the whole diplomatic body had assembled; a motley crowd of uniforms, diplomatic and military, much gold braid, many coloured ribbons of decorations, stars and crosses. There were Highlanders in kilts, Frenchmen in red trousers, German cuirassiers, and Russian Cossacks; there were cocked hats with feathers, helmets with spikes and eagles, képis with plumes, busbies and astrakhan caps. No two men were the same. The high mandarins moved through the throng in their dignified sable coats, wearing the beautiful fur on the outside, and decorated with costly strings of jade beads. Their official hats with red silk tassels and large knobs of coral on the top indicating that they were all of the highest rank, and peacock feathers hanging down from the crown of the hat at the back showing that they had proved themselves distinguished public servants. In a way they were amused at the quaint foreign dresses that were produced for the occasion. I can still hear Ching Hsin, one of the Manchu Ministers of the Tsungli Yamên, laughingly say to a colleague: 'Every kind of funny hat is here.'

William Oudendyk
Ways and By-Ways in Diplomacy, 1939

LOSING HATS

Shortly after the Emperor ordered the three Corean, and the two Dutch Ambassadors to be called, in order that they might approach the throne [in the Hall of Preserving Harmony in 1795]. We were conducted in succession up the steps of one of the sides, and performed the ceremony of adoration near the arm-chair. His Majesty then addressed himself to each of us, and presented us a glass of wine with his own hand. This gave occasion to a repetition of the salute of honour; and after the third prostration each of us rose and retired.

When my turn came to make the salute on account of the glass of wine, I prostrated myself with my head covered as his Excellency had done, but my hat, not fitting me well, fell off. The second Minister who was close to me picked it up, and put it on again. His Majesty laughed at the accident, and asked me if I did not understand Chinese. *Poton,* answered I, which in Chinese signifies I do not understand. At this his Majesty laughed still more heartily, and while I drank my cup of wine looked at me, and seemed to think it whimsical that I should make use of his language so apropos to tell him that I did not understand it.

André-Everard Van Braam
Authentic Account of the Embassy of the
Dutch East-India Company to the Court of
China in the Years 1794 and 1795, 1797

CH'IEN LUNG ABSURD

There is a museum in Peking where, side by side with good Chinese art, may be seen the presents which Louis XIV made to the emperor when he wished to impress him with the splendor of *Le Roi Soleil.* Compared to the Chinese things surrounding them, they are tawdry and barbaric. The fact that Britain has produced Shakspere and Milton, Locke and Hume, and all the other men who have adorned literature and the arts, does not make us superior to the Chinese. What makes us superior is Newton and Robert Boyle and their scientific successors. They make us superior by giving us greater proficiency in the art of killing. It is easier for an Englishman to kill a Chinaman than for a Chinaman to kill an Englishman. Therefore our civilization is superior to that of China, and Chien Lung is absurd.

Bertrand Russell
The Problem of China, 1922

UNCONSIDERED TRIFLES

Tuesday, 3rd March [1914]. They are organizing a Museum of Chinese Art, inside the Forbidden City, near the Western Gate. A very pleasant and efficient little man, a painter and a connoisseur, called Kung Pa King, is doing the work of initial selection. He asked me if I would care to come and watch the opening of the cases as they arrive from Jehol. Today I availed myself of this invitation (I always enjoyed undoing parcels, even if they were not for me).

As I entered the Forbidden City through the vaulted tunnel under the outer wall, I met Mr. Kung coming out. When he saw me he changed his mind and walked back to where his underlings were supposed to be at work. As a matter of fact, they had desisted from their labours and were squatting in the sun with their backs to the wooden cases, all talking at once and laughing at some joke, which of course I did not catch.

As the workmen hurried back to their tasks, Mr. Kung preceded me up the gradient that led to a door in the wall, dividing the central from the lateral courtyards. Underneath the overhanging roofs that protected this doorway, were some bales of sail-cloth, sewn round with stitches of thick string.

'I stopped the workmen,' said Mr. Kung, 'who had begun to open these bales. They are sealed, and the seals are not Chinese. They must have come from abroad.'

I bent down to examine the seals, and exclaimed in genuine astonishment: 'But these are the lilies of France!'

'You mean the arms of the French royal family?'

'Yes. Of the Bourbons.'

'That is what I imagined, but I was not sure. The seals are intact, as you see. Indeed, they were protected by an outer cover that had been taken off.'

'That means that the bales have never been opened.'

'Evidently not.'

'And you are going to open them now?'

'If you like. As you are here, we may as well do it together.'

With his own hands Mr. Kung began to cut the stitches in the sail-cloth. He used a razor-blade, set in a small handle of Chinese make, similar to what we call a 'jigger.'

Twenty minutes later, the contents of the bales was spread out on the flags of the courtyard. They were pieces of Gobelin tapestry, representing birds, larger than life size.

'What do you make of all this?' asked Mr. Kung.

'A present, in all probability, from the King of France to the Emperor of China. I should say in the days of Louis XV.'

'I have no doubt you are right. And nobody took the trouble to see what the bales contained. Possibly the Emperor never even heard of their arrival. Perhaps one of the bales *was* opened and the contents considered of no interest. This kind of tapestry was never appreciated in the East. The gift was taken as an insignificant offering from some vassal state, and put aside and forgotten.'

And so it happened I had the unusual experience of being present in Peking at the opening of a parcel that had been done up in France in the eighteenth century.

Daniele Varè
Laughing Diplomat, 1938

DEATH BEFORE DISHONOUR

24 February [1913]. There are two old 'Empresses' still living in the Forbidden City, who are widows of the Emperor Tao-kwang. He died in 1850, so they must be pretty ancient, even if they entered the harem at 13 or 15 years of age. Since the Republic was proclaimed, these old ladies are in a great state of mind. I am told that they have prepared a pavilion for themselves, with two thrones in the middle. All around the sides of the room they have placed wood shavings and tins of gasolene. If anyone should suggest that they leave the palace, they intend to put on their robes of state (the colour worn by the secondary wives of an Emperor is bright orange), set fire to the wooden shavings, and then take their places on their two thrones and perish among the flames. There is something grand in such sublime pig-headedness. Those poor old ladies would rather die as Empresses than live on as common people, outside the palace walls.

Daniele Varè
Laughing Diplomat, 1938

HOUSEWARMING

The 27th day of Moharram His Worship the Kazi sent a message to the ambassadors: 'To-morrow is the New Year. The Emperor is going to visit his New Palace, and there is an order that none should wear white clothes' (for among these people white is the colour of mourning). The 28th, about mid-night, the *Sekjin* arrived to conduct the ambassadors to the New Palace. This was a very lofty edifice which had only now been finished after nineteen years of work. This night in all the houses and shops there was such a lighting up of torches, candles, and lamps, that you would have thought the sun was risen already. That night the cold was much abated. Everybody was admitted into the New Palace. . . . It would be impossible to give a just description of this edifice. From the gate of the hall of audience to the outer gate there is a distance of 1985 paces. . . . To the right and left there is an uninterrupted

43

succession of buildings, pavilions, and gardens. All the buildings are constructed of polished stone and glazed bricks of porcelain clay, which in lustre are quite like white marble. A space of two or three hundred cubits is paved with stones presenting not the very slightest deflexion or inequality, insomuch that you would think the joints had been ruled with a pen. In the arts of stone-polishing, cabinet-making, pottery, brick-making, there is nobody with us who can compare with the Chinese. If the cleverest of our workpeople were to see their performances they could not but acknowledge the superiority of these foreigners. Towards noon the banquet ended.

Ghaiassudin Nakkash
*An Embassy Sent by Shah Rukh to the Court
of China AD 1419–1422*, 1836

NOT EASILY FORGOTTEN

During this part of the ceremony, which was not long, the retinue continued standing without the hall; and we imagined, the letter being delivered, all was over. But the master of the ceremonies brought back the ambassador; and then ordered all the company to kneel, and make obeisance nine times to the Emperor. At every third time we stood up, and kneeled again. Great pains were taken to avoid this piece of homage, but without success. The master of the ceremonies stood by, and delivered his orders in the Tartar language, by pronouncing the words *morgu* and *boss*; the first meaning to bow, and the other to stand; two words which I cannot soon forget.

John Bell
*A Journey from St Petersburg to Pekin
1719–22*, 1763

44

WORK IN PROGRESS

They [Shah Rukh's envoys in 1420] obtained sight of a very large and magnificent city entirely built of stone, but as the outer walls were still being built, a hundred thousand scaffoldings concealed them. When the ambassadors were taken from the tower, which was being constructed, to the city, they alighted near the entrance to the Emperor's palace, which was extremely large; up to this entrance they proceeded on foot by a pavement formed of cut-stone, about 700 paces in length. On coming close they saw five elephants standing on each side of the road with their trunks towards it; after passing between the trunks the ambassadors entered the palace, through a gate near which a crowd of about a hundred thousand men had assembled.

Ghaiassudin Nakkash
An Embassy Sent by Shah Rukh to the Court
of China AD 1419–1422, 1836

BRASSBOUND

To introduce order amongst the immense crowd, which collects at every audience, brass plates nailed upon the pavement, with an inscription indicating the name and rank of a certain officer, point out to each individual his proper place, so that every one has space enough to lie down prostrate, and ko-tow (knock head) without injury to his neighbour.

Revd Charles Gutzlaff
China Opened, 1838

FUTURE SHOCK

Surrounded with so many sycophants, it is very natural that unbounded pride should fill the breast of such a very powerful monarch as the emperor. The erect attitude of man, which distinguishes him from the beast, is here confounded; he alone surveys so many crawling worms before him. Every one of his actions is sacred, and lauded by some minion or other. His reign bears the most glorious epithets—Reason's lustre, splendid happiness, repose and prosperity—expressions added to each state-paper, to number the years. Having swayed millions, always realized his wishes, and forgotten that he was a mortal, he is finally called before the bar of the Judge of all mankind, to give an account of his stewardship. What scenes will then burst upon him! what will then be his situation!

Revd Charles Gutzlaff
China Opened, 1838

COVERED VESSELS

I must not omit to tell you of the orderly way in which the Kaan's Barons and others conduct themselves in coming to his presence. In the first place, within a half mile of the place where he is, out

46

of reverence for his exalted majesty, everybody preserves a mien of the greatest meekness and quiet, so that no noise of shrill voices or loud talk shall be heard. And every one of the chiefs and nobles carries always with him a handsome little vessel to spit in whilst he remains in the Hall of Audience—for no one dares spit on the floor of the hall—and when he hath spitten he covers it up and puts it aside.

Marco Polo
(trans. Colonel Sir Henry Yule)
The Book of Ser Marco Polo the Venetian . . . ,
c.1300

SWEET DREAMS

You must know that there is a tribe of Tartars called UNGRAT, who are noted for their beauty. Now every year a hundred of the most beautiful maidens of this tribe are sent to the Great Kaan, who commits them to the charge of certain elderly ladies dwelling in his palace. And these old ladies make the girls sleep with them, in order to ascertain if they have sweet breath and do not snore, and are sound in all their limbs. Then such of them as are of approved beauty, and are good and sound in all respects, are appointed to attend on the Emperor by turns. Thus six of these damsels take their turn for three days and nights, and wait on him when he is in his chamber and when he is in his bed, to serve him in any way, and to be entirely at his orders. At the end of the three days and nights they are relieved by other six. And so throughout the year, there are reliefs of maidens by six and six, changing every three days and nights.

Marco Polo
(trans. Colonel Sir Henry Yule)
The Book of Ser Marco Polo the Venetian . . . ,
c.1300

TIGHTLY HELD

In amusing proximity was the Emperor's seraglio. The gate was closed during the allied occupation [in 1900], and on it was a notice to the effect that 'the custodian has strict orders not to admit any person. Do not ill-treat him if he refuses to open the gate for you. He is only obeying orders.' It was signed by General Chaffee, United States Army, and was significant of many things.

Capt. Gordon Casserly
The Land of the Boxers, 1903

IMPERIAL CONSTELLATIONS

The installation of an emperor is very solemn. Shun-che was carried on a board by his Tatar subjects, and proclaimed emperor. But when Kang-he, being of age, ascended the throne, all the mandarins were ranged on both sides, dressed in silk, flowered with gold in the form of roses. There were fifty men who held great umbrellas of gold brocade and silk, with their staves gilt, divided into two rows. On the side of them were fifty other officers, having large fans of silk, embroidered with gold, and near these were twenty-eight large standards, embroidered with golden stars, and the figures of the moon in all its changes, &c. In order to represent its twenty-eight mansions in the heavens, and its different conjunctions and oppositions with the sun, as they appear in the intersection of the circles, which the astronomers called nodes, these things were delineated with considerable accuracy. A hundred standards followed these, and the rest of the mandarins carried maces, axes, hammers, and other instruments of war or court ceremony.

Revd Charles Gutzlaff
China Opened, 1838

ALL RIGHT ON THE NIGHT

Yuan Shih-k'ai sitting with his Crown [at a dress rehearsal for his enthronement as first Emperor of the 'Hung-hsien' dynasty]; 3 thrones at his side for the 1st, 2nd and 3rd wives on descending levels. First wife came in arrayed; kowtowed; took her proper seat. Long delay and 2nd wife the Korean wife, failed to come. Sent for peremptorily. She came in but refused to take her seat, saying Yuan had promised her a throne on the same level as the No. 1. Hearing this, No. 1 jumped down from the Throne and went for No. 2 with her fingers. The Master of the Ceremonies, Wang Kan-nien was supervising the Enthronement, but he could not lay impious hands on the struggling Empresses, where upon Yuan waddled down from the Throne and tried to separate the two combatants. Order was finally restored but the rehearsal was postponed. . . .

G. E. Morrison
Diary, January 1916

A PASSION FOR CLOCKS

The interior of the Emperor's abode consisted of low, rather dingy rooms opening off each other. The appointments were of anything but regal magnificence. The furniture was of carved black-wood, with an admixture of tawdry European chairs and sofas. On the walls hung a weird medley of Chinese paintings and cheap foreign oleographs, all in gorgeous gilt frames. The latter were such as would be found in a fifth-rate lodging-house—horse races, children playing at see-saw, conventional landscapes, and farmyard scenes. Jade ornaments and artificial flowers in vases abounded; but all around, wherever one could be hung or placed, were European clocks, from the gilt French timepiece under a glass shade to the cheapest wooden eight-day clock. There must have been at least two or three hundred, probably more, scattered about the pavilion. The Chinese have a weird and inexplicable passion for them, and a man's social respectability would seem to be gauged more by the number of timepieces he possesses than by any other outward and visible signs of wealth.

Capt. Gordon Casserly
The Land of the Boxers, 1903

MEAN TIME

At the back of the bed along the wall [of Ci Xi's apartment] ran a wooden ledge, on which stood no less than five European travelling clocks, all ticking vigorously. Her Majesty quaintly informed us that as none of them kept very good time, she drew a sort of mean between them all, and so was able to tell approximately what time it was.

Lady Susan Townley
My Chinese Notebook, 1904

CUSTODIAL SENTENCE

All the beautiful things of China are drifting into museums: the Dragon Throne on which mighty emperors sat in state, the golden gods to whom they prayed in all humility, the weapons of their hours of peril, the trinkets of their hours of peace. Bronzes so massive they seem cast for all eternity, sacrificial vessels whereon the sodden meat or the unhusked rice was offered to ancestral spirits, libation-cups from which the dark-coloured liquor was poured in honour of immortal presences—the altars for which they were fashioned, the temples wherein they were placed, the faith by which they were needed, having crumbled away, life felt no further use for them, embalmed them into curios, classified them in catalogues, coffined them in hermetically sealed glass cases. Bowls, vases, platters, perfume-boxes of cloisonné with blues of lazuli, greens of malachite and jasper, worked into patterns ranging from the antique and austere thunder-scroll to the later and softer arabesques of flowers, interlacings of plum-blossom, undulations of waves and clouds and wind-swept reeds, of coils of great dragons in endless pursuit of the night-shimmering pearl; flights of storks and ducks and bats; miniature pleasure-gardens with grapes of amethyst, pomegranates of coral, peach-trees of rose-quartz; toy rockeries of agate, chrysoprase, and turmaline; seals of emperors and high officials carved out of all manner of precious stones; snuff-bottles of crystal, jade, and ivory; jewelled mirrors, painted fans, intricate embroideries—the palatial luxury which required all these lovely trifles to amuse and decorate its leisure, having been exiled to poverty and feebleness, pawned them, sold them, betrayed them into alien hands. Torn from the semi-sacred seclusion of dainty alcoves hidden as something very precious within the maze and the mystery of innermost apartments, damaged, looted, exposed to the ignorant stare of the vulgar, tossed about between dishonest dealers and greedy collectors, what could these orphans of a vanished splendour do but die, glad to come to some sort of rest in the chilly silence of museums? And one fancies that when the doors are closed against all visitors and only a sleepy custodian or two go the round of the dim rooms, whispers pass from case to case, and there occurs a ghostly resurrection of the glories of all the dazzling hours to which these beautiful remnants once added the lustre of their loveliness.

A. E. Grantham
Pencil Speakings from Peking, 1918

SIC TRANSIT

Utter emptiness as in a splendid deserted hive: and the sense of squalor which always accompanies such desertion. Something in the atmosphere of a palace or temple starts to putrefy when the human occupants vanish. And they had all gone; a lounging soldier at the gate, who wore the badge of the Nationalist government in Nanking, watched the foreign intruders with vague insolence. A spectacled person sold tickets from a box; an aged dwarf came toddling up to tear the counterfoils ... *Sic transit.* The tag slips out so easily; there was a time when the past glories of the world went up in smoke at the touch of change. Nowadays we are more conservative of fallen splendour and empty palaces, from Peking

to Madrid, are handed over to a dim rabble of custodians who
punch tickets, jingle coins and erect notice boards.

Peter Quennell
A Superficial Journey Through Tokyo and
Peking, 1932

UNDER SNOW

I have been fortunate enough to see the Forbidden City under
snow, and it was a sight unforgettably lovely. The huge buildings
floated upon clouds, were borne up by them. . . . The glory that
shone from the ground (for it seemed now as if more light came
up from the earth than down from the sky) imparted a brilliance
beyond belief to the interiors, to the great red pillars, up the length
of which golden dragons clawed their way, to doors and frescoed
walls; and still more glittering was it outside, where it reverberated
up against the flashing eaves which supported the quilted tents of
snow covering the roofs. Below, the white terraces were now whiter
still, beneath their soft loads of swansdown: and this expanse of
whiteness still further exaggerated the size of hall and of court.
Even the moats beyond were padded out of sight, the canals
extinguished; and in the gardens, the dark foliage of cypress and
cedar made startling patterns, of lace and fans and cubist needles,
over the light ground. From the walk and round the top of the
Guard-House, floating high above walls and roof—a walk like that
in the gallery of an Italian Romanesque cathedral, just wide
enough for one person—the more distant towers and gateways
of the Forbidden City appeared sombre and isolated by this
whiteness. . . . But astonishing as were the reversals of appearance
undergone by the great buildings, it was the delicacy of the nearer
details that, by this new emphasis placed upon them, triumphed;
the flowers painted upon a shutter, the bird or crag upon a panel,
were now luminous and melting as the snow itself.

Osbert Sitwell
Escape With Me!, 1939

CHAPTER 3

THE IMPERIAL CITY

Only on rare occasions, and those almost exclusively occasions of ceremony, does the emperor pass out of the palace grounds. These no doubt present a microcosm of the empire.

R. K. DOUGLAS
Society in China, 1901

The Forbidden City was the Emperor's preserve. It is hard to believe that anyone else regretted that very much, for the lifestyle there must always have been a little restrictive, even for nobles and courtiers. Better to live in the larger enclosure of the Imperial City, a separate walled compound surrounding the Emperor's palaces but excluded from them.

Like the palaces that lay at its centre, the Imperial City changed shape from the Yuan to the Ming. Two lakes became three, with the excavation of Nan Hai to the south. The spoil from that, and from the digging of a palace moat, created Coal Hill, to take over the protective role formerly performed by the dagoba-topped island behind it (Marco Polo's Green Mount).

Not only did the Imperial City offer lakes and green spaces, it was, if early accounts are to be believed, home to a wide variety of bird and animal life, up to and including the elephants which at times graced the court. In summer one could boat, in winter skate on the frozen lakes. Small wonder that even royal personages like the Dowager Empress Ci Xi chose occasionally to leave the Forbidden City for the charms of this urban park.

The Imperial City contained a number of lesser buildings of state. It was there, in the Hall of Purple Light (*Ze Guang Ge*), that the envoys of the foreign powers presented their credentials after having established permanent residence in Peking. The discovery that the hall had been chosen because it was traditionally the spot where the Emperor received tribute-bearers from vassal states caused much diplomatic heart-burning, and at last a hard-won agreement that the Emperor would receive foreign representatives once a year in a minor hall actually within the Forbidden City.

It was in the buildings at the southern end of the lake complex that Yuan Shikai and subsequent presidents of the Republic of China established their democratic presence. In the same buildings, after 1949, the new rulers of China set up their inner court. Thus, while the holy of holies, the central palaces of the Forbidden City, have become open to the public gaze, there remains a part of the Imperial City dedicated to the conduct of state affairs, and accessible only to the successors to Imperial power.

EXAGGERATED RESPECT

The principal city wherein the king always lives is called Suntien, which is to say 'Heavenly Abode', and here likewise this same city is also called by the name of the province Pacquiaa [Peking]. . . .

The palaces of the King there are so vast that it is said they occupy the space of a city, where he has every kind of pastime. And they say that he never leaves his palace, neither does anybody see him, save only those who serve him and a few very important people; and there they regard him like a demi-God, and they tell some fables such as that no bird or animal drops dung on the roof or in the grounds of the royal household.

Martin de Rada
*Relation of the things of China which is
properly called Taybin*, 1576

NATURE'S BOUNTY

In this city is the siege and the see of the Great Caan in a right fair palace, of which the walls about are two mile and more; and within these walls are many other fair palaces. And in the garden of the great palace is a hill upon which is another palace, a fair and a rich; there is not such another in all the world. And all about the palace and the hill are many trees bearing divers manners of fruit; and without them are deep dykes and broad, and without them are many vivers [ponds] and stanks [lakes], whereon are many fowls of river, as swans and cranes, herons butours [bitterns] and mallards and such other. Without them also are all manner of wild beasts of venery, as harts and hinds, buck and deer and roe and many other. And aye when the Great Caan will have his disport in ryvaying or hunting, he may [have] wild fowl slain with hawks, and deer slain with hounds or other gins, and pass not his chamber.

Sir John Mandeville
Mandeville's Travels, 1366

DRESS FORMAL

Thursday, 1st January 1914.—This morning Yuan-shi-kai received the Diplomatic Body at his official residence in the southernmost of the Lake Palaces (the Nan-hai). The gate we went in at is called the Hsi Hwa Gate. There used to be a tower there, whence, in the days of Ch'ien Lung, the famous Fragrant Concubine [a Muslim princess, the object of the Emperor's unrequited love] used to look down on her relatives congregated below.

The threshold of this gate is raised above the level of the road, so that we had to get out of our carriages and motors in order to enter. Inside there were other motors to drive us up the road that runs along the western shore of the lake.

The lake itself was frozen and the trees white with hoar-frost. The Ocean Terrace, where Kwang-hsu was imprisoned, was half-hidden by the morning mist, but the roofs rose above it, many-hued in the sunlight. A little procession was coming across the ice towards us; sleighs of red lacquer and gold, with lap-robes of leopard skins; brilliant touches of colour against the background of ice and snow. Yuan-shi-kai was in the second sleigh. As he drew nearer the usual incongruous note became apparent. The servants who pushed the sleighs over the frozen surface of the lake wore frock-coats and top-hats! A mid-winter night's dream.

Daniele Varè
Laughing Diplomat, 1938

SPRING FLOWERS

Various amusements were organised in the Palace to mark the holiday [the Sun Festival] in olden times. The Court assembled to witness cock-fights, such as are still popular among the Malays. Meanwhile, the ladies withdrew to make merry tumult among themselves, swinging on swings decorated with bright silk streamers. It must have been a pretty sight to see Ming Huang's three thousand concubines—'half angels' as he called them—floating to and fro like brilliant flowers on a vine, clad in their costly robes of gauze, girdled like queens, their beautifully dressed hair decked with mock flowers, wonderful combs, pins, and ornaments of pearls and jade.

Juliet Bredon and Igor Mitrophanow
The Moon Year, 1927

WINTER SPORTS

The emperor made his appearance [on the frozen Nanhai] on a sort of sledge, supported by the figures of four dragons. This machine was moved about by several mandarins. The four principal ministers of state were also drawn upon the ice in their sledges by inferior mandarins. Troops of civil and military officers soon appeared, on sledges or skates, and others playing at football on the ice, while he that picked up the ball was rewarded by the emperor. The ball was then hung up in a kind of arch, and several mandarins shot at it, in passing on skates, with their bows and arrows.

André-Everard Van Braam
*Authentic Account of the Embassy of the
Dutch East India Company to the Court of
China in the Years 1794 and 1795*, 1798

ELEPHANTS AND INSECTS

That huge animal the elephant, remarkable for its strength and docility, was seen about the palaces of the Emperor. Several, both male and female, have been brought to China from the vicinity of the equator, and some few of them were bred to the northward of the tropic. They are of a lighter hue and smaller than those at Cochin-china. The elephant is the only quadruped that has a proboscis, though instances of it are frequent in the insect tribe.

Sir George Staunton
*An Historical Account of the Embassy to the
Emperor of China*, 1797

BEARING GIFTS

The foreign sovereigns, under the dominating influence of the China empire, repair to Peking; first, as an act of obeisance and submission: secondly, to pay certain rents to the Emperor, whose vassals they consider themselves. These rents, which are decorated with the fine name of offerings, are, in fact, imposts which no Tartar king would venture to refuse the payment of. They consist in camels, in horses remarkable for their beauty, and which the Emperor sends to augment his immense herds in the Tchakar. Every Tartar prince is, besides, obliged to bring some of the rarer productions of his country; deer, bear and goat venison; aromatic plants, pheasants, mushrooms, fish, &c. As they visit Peking in the depth of winter, all these eatables are frozen; so that they bear, without danger of being spoiled, the trial of a long journey, and even remain good long after they have arrived at their destination.

One of the Banners [military subdivisions] of the Tchakar is especially charged with sending to Peking, every year, an immense provision of pheasant's eggs. We asked the minister of the King of the Alechan, whether these pheasant's eggs were of a peculiar flavour, that they were so highly appreciated by the court. 'They are not destined to be eaten,' he answered; 'the Old Buddha uses them for another purpose.' 'As they are not eaten, what are they used for?' The Tartar seemed embarrassed, and blushed somewhat as he replied that these eggs were used to make a sort of varnish, which the women of the imperial harem used for the purpose of smoothing their hair, and which communicates to it, they say, a peculiar lustre and brilliancy. Europeans, perhaps, may consider this pomatum of pheasant's eggs, so highly esteemed at the Chinese court, very nasty and disgusting; but beauty and ugliness, the nice and the nasty, are, as everybody knows, altogether relative and conventional matters, upon which the various nations that inhabit this earth have ideas remotest from the uniform.

Abbé Huc
Travels in Tartary, Tibet and China, 1851

NOBLESSE OBLIGE

Within the walls and at the gate of the Empress Dowager's Palace, with the usual Chinese tolerance, the consideration of the great for the poor, beggars are allowed to come at certain times each day, to receive remnants from the Imperial kitchen. The poor are also permitted to examine the garbage of the Palace, before it is carted away.

Katharine A. Carl
With the Empress Dowager of China, 1906

NO LICENCE

Except the automobiles used inside of the palace enclosure, few were then to be found in Peking; soon, with improved roads, many hundreds came. The Empress Dowager before her death had acquired a large collection of these foreign vehicles, which interested her greatly; but up to the time of her death the Board of Ceremonies had not succeeded in solving the problem how she might ride in an automobile in which there would also be, in sitting posture, one of her servants, the chauffeur. If they had had more time, I imagine that they might have found some way by which the chauffeur could kneel in driving the Imperial car, but, as it was, the poor Empress Dowager never had the pleasure of the swift rides she so much coveted.

Paul S. Reinsh
An American Diplomat in China, 1922

FREE SEATING

During the summer of 1897 the Dowager-Empress gave one or two garden-parties. Her brother-in-law, the late Prince Kung (the Emperor's uncle), stood by her side as her henchman, and several farces were acted before the company. Besides the ordinary paper

Prince Kung

lanterns, the electric light was introduced for the first time; the chief of the *tatan* (certain 'male' officials in attendance on harem duty in Eastern countries) introduced the leading statesmen in turn to the Empress, who was graciously pleased to 'accord rice.' After this banquet they were conducted 'in fish line' (Indian file) round to the theatre, the Empress herself being carried in an eight-bearer open chair, wearing her 'easy costume.' Only forty-six persons were allowed to sit, and only two of these on stools. As to the other forty-four, it is presumed they sat on what the Shah of Persia once told a British Minister to sit, when his Excellency, looking round, inquired: 'On what am I to sit, your Majesty?'

E. H. Parker
China: Past and Present, 1903

SPITEFUL

The Northern Garden is separately walled, and is divided from the actual palace inclosure by a broad highway, continued as a causeway or long bridge across its lake. Until quite recently this road and bridge were freely used as a direct route from one side of the Imperial City to the other. For more than twenty years foreign residents greatly delighted in this one green and beautiful prospect, this one breath of fresh, imperial, purple air, and drove frequently over the marble bridge of nine arches and picnicked in the deserted pleasure-grounds around the lake. Suddenly the gates were slammed in their faces, and no foreigners were permitted to pass through. At the sight of a foreigner looking from a passing cart now, the guardians run to shut the gates, and to emphasize their spite hold boards against the cracks.

E. R. Scidmore
China: The Long-Lived Empire, 1900

PAVILION OF PURPLE LIGHT

The famous Pavilion of Purple Light is in this outer garden [of the Imperial City] also—a building where Korean, Mongol, and Loochoo envoys used to be entertained with feasts and games when they had offered their annual tribute, quite as the Great Father at Washington used to receive delegations of noble red men, give them presents of blankets and tobacco, and pretend to whiff at the pipe of peace.

E. R. Scidmore
China: The Long-Lined Empire, 1900

THE CELEBRATED
BURNING-GLASS

In the imperial palace at Pekin is deposited the celebrated burning-glass [magnifying lens], which was presented in our king's name, by Lord Macartney, to the Emperor of China in the last century. This glass, with the other presents from the king of Great Britain to the monarch of the Celestial Empire, was exhibited at the palace of Pekin, and the glass was believed to be a talisman which the English monarch had sent to enable him to take possession of China. In vain were the Emperor, mandarins, and astronomers assured that this glass possessed no magical powers and in vain were its peculiar properties explained to them—they neither could nor would comprehend what was said, and the unfortunate burning-glass, which had cost £800 sterling, was ordered to be destroyed—'The talisman of the red-bristled barbarians was to be shivered into ten thousand million atoms— no one piece larger than a grain of rice was to be left entire.' Every effort was made to break the burning-glass, but the toil of the would-be destroyers was futile; and, in despite of the innumerable blows which were inflicted with heavy hammers the magic glass remained *in statu quo*—positively refusing to be demolished!

All was consternation in the imperial palace; the most learned astronomers and profound sages declared . . . that, as the talisman would not be broken, it might perchance consent to be buried. The question then arose where the talisman was to be buried? and after a lengthy consultation, it was resolved, to bury the talisman in the grounds which are attached to the palace, as the eunuchs would then be answerable for its safe keeping. To the amazement of the Emperor of China, mandarins, astronomers, and sages, the talisman was not contumacious, and did not refuse to be interred with all due honors. Consequently, the finest and most powerful burning-glass that ever was constructed, is at Pekin in the possession of Taou-kwang, the Emperor of the Celestial Empire; but as it serenely reposes in the bosom of mother earth, we fear that it is lost to earth's sons for ever.

Henry Charles Sirr
China and the Chinese, 1849

DEATH OF AN EMPEROR

When he [the last Ming Emperor, Chong Zhen] was first told of the Enemies being within his Court, he was astonished with admiration at the unexpected hearing of such direful news; but after a small Pause, seeing there was no hopes to escape, he took his Pen, and writing a Letter with his own Blood accuses his Officers therein of most horrid Treason. . . . Having finished this

Letter, as a Man Distracted he kills his Daughter in his Chamber, being a young Virgin of seventeen or eighteen years of Age, that she should not be mishandled or abused by the Rogues; and then with a settled resolution not to survive this dismal misfortune, going into the Garden, with one of his Garters he Hanged himself upon a Plum Tree. This was the miserable catastrophe of the Emperour Zungchinius.

John Nievhoff
An Embassy from the East India Company of
the United Provinces to the Grand Tartar
Cham, Emperor of China, 1669

ABJECT TERROR

The Ministers [presenting credentials to the Emperor Tong Zhi in 1873] were introduced into the Presence by the higher officials of the Tsung-li Yamen. They wore swords. When they had all entered, the doors were closed. They saluted the Emperor without prostrating themselves, but only bending the head. On one side of the throne was a small table, near which each Minister in turn was told to stand, while he read out his credentials. The British Minister came first. But he had not spoken more than a few words when he was seized by a fit of trembling which prevented him continuing his speech. The Emperor kindly asked him some questions, but it was no use, there was no answer. Then the other Ministers came up, each in his turn, but they were all seized with a panic and dropped their credentials, without being able to read them. Prince Kung gave orders to the Palace servants, to help the Ministers down the steps, holding them under the arms. So abject was their terror that they were incapable of standing up, and sank to the ground, damp with perspiration and gasping for breath. They could not even partake of the banquet that had been prepared for them.

Prince Kung said: 'I warned you that the act of entering the Emperor's presence should not be taken lightly. You would not believe what I said. Now you realize that I was right!'

And yet the reception had been prepared without much pomp. The foreign Ministers now admit that a transcendent virtue

emanates from the Emperor, filling humbler mortals with alarm.
. . . Such are these vainglorious men, braggarts from afar, cowards
when at hand!

Chinese broadsheet
quoted in Varè, *The Last of the Empresses*,
1936

THE NEW EMPERORS

On days when I stayed in the city I frequently walked or went
for my lunch in the park of the Winter Palace whose walls
overshadowed my house to the west. This immense enclosure, with
its handsome lake and numerous restaurants and tea-houses, had
been a popular summer holiday spot for the Pekinese, but beside
it lay one of the big barracks taken over by the invaders and it was
now becoming a favourite place of Japanese recreation. Late in
the morning whole companies of the chunky little warriors
marched up to its crenellated gate, double-timed past the ticket-
office, and scattered to their amusements. They collected in
raucous groups before the parrot cages, or walked in awe among
the wooden tubs full of goggle-eyed, fantailed Imperial goldfish.

They packed into rowboats and barges and paddled out among the lotus, or sat in the five lakeside pavilions, drinking beer and experimentally nibbling on jou-dzah, bow-dzah, and other Pekinese snacks. The Chinese boatmen and waiters in the park were already learning a smattering of Japanese, and would have been riding on a wave of prosperity if it weren't that they were paid with Japanese military notes—'monkey money' as it was already known, which could be used effectively as cash only when passed from a Japanese to a Chinese.

An extraordinary number of the holiday soldiers carried kodaks, and it was their pleasure to snap their comrades piling in acrobatic pyramids on the marble bridges or shouting 'Banzai' and waving their arms over their heads in the shrubbery of the Empress Dowager's rock-garden.

Graham Peck
Through China's Wall, 1945

PEACE AND QUIET

8th Day of the 6th Moon, 11 a.m. (July 4th) [1900]

Yesterday afternoon the Empress Dowager crossed over to the Lake Palace for a water picnic, attended by several ladies of the Court. The continuous bombardment of the French cathedral [at the time of the Legation Siege] eventually made her head ache, so she despatched a chamberlain to the officer commanding at the Hsi-Hua Gate, ordering them to cease firing until her return to the Forbidden City.

J. O. P. Bland and E. Backhouse
China Under the Empress Dowager, 1910

MICROCOSMIC

Only on rare occasions, and those almost exclusively occasions of ceremony, does the emperor pass out of the palace grounds. These no doubt present a microcosm of the empire. There are lakes, mountains, parks, and gardens in which the imperial prisoner can amuse himself, with the boats which ply on the artificial water, or by joining mimic hunts in miniature forests; but it is probable that there is not one of the millions of China who has not a more practical knowledge of the empire than he who rules it.

R. K. Douglas
Society in China, 1901

MACARONI SOUP

Being partial to macaroni soup, he [the Emperor Dao Guang] gave orders that some should be prepared for him every day; but the eunuchs objected that this would be possible only if a special kitchen were built, at the cost of 600,000 taels. They added that the yearly expenditure of such a kitchen would amount to 15,000 taels. The Emperor replied that, according to reliable information, a bowl of macaroni soup could be bought outside the Ch'ien Mên for forty copper cents, and he ordered the eunuchs to send out and buy him a bowl every day. A week later, he was told that the only restaurant outside the Ch'ien Mên where the soup could be procured was closed, the proprietor having gone out of business.

Daniele Varè
The Last of the Empresses, 1936

VERY GREEN

Moreover on the north side of the Palace, about a bow-shot off, there is a hill which has been made by art; it is a good hundred paces in height and a mile in compass. This hill is entirely covered with trees that never lose their leaves, but remain ever green. And I assure you that wherever a beautiful tree may exist, and the Emperor gets news of it, he sends for it and has it transported bodily with all its roots and the earth attached to them, and planted on that hill of his. No matter how big the tree may be, he gets it carried by his elephants; and in this way he has got together the most beautiful collection of trees in all the world. And he has also caused the whole hill to be covered with the ore of azure, which is very green. And thus not only are the trees all green, but the hill itself is all green likewise; and there is nothing to be seen on it that is not green; and hence it is called the Green Mount; and in good sooth 'tis named well.

Marco Polo
(trans. Col. Sir Henry Yule)
The Book of Ser Marco Polo the Venetian . . . ,
c.1300

CHEATING TIME

The whole sober, magisterial plan of Pekin was apparent, from this point [the summit of Coal Hill], set out with the abstract precision of a diagram. Straight before me was a rectilinear enclosure which contains the Forbidden City. Another immense enclosure contains the whole of Pekin, though it is cut in two by a wall which separates the Chinese city from the Tartar city. These enclosures are orientated with complete exactitude; each of their faces looking towards a cardinal point, and no other city in the world is constructed so obviously and patently according to the ordinance which rules the universe. The palaces which rise up closely pressed together in the Imperial City have the same rigorous orientation. They face each other and respond to one another. There is some relation to the fields of agriculture in their great simple forms, and their glorious yellow roofs are dazzling like fields of ripe corn, and seen to be lifting a symbol of the fecundity of the imperial soil up into the sky. They make no attempt to conquer Time by the defiant haughtiness of their materials, nor to dispute with it the durability of their wooden pillars or their earthen tiles; but they cheat Time of its victory, by simply replacing what it destroys as it destroys it, and disdainful of the days that wear them away they endure by force of an unchanging spirit, not by the resistance of matter. The Imperial City stands alone. All that is around it is as nothing. You may and do perceive a whole multitude of lowly roofs, a prostrated town, but even this nullity is according to the ordinance. The different quarters are divided from each other by the straight undeviating avenues, and even the walls of the meanest dwelling are built to face the cardinal points, just as the enclosures and the palaces contemplate them from their august *façades*. The order reigning here is very different from that which we are accustomed to; instead of encouraging man to develop and carry forward new order, it fixes man to the spot, binds him with unbreakable bonds and effaces him.

Abel Bonnard
(trans. Veronica Lucas)
In China, 1926

CHAPTER 4

THE TARTAR CITY

*They are very much alike, temples and palaces. There is no such
deep cleavage between lay and religious architecture as prevails in
Christian countries, because the idea that religion is a thing to be
put on and off regularly once a week with one's Sunday clothes
never occurred to the Chinese.*

A. E. GRANTHAM
Pencil Speakings from Peking, 1918

Before the advent of the Qings, the Tartar City was called the Inner City, although it was strictly the outer city of the ideal capital. It held the Forbidden and Imperial Cities at its centre, and it lay squarely on the same north/south axis, so that Peking people have always defined direction by the four points of the compass, rather than by referring to left and right.

The Manchus, or Tartars, who established the Qing Dynasty, were a non-Han people from the north-east. They were happy enough to take over the Ming Dynasty capital, but less confident that they would keep it for very long if it continued to be populated largely by Han Chinese. This fear lay behind the creation of the Tartar City. With few exceptions, all Chinese inhabitants were expelled from within the city walls. In their place the army and camp-followers of the eight Manchu banners moved in, and stayed for 250 years.

It was the Tartar City walls that defined Peking on first approach. Nine gates controlled access, and right into the twentieth century those gates shut firmly at sunset. Only one, Qian Men, reopened for a short time at midnight to admit late revellers from the Chinese City.

The main public buildings of the government were inside the Tartar City. Towards the north, but defining the centre of the old Yuan capital of Dadu, were set the Drum and Bell towers. Further south stood the halls of the six tribunals, the central government offices. The Astronomical Observatory was placed near the south-east corner of the wall (and remains there though the wall itself has gone). Just north of the Observatory is the site of the Examination Halls, scene of the final testing under the old Imperial examination system.

Travellers found much to describe in the Tartar City—the temple fairs, the horsemarket at what has become Tiananmen Square, even the elephant stables near the southwest gate. Foreigners established their homes within the City's boundaries, in courtyard houses approached along *hutungs* (narrow lanes leading off the main thoroughfares). There they had as their neighbours ordinary Chinese such as the exemplary Young Wu (whose adventures appeared week by week in the *Peking Chronicle*). For people such as Young Wu's family, Peking was the Tartar City, and the Tartar City Peking.

MANY CURIOUS SIGHTS

To describe the celestial capital is not difficult. One street is so exactly like another, that when you have seen a bit of the place you have seen the whole of it. The principal street of the Tartar city may be described in very few words. A broad, straggling thoroughfare, knee deep in dust, with low, tumble-down houses on either side, hidden at intervals by dirty canvas booths, wherein fortune-tellers, sellers of sweet-meats, keepers of gambling-hells, and jugglers ply their trade. Deep open cess-pools at every fifty yards; crowds of dirty, half-naked men and painted women; mandarins and palanquins preceded by gaudily-clad soldiers on horseback and followed by a yelling rabble of men and boys, armed with flags, spears, and sticks, on foot; Tartar ladies in mule litters, hung with bells, and bright cloths; dark, savage-looking Mongolians from the desert, leading caravans of camels; Chinamen in grey, green, or heliotrope silk, Chinamen in rags, and Chinamen in nothing at all; water-carriers, soldiers, porters, sellers of fruit and ice, the latter coated with dust, like everything else, and looking singularly uninviting; Chow-chow and sweetmeat sellers; camels, mules, ponies, oxen carts thronging the ruined roadway; a deafening noise of bells, cymbals, shouting and cursing; indecency, and filth everywhere, with a dusty, gloomy glare over everything, even on the brightest day, while the air everywhere around is poisoned with the hot, sickly smell

peculiar to Pekin. . . . We saw many curious sights, but most were of such a nature that I cannot describe them.

Harry de Windt
From Pekin to Calais by Land, 1889

WAYS THAT ARE DARK

The Tartar city contains the residences of all the grandees of the court, the halls of the Six Tribunals, the Hanlin College, several superb temples, a Mohammedan mosque, and many other public buildings. The principal streets are very long and wide, and contain numerous shops, as well as private houses; but they are not paved, which is a great inconvenience in wet weather; neither are they lighted at night: but as no one is allowed to be abroad after dark, unless on some very particular occasion, it is not of much importance that they should be so.

Miss Corner
*The History of China and India, Pictorial
and Descriptive*, c.1850

PASS RATE

Then there is the Examination Hall. The Government of China is a vast system of competitive examination tempered by bribery, and this *Kao Ch'ang* is its focus. It is a miniature city, with one wide artery down the middle, hundreds of parallel streets running from this on both sides, each street mathematically subdivided into houses, a big semblance of a palace at one end of the main street, and little elevated watch-towers here and there. . . . An idea of the part this Examination Hall plays in the contemporary life of China may be gained from the fact that in June, 1894, no fewer than 6,896 candidates presented themselves in Peking, of whom 320 were successful.

Henry Norman
The Far East, 1895

COLD COMFORT

The Chien-mên enceinte is a spot specially selected by poor homeless beggars, who find a comparative shelter within the walls and under the arch of the gateway after the doors have been closed. In winter many of these beggars succumb to the cold, for the thermometer often falls to 8 degrees (fahr.) below zero, and a cart comes round as a matter of course in the mornings to collect the frozen bodies of victims. It is considered by rich Chinese a specially lucrative act of virtue to provide coffins for these poor wretches, who would otherwise have to be buried without.

Lady Susan Townley
My Chinese Notebook, 1904

WASHING THE ELEPHANTS

During the time when the elephant stables still contained elephants, the elephants on the sixth day of the sixth month used to be led outside Hsüan Wu Men and into the moat to be washed, at which time spectators would stand lined-up like a wall. But later, because one elephant went mad and injured a man, they were no longer kept. Before the tenth year of Kuang Hsü (1884), however, they were still to be seen.

The elephant stables are inside Hsüan Wu Men, following the city wall westward, and were under the control of the Imperial Equipage Department. When spectators would enter, the elephants could make a sound through their trunks as of conch shells. And when the onlookers laid down some copper coins, the elephant keeper would make the elephants do tricks at his commands, they looking at him sidewise the while. Only after the full number of copper coins had been received, would they raise their trunks, incline their heads, and let forth a sound.

Tun Li-Ch'en
(trans. Derk Bodde)
Annual Customs and Festivals in Peking,
1936

TRUMPET VOLUNTARY

Having then seen them [the elephants], that was not enough, but
that they must shew several Tricks, and, at the command of the
Master of the Stable, they roared like a Tiger, so dismally loud that
their very Stable seemed to tremble! Others lowed like an Ox,
neighed like a Horse, and sung like a Canary Bird; but which was
most surprising of all, some of them imitated a Trumpet.

E. Ysbrants Ides
*Three Years Travels from Moscow Over-land
to China*, 1706

HOUSE CALL

In those days, when a minister's wife went out to pay calls or to
leave cards, she did so in a carriage with outriders. The coachman
and the grooms wore the so-called 'official' hats. There was a story
in Peking that Lady Jordan's outriders once made a mistake in the
address of some exalted personage, who was supposed to live
somewhere at the back of the Austrian glacis. Chinese servants
are often vague about addresses, and never know people by their
real names, preferring to invent a nickname based on physical
characteristics. Their idea of taking a Minister's wife to call on a
colleague of her husband's (in the Tartar City) is to proceed to
the neighbourhood where he is known to reside and then shout
down the street for information as to the whereabouts of the fat-
bellied foreign-devil with the glass eye. So it happened that, owing
to some muddle of her *ma-fus* [grooms], Lady Jordan's carriage
stopped by mistake at the door of an establishment of ill fame,
fronting the Austrian glacis, and known locally as 'the White
House.' The visiting-cards of His Britannic Majesty's Minister and
Lady Jordan were handed in. I wonder what the ladies of the house
thought about it?

Daniele Varè
Laughing Diplomat, 1938

THE LEISURED CLASSES

They [members of the Manchu Imperial clan] are not only studiously kept from all public business, but are held under such control, that the life of a common private gentleman is far more enviable. It has been the custom of several emperors, to expose their vices in long edicts to the whole nation, and to punish them like common criminals. They possess no liberty, no respectable establishment, no consideration. Whatever they possess may be taken from them on the least suspicion. To console them, however, under such disgrace, titles are conferred upon them, at once high sounding, and imposing. . . . It would be scarcely credible in Europe, that several of these illustrious personages live like porters, and hide their birth in order to cover their shame. If there is somebody amongst them, who shews a superior genius, and does not conciliate the imperial favour, he is sure to be degraded, and either thrown into prison, or sent into exile. Confined to Peking, and not even permitted to carry on a free intercourse with the mandarins, without any occupation, they indulge in a life of vicious ease, and render themselves odious. It is then not uncommon to punish them for their effeminacy, and transport them to the deserts of Mantchouria, that they may again inure themselves to a hardy life.

Rev. Charles Gutzlaff
China Opened, 1838

THE MANCHU PAYROLL

An imperial relative of the first rank receives . . . 10,000 taëls annually from the exchequer, with a large allowance of rice, and as many as three hundred and more servants. As the multiplication of these expensive idlers would soon ruin the Government, their rank descends by one degree in each generation, until after five descents their heirs retain the simple privilege of wearing the yellow girdle, with a bare subsistence. . . .

The expense to the state of a *wâng* [prince] of the first rank is about 60,000 taëls, or £20,000 annually, and this diminishes through the several grades down to the simple inheritors of the yellow girdle, who receive only three taëls a month, and two sacks of rice. But they are allowed 100 taëls when they marry, and 120 for a funeral; from which (says Serra) they take occasion to maltreat their wives, because, when they have killed one, they receive the allowance for her interment, as well as the dowry of the new wife, whom they take immediately!

John Francis Davis
The Chinese, 1836

HOLDING COURT

Besides the Seven Councils in Peking there are the six famous Courts, among whom all the Business of the Empire is divided. The third of these Courts is Li Pu, the Court of Rites and Ceremonies, whose care it is to examine the Doctrines that are preach'd, the Business of Embassadors, and to regulate Court-Funerals. The Court of the Mathematicks is subordinate to this; and here our Cause was try'd.

The Ground each Court takes up is very much. The Shape and Structure of them is all the same, all the difference is, that some are bigger than others. They all look towards the South with their Backs towards the North where the Emperor resides. Each Court has three Doors, on which are painted horrible Giants, ghastly to look at, all to terrify the Multitude. That in the middle is very large, and none but Mandarines, or Persons of great Note come in at it. The two little ones are on the sides of it, at which those that have Causes depending, and the Commonalty come in. Next is a great Court big enough to bait Bulls in. In it are three Causways, each answering to one of the Doors; but that in the middle is rais'd above a yard higher than the others, with a stone Arch, and another Gate in the middle of it. On the sides are a vast number of Rooms, under Piazza's, for Clerks, Sollicitors, and other Officers. A Temple is never wanting. Opposite to the Doors are very orderly great Halls, and within them others as good; Courts are kept in both of them.

Domingo Navarrete
*The Travels and Controversies of Friar
Domingo Navarrete*, 1676

TRADESMAN'S ENTRANCE

The Chinese Foreign Office, the Tsung-Li Yamên, is almost as bad a place for receiving in as our old building in Downing Street. In order to be met at the great gates, which on grand occasions is *de rigueur*, we have to pass into the reception-room through the back kitchen, where we see all the little dainties which we are to eat being cooked by very dirty natives.

A. B. Freeman-Mitford
The Attache at Peking, 1866 pub. 1900

POLITICAL FOOTBALL

On my return to Pekin some years later I accompanied Sir R. Alcock to the Tsung-li-yamen to discuss a project for a code regulating commercial differences between Chinese and foreigners with the Ministers. The Tsung-li-yamen is not a Foreign Office as we understand Departments of State so called in Europe. It is simply a Committee or Board of Ministers taken or selected from either of the State departments to discuss foreign affairs with foreign Ministers. Prince Kung is, or rather was, the Chairman or President of this Committee. I cannot say I was struck with the magnificence of the apartment set apart for the reception of Foreign Ministers and the discussion with them of foreign affairs. Indeed I have a shrewd suspicion that this building was designedly selected, first because it is at some considerable distance from all the departments of State, secondly because it is in an infamous state of repair, very small and inconvenient, and only approachable through streets which have very much the appearance of being the back slums of Pekin, and thirdly because it shows the estimation in which Foreign Ministers are held and the utter unimportance of foreign affairs, when so poor accommodation is thought good enough to receive the one and discuss the other. . . . Perhaps I am over-sensitive on the score of being insulted and am not quick at gulping down what I conceive to be an intentional rudeness; but if I had been Her Majesty's Minister I should on my first introduction to the Tsung-li-yamen have declined altogether transacting anything like business therein, except that of kicking the Committee all round.

Sir Edmund Hornby
An Autobiography, 1929

MATERIAL ADVANTAGE

The ruins of the old Examination Hall may be surveyed from the walls a few hundred yards north of the observatory. This structure, known to the Chinese as the Kung Yuan, was built by the Ming Emperor, Yung Loh, who moved the national capital from Nanking to Peking early in the 14th century. . . .

All of the Legations, after the Boxer trouble, were in serious need of repairs and bricks were at a premium, so the examination hall was torn apart and a vast quantity of its bricks and other building materials were used in rebuilding the various legations. Nothing remains but a labyrinth of low walls and a few stone foundations of pavilions.

Thos. Cook and Son
Peking and the Overland Route, 1920

SKY-GAZING

There is in Peking a very noted Tower, call'd of the Mathematicks; in it are sundry very antient Instruments, with admirable graving on Brass-plates; with them they observe the Eclipses, and other

Observations belonging to this Science. Some Mathematicians always watch atop of it, who observe the Motions of the Stars, and remark any thing particular that appears in the Sky, whereof the next day they give the Emperor an Account. When anything unusual occurs, the Astrologers meet, and make their Judgments whether it portends Good or Evil to the Imperial Family.

Domingo Navarrete
The Travels and Controversies of Friar
Domingo Navarrete, 1665

TREATY BENEFIT

Kublai removed his capital from Kara Korom in Mongolia to Peking. He built walls like those which still surround the city, and established on the walls an observatory which is preserved to this day. Until 1900, two of the astronomical instruments constructed by Kublai were still to be seen in this observatory, but the Germans removed them to Potsdam after the suppression of the Boxers. I understand they have been restored in accordance with one of the provisions of the Treaty of Versailles. If so, this was probably the most important benefit which that treaty secured to the world.

Bertrand Russell
The Problem of China, 1922

COURTYARD DWELLINGS

Such a court was a home which fitted man as comfortably as the cocoon fits the caterpillar or the shell the snail. Though it was a square of perfect living space in all except the coldest months, I think late spring and early summer saw it at its best. When the fine weather came, its walls seemed to change their significance; they were no longer the outer walls of the houses, but became the inner walls of the court, and then the courtyard existed simply as a cube of the marvellously liquid North China air. The floor of the cube was a neatly swept stretch of hard-beaten earth, dappled with the trembling shade of leaves. Its sides were the cool grey walls of the buildings, varied by the red-and-white patterns of the latticed windows. It was garnished by rows of potted flowers and shrubs, and from the green branches of the trees and flowering vines, which seemed afloat in its aerial solidity, cages of singing birds were hung.

After a while it seemed to me that the Peking courtyard was not only an architectural contrivance; it was also a state of mind, a private world to be shaped as its owner inclined.

Graham Peck
Through China's Wall, 1945

MODERN TIMES

There is no character to the selection of plants and courtyard decorations, you will say. But, no, the Chinese have their own ideas of a scheme of floral decoration. For summer, it provides for pomegranate trees in pairs, two, four, or six flanking a big pottery aquarium in which, it is ordained, goldfish should be kept. A saying goes: 'Matshed, fish bowl and pomegranate trees; a fat watch-dog and a fatter slave-girl' as the Chinese describe their proverbial courtyard decorations. Mr. Wu does belong to that school of thought, but he is modernistic enough to discard the slave-girl idea.

H. Y. Lowe
The Adventures of Wu, 1940

EXCELLENT LIKENESSES

The people of China of all mankind have the greatest skill and taste in the arts. This is a fact generally admitted; it has been remarked in books by many authors, and has been much dwelt upon. As regards painting, indeed, no nation, whether of Christians or others, can come up to the Chinese; their talent for this art is something quite extraordinary. I may mention among astonishing illustrations of this talent of theirs, what I have witnessed myself, viz., that whenever I have happened to visit one of their cities, and to return to it after a while, I have always found my own likeness and those of my companions painted on the walls, or exhibited in the bazaars. On one occasion that I visited the Emperor's own city, in going to the imperial palace with my comrades I passed through the bazaar of the painters; we were all dressed after the fashion of Irák. In the evening on leaving the palace I passed again through the same bazaar, and there I saw my own portrait and the portraits of my companions painted on sheets of paper and exposed on the walls. We all stopped to examine the likenesses, and everybody found that of his neighbour to be excellent!

Ibn Batuta
The Travels of Ibn Batuta in Bengal and China, c.1347

BLUE TROWSERS

Near the wall of the imperial town—there is a row of doors—near a door there stands a small girl—she is really nice—with a shirt of white cloth and trowsers of blue cloth—she wears round earrings—and has a great chignon on her head—on the face she has rubbed red powder—and white powder—who shall be my little bridegroom?

Trans. Guido A. Vitale
Pekinese Rhymes, 1896

BOXER MEMORIAL

The Chinese Government erected an expiatory monument, in the form of an arch of white marble (*pai-lo*), in honour of the German Minister, von Ketteler [killed during the Boxer uprising]. It was put up over the Hata Mên street, at the point where the Minister had been killed. The Republican Government of China hastened to demolish the arch, when they saw fit to join the Allies and declared war on Germany, in 1917. The arch was then reconstructed elsewhere, after the inscription (in Chinese, German and Latin) had been removed. But even before it was taken down, and passers-by might still read how Baron von Ketteler had been traitorously done to death, the actual value of this monument as an object lesson was doubtful. If one asked one's rickshaw-coolie, for example, to whom that monument had been erected, he was almost sure to answer that the *pai-lo* had been set up to honour the memory of the Chinaman who had killed the German Minister.

Daniele Varè
The Last of the Empresses, 1936

THE MINISTER'S WRITER'S SPECTACLES

One morning Old Lew came in [to the British Legation, where he was employed as a writer], flushed with indignant excitement, to say that he had been robbed of his spectacles by a fob-snipper (=pickpocket, but the Chinese hang their various purses, pouches, and cases to the belt), and wished the Foreign Office to be informed at once. This seemed rather a large order, but we sent him in to interview Sir Thomas (then Mr.) Wade himself, feeling on our own part much like a couple of schoolboys who despatch a greenhorn into a fierce grocer, in order to enquire the price of pigeon's milk or strap-oil. To our surprise he succeeded in his mission, having explained to the Minister's satisfaction that it was customary with all 'genuine' thieves to take their plunder to the Captain-General's *yamén* for three days, so that, in case any person of influence should complain, it might be rescued from the hotchpot, in which the police shared. Accordingly, a note was sent in to His Imperial Highness, Prince Kung 'and others,' couched much as follows:

'H. M. Minister has received a petition from his writer Lew to the effect that at nine o'clock this morning, as he was passing the Palace Gate near Coal Hill to come to his work, a fob-snipper snatched hold of his crystal spectacles and made off. H. M. Minister opines that violent robberies of this sort under the very "wheels of the chariot" cannot possibly meet with the toleration of H. E. the Captain-General; moreover, Mr. Lew cannot do his work without those spectacles; and he therefore begs that the Prince and Ministers will kindly bring the matter to the notice of the high functionary named. He takes this opportunity to renew the assurances of his highest consideration.'

McLeavy Brown and I lost no opportunity during the day in 'chaffing' Old Lew, who, however, adopted a 'he-laughs-best-who-laughs-last' attitude, and nodded or snorted defiantly, as much as to say: 'A time will come.' Sure enough that very evening, or the next morning, a note arrived from the Tsung-li *Yamên* running somewhat in this fashion:

'They who respectfully open out in reply, beg to state that they have received etc., etc. That in broad daylight a fob-snipper should extend his gall to such dimensions as to snatch the spectacles of H. M. Minister's writer is indeed a practice which cannot be allowed to grow. Exclusively of having sent on the petition to H. E. the Captain-General of the Nine Gates, requesting him to instruct the division, to command the etc., etc., one and all to *ch'a* (enquire) and to *ts'wei* (hurry) [everybody everywhere]——. Just as these lines were being written, lo and behold! a note is received from the Captain-General, stating that one of his gendarmes had found a pair of spectacles on the ground, and had honestly brought them to the office, etc., etc.'

In concocting their little stories, the Chinese nearly always manage to leave something out: in this case, I think it was, they omitted to say why the Captain-General had spontaneously sent to the Foreign Office. I forget exactly how it was put, but the principle is there in any case, and the letter is on record too (unless the 'Boxers' burnt it); so that it is immaterial what particular form of make-believe was employed. Old Lew got his spectacles, whilst Brown and I accepted a second place in knowledge of mankind.

E. H. Parker
John Chinaman and a Few Others, 1901

TIME AND THE BELL

Another order of ideas is embodied in the Drum Tower and the
Bell Tower, once the centre of Khan Baligh, and still so strongly
reminiscent of mediæval alarms and excursions. Much hard
stone went into their making. They were built for hard men in
the bitter days of conquest. They were watch-towers whence to
keep an eye on the citizens given to subterraneous discontent,
to mark for them the hours of their rising and their lying down.
Now they are given over to crows, forlorn caretakers, and the
occasional gaze of hurried tourists.

A. E. Grantham
Pencil Speakings from Peking, 1918

WHITE PAGODA TEMPLE

In the Temple of the White Pagoda the altars are quite empty,
the priests gone, and the worshippers. There are no candles,
no incense-sticks, no offerings, no prayers; the red lacquer
peels off, and the gilding. Crows settle their loves and their
disputes round the lofty stupa; trees shoot up between the slabs
of polished marble which once made it a glittering sepulchre
for the two thousand clay models of pagodas, the twenty
precious pearls, the five sacred manuscripts believed to protect
the neighbourhood from evil, and which actually did lure
strong men away from active life to become their consecrated
priests—secured rich endowments from long lines of emperors
and fervent worship from many generations of believers. Yet
who cares about them now? So much is all power a matter of
faith.

In what is left of the sacred courtyards, fairs are held to
supply the household wants of common folk—indestructible in
their extreme humility—brooms, combs, scissors, spoons,
brushes, peanuts heaped up in little piles, the frailest of toys,
the cheapest of glass jewellery, displayed round the pedestals
on which huge marble tortoises bear the weight of memorial

tablets, beautifully carved with an inscription nobody now troubles to decipher.

And the great Buddha, utterly forgotten by the living, sits in mournful state with his eighteen Lohans, dead over two thousand years; gazes into the cobwebby silence, as if waiting for an echo of all the fervour of faith and prayer that once poured itself out before him here, as if wondering at all the dust and dimness and oblivion that is gathering around him now.

A. E. Grantham
Pencil Speakings from Peking, 1918

COOKING THE BOOKS

There is the Hu-pu, or Treasury . . . in the street to which it gives its name. Tribute, taxes, custom houses, the grain and rice of the Government are all under its control, also the treasure of the Empire and the Mints. A Manchu official, specially appointed to pay the pensions upon which his countrymen subsist—till lately no Manchu was allowed to engage in business, or try to earn his own living in any way—is attached to this office, which was burnt down in 1903 for the third time in eight years. On the last occasion the accounts were saved by two young men attached to the US. Legation, who did not feel sure afterwards that any one was glad of this.

Mrs Archibald Little
Round About My Peking Garden, 1905

UNAMERICAN ACTIVITY

At night the fact of all the gates being locked and barred against the bandits, as in the European Middle Ages, in no way impeded the general gaiety of restaurants, streets and theatres, induced no depressing sense of being imprisoned for your own safety —though, in this connection, I recollect an American visitor enquiring of a friend of mine, resident in Peking, whether it was

true that the city gates were shut every evening at nine, and, on
this statement being confirmed, exclaiming, 'Well, I can tell you
here and now, we wouldn't stand for it in Detroit!'

Osbert Sitwell
Escape With Me!, 1939

A BREAKFAST INVITATION

We were introduced to the lay brother of the [Lama] monastery,
the confidant of the Grand Lama, and factotum in all secular
affairs. A fine, hard-headed, swarthy complexioned, rough-and-
ready burly fellow he was, and he received us with his rude native
hospitality, showing us into the room, and making us sit on the
very *kang* used by the absent Bhudda.

When . . . we rose to leave, the old fellow, on hospitable thoughts
intent, protested, seized our hats, and by main force pushed us
back to the seat of the Grand Lama. To keep us in play he put fruit
before us, but we did not know what it was all about until our
breakfast was brought in in a large basin. It consisted of about
twenty pounds of plain boiled mutton, without bread, rice,
potatoes, or vegetables of any kind. All we had to eat with it was a
solution of salt, soy, vinegar, and sugar. Eat we must, there was no
help for it, and we honestly set ourselves to do as full justice to the
unsavoury meal as we were capable of, although we had a good
breakfast waiting us at home, that is, at our restaurant, our host all
the while standing over us like a taskmaster to keep us up to our
work. When no entreaties would make us eat more, with looks and
expressions of pitying regret, our uncouth friend showed us how
Mongols eat mutton by taking out a good-sized piece with his
fingers, and dropping it down his throat. Then turning to the
youngsters who crowded the room he pitched lumps of mutton
to each of them, who, in like manner, gobbled it like hungry
eagles. Our reception at the Lama temple gave us a fair idea of
Mongol hospitality and habits, and impressed us favourably with
the former.

Alexander Michie
The Siberian Overland Route, 1864

A PITY

[At the time of the Allied occupation in 1900] no less than ten
conflagrations were seen in the Imperial City, and the great Lama
temple—the most infamous place in Pekin, where, even in times
of peace, foreigners were always insulted and shockingly ill-treated
by the Buddhist priests—was entered by looting parties, who
scattered the valuable library said to be contained within its walls.
This was a pity.

A. Henry Savage-Landor
China and the Allies, 1901

DISAPPOINTING

Here [Great Buddha's Hall in the Lama Temple] used to be kept a large number of idols, especially of the kind called *Huan Hsi Fo* (Joyful Buddhas), in all stages of crude animalism, said to be symbolical of fecundity. These have now been moved to other places. The lama guides make a great to-do about showing these figures to tourists and demand an extra tip before doing so. Visitors are recommended to save their dollars. The figures are very crude indeed and, as a pornographic exhibition, disappointing.

L. C. Arlington and William Lewison
In Search of Old Peking, 1935

YOUNG BLADES

Had there been any of what is called 'rank, beauty and fashion' at Peking, its favourite promenade would have been the wall. There we found peace and quiet—for the public invaded it not—and comparative immunity from the demon dust. It was wonderful to look over the great city—the two great cities—to gaze upon the roofs of the inviolable Palace Grounds, and wonder what mysteries they were hiding. At the southern corner of the wall were the beautiful astronomical instruments, masterpieces in the interest of which European science entered into a happy alliance with Chinese art—the great Emperor Kang Hsi with the Jesuit Father Verbiest—in order to furnish after two hundred and fifty years a prey for Prussian burglary. At intervals rose the great fantastic towers, threatening, cruel—suggesting unspeakable horrors; for in one of them, as we were told, dwelt the chief executioner, like Mauger the headsman in George Cruikshank's etching, watching over the Five Lords—broad choppers like butchers' instruments, on the handle of each of which is carved a grotesque human head.

Those who have wandered on the walls in the witching hours of night are said to have heard the sound of weird and unearthly strains, songs in which the Five Lords are wont to celebrate the bloody deeds in which for centuries and more they have played their part. Pray that you be not dealt with by the Benjamin of the

Five Lords, for he is still young and skittish, not more than two hundred years old, loving to dally and toy with the heads of his victims, unlike his more reverend elders who will strike off your head at one blow, impressed with the serious nature of their duties.

Lord Redesdale
(A. B. Freeman-Mitford)
Memories, 1915

ON THE BEAT

The police is singularly strict. It is indeed stretched to an extent unknown I believe in any other city, and strongly marks the jealousy of the Government, and their unceasing apprehension of danger. At night all the streets are shut up by barricadoes at each end and a guard is constantly patrolling between them so that no person can pass after a certain hour without assigning satisfactory reasons or being liable to punishment if disapproved of. A number of watchmen are also stationed at short distances who carry a rattle and every two or three minutes proclaim their vigilance by the exercise of their instrument. One or two of these guardians of the peace had their stands so near to my house that I could not sleep a wink for the first three or four nights.

Lord Macartney
Journal, 7 October 1793

POLICE METHODS

So summary is the mode in which the objects of the police are effected, that it is no light matter to be once in their hands. The Chinese emphatically express their sense of this unfortunate condition by the popular phrase, 'The meat is on the chopping-block.'

John Francis Davis
The Chinese, 1836

DEATH BY DROWNING

The Tartar City is pierced by broad roads running at right angles to the walls. From them a network of smaller lanes leads off, usually extremely narrow and always unsavoury, being used as the dumping-ground of all the filth and refuse of the neighbouring houses. The main streets even are unpaved and ill-kept. The centre portion alone is occasionally repaired in a slovenly fashion, apparently by heaping on it fresh earth taken from the sides, which have consequently become mere ditches eight or nine feet below the level of the middle causeway and the narrow footpaths along the front of the houses. After heavy rain these fill with water and are transformed into rushing rivers. Occasionally on dark nights a cart falls into them, the horse unguided by a sleepy driver, and the occupants are drowned. Such a happening in the principal thoroughfares of a large and populous city seems incredible. I could scarcely believe it until I was once obliged almost to swim my pony across a main street with the water up to the saddle-flaps, and this after only a few hours' rain.

Capt. Gordon Casserly
The Land of the Boxers, 1903

CHAPTER 5

THE LEGATION QUARTER

My first impression of the foreign Legations in Peking was one of astonishment at their size. I could not help asking: 'Why so enormous?' If our embassy in London had been on the same scale it would have included all the houses in Grosvenor Square as far down as Claridges.

DANIELE VARÈ
Laughing Diplomat, 1938

The story of the Legation Quarter in Peking falls into two parts, divided by the violent episode of the Boxer uprising and the Siege of the Legations in 1900.

The 1860 Treaty of Tientsin gave foreign nations the right to establish permanent diplomatic representation in Peking. Most (there were never very many—eleven in 1900) chose to set up in the same general area, in the southeast part of the Tartar City. Because, in the arcane world of diplomatic practice, China was regarded as a 'power with limited interests' (as distinct from the 'great powers' of Europe), these establishments were called legations, not embassies, and the foreign representatives ministers, not ambassadors.

It was this small community which became a focus for anti-foreign feeling at the time of the Boxers. The bizarre episode of the fifty-five-day siege, and the relief of the legations by the forces of the eight allies, focussed the world's attention on Peking. Among the more lively accounts is that of Mary Hooker, who as Polly Conduit Smith, was the (possibly somewhat regretful) guest of the United States First Secretary at the time of the conflict. The destruction and looting that followed the relief was less extensively reported, although the renegade customs official, Putnam Weale, made some widely resented efforts in that direction.

Asserting the rights of conquest after 1900, the allied representatives set themselves up considerably more comfortably than had been the case previously. Only Sir Robert Hart, the Inspector-General of Customs, missed out. As an employee of the Chinese Government, he was forced to surrender his rose garden to the greater glory of the Italian Legation. All the missions expanded their premises. Moreover, they set up their own walled enclave within the Tartar City, excluding the Chinese and placing armed guards on the gates. The Legation Quarter became a self-administering, exclusive island of foreigners.

When, in 1928, the Chinese Government decided to move the national capital to Nanking, the foreign ministers made the surprising decision not to accompany the government to which they were accredited. China's leaders would in due course, they thought, see the error of their ways. And so, in due course, they did, although by then they were different leaders, and the old Legation Quarter had largely ceased to exist.

MELTING INTO THE LANDSCAPE

It was a far cry from the well-upholstered comfort of a European Embassy to the diplomatic life of Peking. There, the rude virtues of the frontier were still in demand. Conditions of work, with no operas, no duchesses, no levees, scarcely merited the name of diplomacy at all. A diplomat tries to melt into the landscape of any capital where he may happen to be, as an Arctic fox turns its fur white in winter. But at Peking! He could not be expected to grow a pigtail.

E. V. Kiernan
British Diplomacy in China 1880–1885,
1939

THE PRICE OF A HAIRCUT

It is not only the health and physical enjoyment of their sojourn that people remember wistfully in after-years. Peking society—at any rate, till quite recently—had also its special charm. The capital not being 'open to trade,' the community practically consisted of the diplomatic corps and the inspectorate-general of Chinese maritime customs, amounting in all to about a hundred, of whom about fifteen were ladies. The social atmosphere was as genial as it was refined. Old friends met again who had last known each other in Rome or Washington, Vienna or The Hague. Outside his *chancellerie*, no one was Russian or British or Spanish, but only one of a little band of foreigners isolated in a semi-hostile country . . . A talented student might be, for the time, a greater personage in the *salon* than a dull plenipotentiary, and a brilliant cotillon leader eclipse even a *chambellan de l'Empereur* (but gouty) while the music lasted. Neither was there any incentive to vain display where ranks and incomes were so clearly defined. If any stranger were in doubt as to his exact status, it was only necessary to send for the old Peking barber and see what position he was assigned in that artist's rigid scale of charges: hair cutting, $1 for a plenipotentiary and envoy extraordinary, 80 cents for a *chargé d'affaires*, 30 for an *attaché*, 20 cents for a student, and 10 for a missionary, with all intermediate and subtle graduations.

Archibald Colquhoun
Overland to China, 1900

PICK-A-BACK

Foot-passengers pick their way along the shop fronts, by an uneven track beaten in the mud or dust, as the case may be. During the summer rains these thoroughfares become sloughs of unimaginable despond. Men and mules have been drowned in the cesspools which form between the houses and the embankment, and even the street in which the foreign legations are situated is not much better . . . Fishing 'waders' would form a useful adjunct to evening dress for any one rash enough to venture out on foot when the rains are at their worst. A Russian *chargé* has been known to ride out to dine with his United States colleague 'pick-a-back' on a Cossack of the Escort.

Archibald Colquhoun
Overland to China, 1900

PRIVATE PURPOSES

The sunny side of a legation wall, at noon, within two feet of a frequented path, is by the Pekinese considered sufficiently private for any purpose.

Archibald Colquhoun
Overland to China, 1900

SPECIAL PUNISHMENT

The [British] Legation is really deserving of some attempts at description. Not but what it must be to those who live in it a species of prison. I would suggest that the appointment of Minister to China should be converted into a special punishment for diplomatic criminals—men who have systematically neglected to endorse or number their despatches, or who have insisted upon having an opinion of their own, or who have persisted in sending home true reports of what they have seen and heard with their own eyes and ears, and not reports written to please the Cabinet for the

time being at home. Men, in short, whose whole official life has been a terror to their employers—for such men no one can entertain sympathy, and Pekin would be a fitting penal settlement where they might ponder over their mis-spent life, and if young and of herculean constitution might even live long enough to repent.

Sir Edmund Hornby
An Autobiography, c.1870 pub. 1929

HOME SWEET HOME

If in those days you were to pay a surprise visit to the Japanese legation you would find the minister in a *kimono*, drinking *saké* and eating raw fish—very unlike the correct official who, smothered in gold lace, would, a few hours later, welcome you in his stiff, Europeanized drawing-room. A similar visit to your Russian friend would, nine times out of ten, catch him in a frowsy flannel shirt, playing a masterly game of Russian whist with rather greasy cards, the atmosphere, generally, one of Russian cigarette-smoke, *vodka*, and yellow-backed decadent French novels.

Archibald Colquhoun
Overland to China, 1900

BRILLIANT COMPANIES

All these official European residences are maintained on a scale of considerable splendor, and the sudden transfers from the noisome streets to the beautiful parks and garden compounds, the drawing-rooms and ball-rooms, with their brilliant companies living and amusing themselves exactly as in Europe, are among the greatest contrasts and surprises of Peking. The picked diplomats of all Europe are sent to Peking, lodged sumptuously, paid high salaries, and sustained by the certainty of promotions and rewards after a useful term at Peking—all but the American minister, who is crowded in small rented premises, is paid about a fourth as much as the other envoys, and, coming untrained to his career, has the cheerful certainty of being put out of office as soon as he has learned his business and another President is elected, his stay in Peking on a meager salary a sufficient incident in itself, leading to nothing further.

E. R. Skidmore
China: the Long-Lived Empire, 1900

BLACKBALLED

In general, none know less of Chinese character and life than those officially acquainted with the Emperor of China. No Chinese official dares maintain intimate social relations with the legations, even those who have appreciated and keenly enjoyed the social life and official hospitalities of London, Paris, Tokio, and Washington relapsing into strange conservatism and churlishness, the usual contemptuous attitude of the Manchu official, when they return to Peking. Even then they are denounced to the throne for 'intimacy with foreigners,' blackballed and cold-shouldered at their clubs, and persecuted into retirement.

E. R. Skidmore
China: The Long-Lived Empire, 1900

PENT-UP EMOTIONS

On a day fixed beforehand, the Chinese ministers, presidents of the various boards, and others—forming a formidable column of sedan-chairs and outriders—ran the gantlet of all the legations in one afternoon. No light undertaking this! At each they were regaled with choice vintages and cakes, of which etiquette compelled them in every case to partake. However soberly they might set out for the Belgian legation, the first to be visited, they arrived rumpled and flushed at that of the United States, at the other end of the line. All ceremonial, all stiffness had by that time dissolved, the habitual masks had been discarded, and the real men came forth from underneath. At this stage the Confucians were to be tickled by a straw. Solemn viceroys would evince a disposition to change hats with their foreign hosts, and consequential ex-governors of provinces as large as England would find a source of innocent merriment in the elastic properties of the cords of military epaulettes, which they would pull out and then release, amid peals of laughter. Sweets, comfits, and (one lady maintained) even curios, were stuffed into capacious satin boots— for the children—while occasionally a president of the board of ceremonies would stumble into an alcove and give disastrous vent to his pent-up emotions.

Archibald Colquhoun
Overland to China, 1900

ON WITH THE DANCE

Winter was the season for every sort of gaiety—dinners, balls, concerts, theatricals following in continuous succession, which derived additional piquancy from the surroundings, so far removed from the commonplace of Western cities. For instance, the setting out, in sedan-chair or mule-cart, for the ball; the ladies, unrecognizable bundles of Tibetan sheepskins, terminating in ungainly 'Mongol socks'— loose top-boots of white felt worn over the dancing-shoes, a necessary protection when the thermometer stands below zero. Then the fantastic lantern-lights, revealing for an instant, as one jolted along in ruts and hollows, small impressionist pictures framed in darkness; a moaning beggar curled under a wall, two snarling pariahs, a deserted alley—to be as instantly swallowed up again in shadow. Finally, the entrance, straight from out this medieval horror and darkness into the warmth, light, and music of a ballroom—a hundred tapers reflected from trembling

PEKING.

LEGATION QUARTER'S
OFFICIAL RICKSHAW TARIFF.

as approved by the Diplomatic Body on the 1st of August, 1911.

(*Tourists are earnestly requested not to exceed this tariff.*)

	1 coolie	2 coolies
BY THE RUN		
Up to ¼ of an hour	$0.10	$0.15
Up to ½ of an hour	0.20	0.30
BY THE HOUR		
The first hour	0.25	0.30
Each successive hour	0.20	0.25
Six hours	0.90	1.10
Ten hours	1.50	1.80
SPECIAL RATES FOR		
Run to Temple of Heaven (Tien Tan)	0.25	0.35
Run to Four Eastern Pailous (Tung Si Pai Lou)	0.25	0.35
Run to Pei Tang Cathedral (Pei Tang Tse)	0.40	0.55
Run to Kalgan Railway Station (Hsi Chih Men)	0.50	0.65
Run to Zoological Garden (Nung Shi Shih Yen Chang)	0.60	0.75
Run to Yellow Temple (Huang Sze, Hwang Kung)	0.60	0.75
Stoppage at and return from above places to be calculated BY THE HOUR.		
SPECIAL RATES FOR		
Run to Summer Palace (Wan Shou Shan) and back including time of stoppage at Summer Palace.	2.00	2.30

Hotel Autos $ 4 for 1st hour in City and $ 3 for each succeding hour. Auto trips outside Peking from $ 18 to $ 25 for time consumed or day.

chandeliers in the shining parquet, diamonds flashing, the stream of dancers swaying to the rhythm of the waltz, the ripple of merry laughter . . . who in this scene of fairyland could spare a thought to the frozen squalor of the sleeping city outside, in whose streets, each winter dawn, men are found dead of starvation and cold?

Archibald Colquhoun
Overland to China, 1900

ASTONISHED

I should be astonished to learn that while the Chinese Minister in London was preparing his communication his Legation was under a constant fire from British troops, yet it is in a situation analogous to this that the Foreign Representatives at Peking find themselves placed.

Sir Claude Macdonald
Despatch to Foreign Office, 8 August 1900

IMAGINARY BULLETS

June 23 [1900]

This afternoon we were in Mrs Coltman's room, and her sweet baby was asleep in a funny, old-fashioned, high-backed crib. Although the sound of exploding bullets was to be heard outside the house, we were much startled to feel one—you can't see them, they come so fast—enter the room, hit the headpiece of the baby's crib, detaching it from the main part, and bury itself in the opposite wall. An inch lower and it would have cut through the baby's brain. His mother picked him up, and all of us flew into a room on the other side of the house, where we felt we would be free from shot, at any rate coming from that direction.

We were accompanied by the wife of the Chief, Mrs Conger, conspicuous for her concise manner, and an open follower of Mrs Eddy. She earnestly assured us that it was ourselves, and not the times, which were troublous and out of tune, and insisted that while there was an appearance of warlike hostilities, it was really in our own brains. Going further, she assured us that there was no bullet entering the room; it was again but our receptive minds which falsely lead us to believe such to be the case. With these calming (!) admonitions she retired, and I can honestly say that we were more surprised by her extraordinary statement than we were by the very material bullet which had driven us from the room.

Mary Hooker
Behind the Scenes in Peking, 1900

A MOTHER'S LOVE

July 31 [1900]

M. Pichon, the French Minister, today had a very nice telegram sent him from France, saying: 'You are unanimously voted to have the Legion of Honour. Your mother sends her love and greeting, and 15,000 Frenchmen are on their way to your support.'

Mary Hooker
Behind the Scenes in Peking, 1900

CHAMPAGNE SUPPER

24 June 1900

Today my midday tiffin consisted of a rude curry made of pony meat; and in the evening, because I was busy and had no time to search out other things, I ate once again of pony—this time cold! I will frankly confess that I was not enchanted, and had it not been for the Monopole of which there are great stores in the hotel and the club—a thousand cases in all, I believe—I should have collapsed.

B. L. Putnam Weale
Indiscreet Letters From Peking, 1906

THE RELIEF!

Hark! what is that we hear!
  List, friends!—and list again.
Hark! Now 'tis drawing near—
  Tramping across the plain.

Men! that's no Chinese crowd,
  Men! that's no *heathen* roar!
Hark! Now the tramping's loud—
  Christ! They're at our door!

List to the bugle's blast!
  Rescued by armies brave!
Thank God—they're here—at last,
  Allies are here—to save!

Revd Frederick Brown
From Tientsin to Peking with the Allied
Forces, 1902

OORAH!

The first man through the green door opposite the Counsellor's house was a Sikh. He rushed up to the lawn and then toured the compound: an unforgettable sight, naked to the waist . . . He kept waving his rifle and shouting: 'Oorah!'

Mrs W. P. Ker
Quoted in Varè
The Last of the Empresses, 1936

NAKED DEPARTURE

I have lost everything and possess only two summer suits . . . Man eventually departs naked, of course, but *this* nudity is a bit too previous, confound it!

Sir Robert Hart
Letter to E. B. Drew, 18 August 1900

SAFEKEEPING

August 18 [1900]

Yesterday a very animated generals' conference was held, the great question being whether there should be a unanimous effort to stop all looting and sacking, or whether it should be continued. The Japanese, French, and Russians were absolutely *pro*; English and Americans, *con*, the latter having the strictest orders from President McKinley against any looting. The English, although giving their vote for no looting, added they should continue to place 'in safe-keeping all valuable things' found in the district given them to police.

Mary Hooker
Behind the Scenes in Peking, 1910

CHERCHEZ LE GENERAL

September 1900

What immense quantities of things have been taken! Every place of importance, indeed, has been picked as clean as a bone. Now that the road is well open, dozens of amateurs, too, from the ends of the earth have been pouring in to buy up everything they can. The armies have thus become mere bands of traders eternally selling or exchanging, comparing or pricing, transporting or shipping. Every man of them wishes to know whether there is a fortune in a collection of old porcelain or merely a competence, and whether it is true that a long robe of Amur river sables, when the furs are perfect and undyed, fetch so many hundreds of pounds on the London market. There are official military auctions going on everywhere, where huge quantities of furs and silks and other things come under the hammer. Yet it is noticed that the very best things always disappear before they can be publicly sold. A phrase has been invented to meet the case. '*Cherchez le général*,' people say.

B. L. Putnam Weale
Indiscreet Letters from Peking, 1906

BIDDING AT AUCTION

When I entered the gate of the British Legation a busy scene presented itself. An auction was in full swing in the first *ting'rh*, or open pavilion, in front of the Minister's house. A collection of Chinese things lay spread out on the tiled floor, from silks and furs to blackwood furniture and antique bronzes. All the legation people, amongst them Lady MacDonald [wife of the Minister] sitting on a chair, and a number of other English men and women thronged around this display of valuable articles, taking them up and examining them and discussing their age and merits. There was an atmosphere of happiness and enjoyment. A sergeant held up each article in turn, and the bidding was lively, but prices were low, there was evidently a glut in the market. An officer noted down all the sums in a register, the proceeds going to his regiment's prize fund. While this was going on two Chinese mule carts drove in escorted by some Indian soldiers under an officer. They were heavily loaded with more Chinese valuables destined for auction. This had a bad influence on the bidding.

William Oudendyk
Ways and By-Ways in Diplomacy, 1939

GALLANTRY

When the French general was remonstrated with by his allied colleagues about the frequent occurrence of disgraceful outrages upon women, he replied: 'It is impossible to restrain the gallantry of the French soldier.'

George Lynch
The War of the Civilisations, 1901

MAKING THE BEST OF IT

All the street doors were securely barred, all shops were closed, there was hardly a man walking in the streets; those whom I saw glided stealthily along, pressing closely to the sides of the houses. The Chinese are practical people; the sack of the town with all its horrors was . . . not a surprise to the populace. They had to make the best of it. Many who were able to do so, bought their security from the invaders by divers sorts of bargainings or offering their services. In return they obtained small national flags which they fastened to their door-posts for protection. The Japanese flag was the easiest to make, simply a piece of white cotton with a round red dot in the middle. The British and the American were the most difficult. Japanese therefore predominated everywhere. Notices in English were placed underneath them. Some were very curious. One ran, 'Please do not touch the girls in this house. They belong to the Japanese.' Another: 'This house has been looted by the French, there is nothing left.'

William Oudendyk
Ways and By-Ways in Diplomacy, 1939

JUSTIFIED RETRIBUTION

To be shelled from your own garden wall! To live through eight weeks of a Chinese summer, bathless, with barely a change of clothing, on food that disagreed with nearly every one, some less, certainly, but most more! . . . What would *you* have done?

Mrs Archibald Little
Round About My Peking Garden, 1905

LAST ORDERS

The next day was Sunday, so we went to the Legation Church and were entertained at lunch afterwards by the Ambassador. Two or three of those present had been in the siege, and they showed us some of the sandbags used, a stable into which millions of rifle-bullets seemed to have been fired, and a place where the last order issued was written up in chalk. Underneath were the words, '*Nil desperandum*, two bottles of beer.'

Revd E. G. Hardy
John Chinaman at Home, 1905

GLOOMY BRICKWORK

The Legation quarter! It is a Legation quarter no more, but a rude and ugly semi-fortress split up into a hundred great walled enclosures that are an insult to the eye. It is 1900 and its disastrous consequences projected into infinity and perpetuated in gloomy brickwork—insult upon insult; the sore salted. . . .

No matter if you turn north, south, east, or west, the walls follow you everywhere with their loop-holed eyes, and sternly bring you back to the grimness of the situation. The loop-holes, it is true, are mostly blocked up, but the lighter patches of colour show you when the sun strikes exactly where each rifleman would take his stand; and every Chinese and Manchu in Peking knows this equally well. And then you can enter only through the armoured gates, which are only four in number.

The very Tartar walls seem to have lost their old-time grandeur and appear almost dwarfed by the countless Legation walls and enclosures. The finest Tartar towers have all gone and have not been replaced; block-houses have been built on the Tartar wall itself parallel to the eastern and western face of the fortress, so that no Chinese troops may fire down from this point of vantage on their enemies. And distances, too, have been nicely calculated so that at a given signal howitzers could drop shells from the Legations right on top of the Empress Dowager two miles away. It is a pleasant picture and gives a fine promise for the future.

B. L. Putnam Weale
The Reshaping of the Far East, 1905

INTERNATIONAL ARCHITECTURE

These Legations under the wall are greatly out of conceit with the encircling city. They do not even harmonise with one another. It is as though each first Plenipotentiary of the Powers concerned brought with him a shipload of building material from the homeland and tried to assemble it when he came to his journey's end. The result is interesting, even educative, but not by any way of looking at it architecturally harmonious. The Belgian Legation shews you a tiny slice of Brussels, the Netherlands a morsel of Amsterdam; Italy grows homesick contemplating her broad façades of villaesque stucco, while America echoes, faintly but with palpable intent, the pillared and stepped and State-Departmental porticoes of Washington, D.C.

Gilbert Collins
Extreme Oriental Mixture, 1925

A LACK OF BOOKS

'There's no proper library here, you know—only Lady Aglen's, and we haven't funds enough to keep that very up to date. No, books are very scarce out here—it's one of the troubles. The shortage of them is almost as acute as of unmarried women,' said Anastasia crisply. 'So they just fill up their time with amusing

themselves—Bridge and gossip, and drinks at the Club; and
these endless dreary, dreary parties, and the drab little
flirtations.'

Ann Bridge
Four-Part Setting, 1939

POLYMATH

The Diplomatic Body in Peking met in the house of the doyen,
that is to say in the British or, if Sir John was away, in the
Spanish Legation.

When we met in the British Legation, in warm weather, the
windows would be open on to a small inner courtyard, where
the lilac blossomed in the spring. The Legation parrot used to
sit out there and join in our discussions (sometimes very aptly)
with a hoarse guffaw, or a subdued chuckle, or a sudden
screech. He was a talking parrot, but he only spoke Chinese, so
that his remarks were unintelligible to most of the assembled
diplomats.

Daniele Varè
Laughing Diplomat, 1938

OCCASIONAL MUSIC

The barracks of the Russian Legation Guard were just opposite
our legation. One day in the spring of 1905 I heard their
amateur soldiers' band practising the whole day a most
depressing funeral march to the tune of a certain German
Protestant hymn. Happening to meet a Russian officer, I
inquired whether a death had occurred among his soldiers.
'No,' he said, 'but our Minister, Monsieur Lessar, is not
expected to live much longer, and our band, consisting mostly
of Jews, does not know how to play a funeral march. What they
are playing now is the easiest tune they can pick up.' For two
whole days that dismal, wailing dirge floated across Legation

Street till I could have yelled. Meanwhile M. Lessar was still reading and signing documents to the sound of his own funeral music. I wonder what he thought of it. Evidently he could not stand much of it, for on the second day he died.

William Oudendyk
Ways and By-Ways in Diplomacy, 1939

AN EXCHANGE OF COURTESIES

Our first call was on Prince and Princess Púlun. The Prince, many Chinese thought, should have been the rightful Emperor, but he had been passed over in the succession by the Dowager Empress. We were received with great politeness in a so-called Louis Sixteenth boudoir . . .

After the glasses had been emptied with many appropriate smiles, Princess Púlun opened the conversation by touching my wife's sleeve and muttering *Howw!* 'Her Highness says it is beautiful,' the interpreter translated. My wife, to be no less polite, touched the Princess' skirt, exclaimed *Howw!* and admired the blooms of fresh double jasmine arranged as bangles in her hair. After more touchings of apparel and more exchanges of *Howw*, the audience was over. The Prince had remained silent, and in fact the only English word I ever heard him utter was 'dry' over a glass of champagne. Unlike other members of the dynasty, he seemed for some odd reason to be genuinely fond of foreign society and spent much of his time at the Wagons Lits Hotel playing billiards with a former warrant officer in the German navy.

Lewis Einstein
A Diplomat Looks Back, 1968

CITY OF THE DEAD

Lines, written in dejection, to the Diplomatic Body, at Peking (1906).

A LULLABY

Far, far away, beyond your drowsy peace
Are haunts of toiling men, a bustling world,
Of those who strive and struggle, without cease,
By storm and stress of life all tossed and whirled.
   Hush ye, my weary ones. They shall not mar
   Your lotus-days of rest, your slumbers deep;
   Their clamour and their shouting pass afar.
   Sleep, my pretty ones; sleep, my weary ones—sleep.

Far, far away, the great ships come and go,
Swift news is shouted through the tireless street,
Life, tremulous by day, by night aglow,
Moves, to the beat of drums, on rapid feet.
   Fear not, oh weary ones. Your walls are high,
   The dust that lies between is centuries deep;
   No louder shall ye hear them than a sigh.
   Sleep, my pretty ones; sleep, my weary ones—sleep.

Far, far away, are men who think and feel,
Who speak not smoothly of corrupt decay,
Whom justice and humanity's appeal
Call yet, like shrill-blown clarions, to the fray—
   Ah, heed them not, secure is your repose
   Should they come hither, they could only weep,
   To see the nodding lotus, how she blows,
   Sleep, diplomatists; sleep, my polyglots—sleep.

Far, far away, the great world works and prays,
Peking abides, a city of the dead,
Of still-born protocols, of dust-filled ways,
Dry bones and empty phrases, vainly said;
   Well, be it so, but ye, at least, from care
   Exempt, your souls in drowsiness may steep,

Strife is but vanity and rest is dear.
Sleep, my little ones; sleep, my weary ones—sleep.

J. O. P. Bland
Quoted in Varè
Laughing Diplomat, 1938

COST-CUTTING

My friend McAlpine of the Scotch Colporteur Society, an
eminently practical man . . . recommends replacing the present
expensive and ineffective Diplomatic Body by an ingeniously
constructed set of clockwork figures with appropriate gestures,
phonographic apparatus, and uniforms complete. The set of
twelve (of best materials), in charge of a Scotch engineer (himself,
I think), to be worked at a total cost of not more than £3000 a year,
the figures to be taken to the Waiwupu [Foreign Ministry] free of
charge, singly or collectively according to political emergencies, at
least once a week, and the interviews duly recorded and preserved.

J. O. P. Bland
Houseboat Days in China, 1909

THE DIPLOMATIC WHIRL

Mrs Pavlov [wife of the Russian Minister] used to reproach her
husband. 'Tu etais l'amant de ma mère, tu es le père de ma soeur.'
It was true. Her mother was one of three sisters who used to sing
at the *café chantants*. The eldest sister was the mistress of Cassini,
former Russian Minister in Peking, and bore him a daughter and
came to Peking with him where her daughter passed as Cassini's
niece and the mother as the governess. This niece Marguerite is
now the bosom friend of Alice Roosevelt. The second sister is the
mistress of a Jew in Paris. The youngest sister came to Peking to
see her sister and bore a child to the Italian Minister, who is the
present Mrs Pavlov and then became the mistress of Pavlov to

whom she bore a daughter. Pavlov arrived to espouse the niece of Cassini, but instead married the cousin. . . .

G. E. Morrison
Diary, 1904

PURE PROFIT

October 4 [1916]—I am told that a guest at last night's dinner, a visitor from a distant country, complained because he had not been ranked with the ministers. As I had no information, nor have it now, that he was entitled to such ranking, I shall not worry. This is the first instance of any dissatisfaction with the seating. My predecessor related to me that a secretary of the British Legation once took his sudden departure before dinner for this reason. I have not always closely adhered to rank in seating, particularly at dinners where there are Chinese, in order to avoid a grouping which should make conversation impossible; but in such cases, of course, I always speak to whichever guest is slightly prejudiced by the arangement and explain the reason to him. I have never noticed the least sign of displeasure. At a very formal dinner, it is of course always safer to follow rank and let the conversation take care of itself. Any enjoyment people get out of such a dinner they set down as pure profit, anyhow.

Paul Reinsh
An American Diplomat in China, 1922

DINNER COMPANIONS

Dinners in Peking were peculiar in this way, that as the foreign community was small and our relative importance fixed by protocol, it happened that the same people would sit next to each other night after night, and some of us made no mystery of the fact that we would rather have stayed at home.

Daniele Varè
Laughing Diplomat, 1938

BEASTLY NANKING

Peking is no longer the capital of China, and the seat of government being in Nanking, 600 miles to the south, ministerial or foreign crises lose their significance, as by the time news has reached the Legations the situation has probably changed. It is as if Parliament sat as usual in London and the diplomatic representatives of foreign Powers lived somewhere in the middle of Scotland, with the additional disadvantage of slow train services and no long-distance telephones . . . The reason given for this anomalous state of affairs is that there being no Legation quarter in Nanking, the diplomatists' lives would not be safe; in other words, that they are very comfortable in their well-built houses in Peking, where life is cheap and informal, and they do not want to go to Nanking, which is a beastly place full of hostile Chinamen.

R. V. C. Bodley
Indiscreet Travels East, 1934

The International Train, manned by Detachments of Five Nations, under the Walls of Peking.

AN AQUARIUM

For all its curious beauty, I would not like to live there. An atmosphere of unreality pervades the Legation Quarter. The diplomats drift to and fro with the slow, stately, and mysterious grace of fish in an aquarium. Yes, that is what Peking is like: an aquarium. Round and round they go, serene and glassy-eyed. Their natural surroundings have been artfully reconstructed in a confined space, behind glass. Round and round, round and round . . .

Peter Fleming
One's Company, 1934

CHAPTER 6

THE CHINESE CITY

Here, relieved from the strict discipline that prevails in the palace,
the citizens give themselves up to business, or dissipation.

W. G. MEDHURST
China: Its State and Prospects, 1857

The Chinese City was that part of Peking outside and to the south of the Tartar City. It got its name at the same time as the Tartar City, and as a result of the same events. When the Manchu rulers of the Qing Dynasty decreed that only Manchus could live in the Inner City, they set the Outer City aside for the displaced Chinese.

The Chinese City has some claim to be the oldest part of Peking, for it was upon that part of the plain that successive cities took shape before the Mongols established their new capital, Dadu, a little to the north. Relegated to suburban status with the rise of Dadu, the old town continued to flourish. The main hostels for travellers were clustered there, the centres for many traditional trades, and it was the haven, according to Marco Polo, of more than 20,000 'public women' not welcome within the walls of the capital.

Under the Ming, it was decided to reincorporate the suburbs into the city by building yet another wall. As originally planned, the wall would have gone right round the city at a mile or two's distance, but in the way of governments, money ran out before it had got beyond the built-up area to the south. Thus the Outer (later the Chinese) City came into existence, enclosed by a secondary wall with both ends tacked onto the main city wall, and called 'the hat' for the way it capped the city proper.

The Chinese City, more than the Tartar, has been defined by a single road. Qianmenwai Street, the continuation of the Imperial capital's north/south axis, bisected the outer city, leading at last to two most sacred sites, the Temples of Heaven and Agriculture, and, more prosaically, Peking's first railway station.

The Chinese City was always Peking's pleasure quarter. The lineal descendants of Polo's public women maintained a welcoming presence in the 'Eight Big Hutungs' into the 1930s. All the theatres were here, restaurants, sing-song houses, and hotels. Dance halls sprang up, where sophisticated girls from Shanghai or Suzhou could command twice the fee of their Peking cousins. To the end of the Manchu dynasty, special arrangements had to be set in place to allow libertine courtiers to pass back from the Chinese into the Imperial City in time for the Emperor's dawn audience. In some reigns, the revellers were rumoured to include the Emperor himself.

HAT CITY

What is known as the Chinese quarter of Peking fits on to the South
end of the Tartar City, and from its appearance is known as the
Mao tsu Ch'eng (帽子城), 'Hat City.'

R. W. Swallow
Sidelights on Peking Life, 1927

BUSINESS OR DISSIPATION

The southern division of the city, where the Chinese principally
reside, is the grand emporium of all the merchandize that finds its
way to the capital, and tends to ornament and gratify the adherents
of the court. Here, relieved from the strict discipline that prevails
in the palace, the citizens give themselves up to business, or

dissipation; encouraged and led on by voluptuous courtiers, who
have nothing to do, but to display their grandeur, or to please their
appetites. There is an immense deal of business done in this
southern city, and the broad street which divides it from north
to south, is constantly thronged by passengers and tradesmen.

Chinese shopkeepers are in the habit of advertising their wares, by long projecting signs, hung out in front of their houses, painted in the gayest colours; while the bustling crowd, perpetually thronging the principal avenues, contributes to enliven and animate the scene.

W. H. Medhurst
China: Its State and Prospects, 1857

CH'IEN MEN WAI

To get from the outer gate to the inner entails a drive of nearly an hour under walls of very considerable height and apparent strength, but which I should say very moderate artillery would smash in a few minutes. This intervening space seems dedicated to the flying of kites, to the airing of larks and spectacle thrushes, and to the rolling of mules, all of which operations are superintended by elderly gentlemen of very reverend and respectable appearance —many of them greybeards and wearing gigantic spectacles. One of them is airing his pet bird in a cage which he supports in his uplifted hand, and in this attitude he will remain for hours. I have counted as many as thirty old men standing with their birds in cages apparently watching with the greatest interest their pets flapping their wings, canvassing their beauty and other qualifications with their neighbours.

Sir Edmund Hornby
An Autobiography, c.1870 pub. 1929

MEAN STREETS

Although adjoining the Tartar, there is a Chinese city, it is so squalid and of such mean pretensions that with the exception of a single street it is of but little interest to Europeans.

Oliver G. Ready
Life and Sport in China, 1903

117

LADIES OF PLEASURE

It may easily be imagined, that, in so populous a city, there must be many idle persons of both sexes; though, I believe, fewer than in most other cities of the world, even in those of much less extent than that of Pekin. In order to prevent all disorderly practices, as much as possible, the government have thought fit to permit, or connive at, certain places, in the suburbs, for the reception and entertainment of prostitutes, who are maintained by the landlords of the houses in which they dwell; but not allowed to straggle abroad. I have been informed, that these ladies of pleasure have all separate apartments; with the price of each lady, describing, at the same time, her beauties and qualities, written, over the door of her apartment, in fair legible characters; which price is paid directly by the gallant; by which means, these affairs are conducted without noise in the houses, or disturbances in the neighbourhood. Noisy brawls are very seldom, hardly ever, known at Pekin; those who are found offending, in this way, undergo very severe penalties. It is likewise to be observed, that these houses are calculated for the meaner sort of people only; so that any person, who hath the least regard to his credit or reputation, carefully avoids being seen in them.

John Bell
A Journey from St Petersburg to Pekin
1719–1722, pub. 1763

BEATING THE DRUM

The [1913 National] Assembly soon succeeded in thoroughly discrediting itself. . . . The members led such profligate lives that one Chinese paper reported that a certain Li Lo-keng made a practice of going round to houses of ill-fame in certain districts daily, banging a drum and calling upon legislators within to wake up and attend to their duties.

H. G. W. Woodhead
A Journalist in China, 1934

ACADEMIC SANCTIONS

Many of the older college students are making a practice of visiting these houses. In going through houses of all four classes we saw many students usually in groups of two or three in the rooms of the prostitutes. The practice is so general that it is a distinct problem and certain colleges have had to adopt very strict rules of discipline concerning it. The Army Medical College, for example, deducts 10 per cent from final marks of any student who is seen in the segregated district.

Sidney D. Gamble
Peking: A Social Survey, 1921

NOT MORAL

We had noticed many peepshows being exhibited along the side-walk, with small, pig-tailed urchins, their eyes glued to the peepholes, evidently having their money's worth. Curious to see the spectacles with which the Chinese showman regales his audiences, we struck a bargain with one, and for the large sum of five cents the whole party was allowed to look in through the glasses. The first tableau represented a troupe of acrobats performing before the Imperial Court. Then the proprietor pressed a spring; by a mechanical device the scene changed, and we drew back from the peepholes! The Chinese are not a moral race.

Capt. Gordon Casserly
The Land of the Boxers, 1903

EXECUTIONS

At Peking the autumn executions, as they are called, are carried out about the middle of the Chinese 'winter moon,' or eleventh month, at a place called the 'Entrance to the Vegetable Market,' about one mile outside the 'Easy Government Gate' of the Inner or Tartar city, in the middle of the main street which runs thence through the Outer or Chinese city. The Autumn Revision precedes the executions, and at this revision the Emperor ticks off, or 'hooks off,' as it is termed, a number of those offenders whose crime presents 'solid circumstances' of proof, allowing the remainder to stand over. If a criminal is fortunate enough to pass three such ordeals without being 'hooked off,' he may consider himself reprieved, and he either languishes in gaol, is exiled, or is banished with or without hard labour; or he may even in time bribe himself free.

E. H. Parker
China Past and Present, 1903

MINOR PLEASURES

At all times of the year it was a pleasure to wander round the Forbidden City or poke about in the markets and antique shops, for we never knew what was going to happen. One day . . . walking with the children round the Temple of Heaven, we found pasque flowers (*Anemone pulsatilla*) in full bloom, growing fifteen inches

high between the paving-stones. Another day we met the public executioner going to the execution ground in the Temple of Agriculture with the condemned men trussed up in a cart behind him. On the way there he was playing with the cord which is used to pull forward the kneeling victim's head and make it easy to cut off. On the way back he was chewing dough-nuts.

Sir Owen O'Malley
The Phantom Caravan, 1954

CHINESE LANTERNS

First Day of the Ninth Moon

Two or three nights ago, at dinner, I happened to mention that the door of the pavilion, where King Cophetua [the narrator's husband] has his study, was badly lighted on the outside, and I suggested that a Chinese lantern (or two) might be hung there, with an electric bulb inside. A long discussion followed about Chinese lanterns generally and horn lanterns in particular.

The next day Fédor and Natasha went off to the fair at the Loong-fu Ssèu, and returned later in triumph with two lanterns of the kind that were once carried in the street in front of some important person's palanquin.

King Cophetua expressed our common gratitude and gave orders that both the lanterns should be set up at his study door. For some reason that at first was not apparent, his orders were not carried out. Indeed, he had to repeat them several times before the lanterns were set up.

And this morning the storm burst!

Mr. Tang came, as usual, to give King Cophetua a Chinese lesson, and seeing the lanterns at the door, he stopped to read the characters that were written on them. The next moment, he rushed in to King Cophetua and asked that the lanterns be taken down *kwi-kwi*! I happened to be there, so we all came out and looked at the object of Mr. Tang's indignation.

It appears that the lanterns had once belonged to a most immoral establishment that had flourished in the days of the Empire and was suppressed not long ago. The two inscriptions were identical; they ran as follows:

'Admire the beautiful shapes and moon-like countenances of the Perfumed Boys, in the Garden of Ten Thousand Pleasures, in the Quarter of the Eight Big Hutungs!'

The lanterns were taken down again.

Fédor swears that he had no idea what the characters meant.

Daniele Varè
The Gate of Happy Sparrows, 1937

121

SOUND AND FURY

There are a great many theatres in the Chinese city, their situation being marked by a few masks, lay figures, images of tortoises or dragons, or other queer beasts; though indeed no sign is necessary to indicate their whereabouts, for the infernal din which comes from them the whole day long would guide any one to them.

A. B. Freeman-Mitford
The Attaché at Peking, 1866 pub. 1900

LOVE INTEREST

My first visit to the old Peking Theatre was made in company with my Chinese teacher, Mr. Ts'ui; for it was the custom, as in Europe, for students of the language to learn what they could from the drama of the country. The selection of the play was left to the professor. Mr. Ts'ui's choice, possibly because of the more tuneful music, had fallen on a comedy which for realistic love scenes might have given points to the most outré spectacle of the Paris stage and proved an easy winner. The *mise en scéne* was as scanty and simple as possible and left much to the imagination. The acting, on the other hand, left nothing; and each phase of the would-be co-respondent's amours was carried through to its logical conclusion with a vivacity and realism worthy of a better cause.

Col A. W. S. Wingate
A Cavalier in China, 1940

THE SOOCHOW GIRLS

The oldest restaurants are compelled to close down, the number of tea houses and sing-song girls houses is diminishing, and mah-jong and poker matches, where fortunes were made or lost and wherefrom sing-song girls were having their steadiest income— belong now to history. These establishments and occupations are

being gradually replaced by dancing halls. . . .

Hundreds of sing-song girls have lost their jobs, and they try to make a living with dancing.

Peking girls are not very much successful in this respect because they lack the physical qualities required from a good dancer, being naturally slow and shy. Therefore managers of fashionable dancing halls hire dancing girls from Shanghai, the Soochow girls . . . who are believed to be the most beautiful girls in China.

I. L. Miller
The Chinese Girl, 1932

EXERCISING BIRDS

Down the Chien-mên Wai, silent, grave and dignified, in black or grey gowns, passes a steady stream of middle-aged men, each carrying a cage and a little stick like a wand. On reaching the appropriate spot, the cage doors are opened, and each feathered occupant hops daintily out and perches on the wand: with a quick deft movement, the owner tosses the bird into the air, where amid a crowd of others it flies up into the sunlight: fluttering, wheeling, chirruping, the whole sky is full of wings and song and glad freed creatures: below upturned faces watch the pretty sight, pleased and benevolent smiles on the usually impassive countenances. Then, at some signal, the birds drop down out of the airy throng, each to his proper owner, perch again upon the lifted wands, and hop back, docile and content, each into his own cage.

Ann Bridge
The Ginger Griffin, 1934

CHAPTER 7

THE TEMPLES OF HEAVEN AND AGRICULTURE

Among all the buildings of the city, perhaps in the whole world the richest architecturally, the Temple of Heaven most stirs the eye and the mind.

ANN BRIDGE
The Ginger Griffin, 1934

One reason for the Ming Emperors' building a new city wall to enclose the southern town was that they had established at the south end of the central axis two sites of key religious importance, the Altar of Heaven and the Altar of Agriculture. The Altar of Heaven in particular was integral to the cosmology of the restored Chinese dynasty. Heaven at the top (the south) balanced the Altars of the Earth, the Sun, and the Moon, to the north, east, and west respectively of the Emperor's seat in the Palace City.

The Altars of Heaven and Agriculture were the scene of the most sacred religious observances. It was upon the Altar of Heaven that the Emperor, after purification and fasting, sacrificed to heaven as the priest of his people. The people's representatives, in the form of a host of subsidiary rulers and high officials, attended at the ceremony. At the Altar of Agriculture, the Son of Heaven each year ploughed a symbolic furrow to promote a fruitful harvest.

Despite the official witnesses, these were private ceremonies. The glowing white marble of the Altar of Heaven was surrounded by high walls. It was a source of ongoing frustration to foreign visitors that they were denied access to the grounds. The restrictions lapsed for a time after the military occupation of 1860, and became irrelevant after 1900, when the Allied troops lopped the sacred trees for firewood, and put the Emperor's throne to practical use as a barber's chair.

Perhaps surprisingly, among the sternest critics of the shrines' desecration were two champions of Christianity, the veteran missionaries W. A. P. Martin and Arthur Smith. For them, the Altar of Heaven was 'sublime in its suggestions'—the manifestation of a religious impulse that transcended time and narrowly defined codes of belief.

LIGHT

It is this capture of light from the whole vastness of the horizon, compelling it to flow and splash and sparkle along the curves of three perfect rings of immaculate whiteness laid in a frame of green and lazuli, where the light flows too, but much more softly,

as befits what is only framework and accompaniment; this triumphant kindling of lifeless stone and heavy clay with the swiftest, the airiest, the most vital of all things—light—which makes this Temple of Heaven such a wonderful, such a supremely satisfying, solution of the world-old problem of how architecturally to express man's veneration for the source and uttermost summit of his life.

A. E. Grantham
Pencil Speakings from Peking, 1914

CREDIT WHERE DUE

The whole plan of this splendid monument is nobly conceived, and would do credit to the most advanced nation in the world.

Alexander Michie
The Siberian Overland Route, 1864

IF ONLY

As we stood there, with nothing but the blue sky above us, the world and its turmoil shut out by a triple barrier of blue-tiled wall, the grove, the park, we felt the solemnity of a place designed to force man to turn his whole attention to the sky. If only the Chinese perform their functions reverently, which it is to be feared they do not, to see the Emperor, the High Priest of his people, the Son of Heaven, ascend that altar in state must be a singularly impressive spectacle.

Revd Roland Allen
The Siege of the Peking Legations, 1901

HARK!

Lower buildings reigned with their own dignity around it; in the modest cloisters and little porticoes there was no searching after effect: but the proportions of these buildings are so exact, they defer to each other in such exquisite relationship, that all together they give the impression of some motionless ceremonial. One cannot distinguish how it comes about, but in all these buildings the pleasing is strangely combined with the august. It is an architecture devised for dignitaries and philosophers, and regulated by a harmony so subtle, that after having looked at it, you bend your head as if to listen to it.

Abel Bonnard
(trans. Veronica Lucas)
In China, 1926

HOLY GROUND

Dr Legge, the eminent missionary, before climbing the steps of this altar heard a small, still voice, which others might have heard had they but hearkened, saying: 'Put off thy shoes; for the place whereon thou standest is holy ground.' The students in the British legation, less reverent, were for years wont to play cricket in its shady groves.

Dr W. A. P. Martin
A Cycle of Cathay, 1897

NEW YEAR'S GREETINGS

On the first day of the year, however, there is a solemn ceremony, at which these two hundred monarchs [of tributary kingdoms] are admitted to a sort of contact with their suzerain and master, with him who, as they phrase it, sitting beneath the sky, rules the four seas and the ten thousand nations of the world by a single act of his will. According to the ritual which regulates the state proceedings of the Emperor of China, he is bound to visit every year, on the first day of the first moon, the temple of his ancestors, and to prostrate himself before the tablet of his fathers. There is before the entrance of this temple a long avenue, wherein the tributary princes, who have come to Peking to render homage to the Emperor, assemble. They range themselves right and left of the peristyle, in three lines, each occupying the place appertaining to his dignity. They stand erect, grave, and silent. It is said to be a fine and imposing spectacle, to witness all these remote monarchs, attired in their silk robes, embroidered with gold and silver, and indicating, by the variety of their costumes, the different countries they inhabit, and the degrees of their dignity.

Meantime the Emperor issues in great pomp from his Yellow Town. He traverses the deserted and silent streets of Peking; for, when the Asiatic tyrant appears, every door must be closed, and every inhabitant of the town must, on pain of death, remain silent within his house. As soon as the Emperor has arrived at the temple of the ancestors, the heralds, who precede the procession, cry out, at the moment he places his foot on the first step of the stairs that lead to the gallery of the tributary kings: 'Let all prostrate themselves, for here is the Lord of the earth.' To this the two hundred tributary kings respond in unison: 'Ten thousand congratulations!' And, having thus wished a happy new year to the Emperor, they all fall down with their face towards the earth. Then passes through their ranks, the son of heaven, who enters the temple of the ancestors, and prostrates himself, in his turn, thrice before the tablet of his fathers. Whilst the Emperor is offering up his adoration to the spirits of his family, the two hundred monarchs remain prostrate on the earth, and they do not rise until the Emperor has again passed through their ranks; after this they re-enter their litters and return to their respective palaces.

And such is the entire and sole fruit of the long patience of these potentates, after leaving their distant countries, and enduring fatigues and dangers of every description, and a long journey through the desert: they have enjoyed the happiness of prostrating themselves in the path of the Emperor!

Abbé Huc
Travels in Tartary, Thibet and China, 1851

NO SHOW

The prime minister of the king of the Alechan told us that a sight of the Emperor is not easily obtained. One year, when his master was ill, he was obliged to take his place at Peking, in the ceremony of the temple of the ancestors, and he then hoped to see the Old Buddha, on his way down the peristyle, but he was altogether mistaken in his expectation. As minister, the mere representative of his monarch, he was placed in the third file, so that, when the Emperor passed, he saw absolutely nothing at all.

Abbé Huc
Travels in Tartary, Thibet and China, 1851

WEEDS

The avenues are like a wilderness, and weeds are even taking root in the beautiful blue-tiled roofs, which, if not soon ruined by it, will at all events be twisted out of their symmetrical proportions. It is melancholy to see that what men of large and enlightened ideas have been at such pains to build, the present degenerate race do not consider it worth while to hire half a dozen coolies to keep in order.

Alexander Michie
The Siberian Overland Route, 1864

KITCHEN GARDEN

It is one of those places almost impossible to describe, and leaves upon the mind confused ideas of grandeur and utter ruin— recollections of wonderful blue encaustic tiles, and marble stairs, with rank weeds growing between the slabs—visions of elegant bridges, and rich but broken carvings—vivid impressions of a general covering of dirt and filth, and the surprise of a patch of kitchen garden in an unexpected corner.

Capt. William Gill
The River of Golden Sand, 1883

ARMOUR-PLATED

A few days afterwards, at the winter solstice, Yüan [Yuan Shikai, in 1915 President of the Chinese Republic] took the significant step of reviving the most imposing of Chinese religious ceremonies—the sacrifice to God at the Altar of Heaven. This was a ceremony which could be carried out only by an emperor, and was equivalent to a public declaration to the whole empire that he had already assumed the imperial prerogatives and was about to ascend the dragon throne. Unfortunately, the ceremony was shorn of much of its traditional beauty and stateliness by the fact that Yüan thought it necessary to ensure his own safety by proceeding from the palace to the Altar of Heaven in an armoured car. Evidently he was not so sure of the unanimity of 'the will of the people' as his public utterances signified.

Reginald F. Johnston
Twilight in the Forbidden City, 1934

MAGNIFICENT VIEW

From the marble terrace which surrounds the Temple we had a magnificent view of the city, but then in ruins and flames.

Revd Roland Allen
The Siege of the Peking Legations, 1901

READY ACCESS

Across the wide street opposite the Temple of Agriculture is the vast area, at least a mile on each face, inclosing the Temple of Heaven. For many years it was absolutely inaccessible to foreigners, and even during the minority of the present Emperor it was difficult to set one's foot inside. Now there is not a single Chinese anywhere to be seen, the keepers having been all driven away by the British when they took possession immediately on reaching Peking. One can drive his cart quite up to the lofty terrace leading to the triple cerulean domes denoting the threefold heaven. Each gate was sentried by a swarthy Sikh soldier—the personification of the domination of a greater empire than that of Rome in its best days—who merely glanced at you as you passed or asked unintelligible questions in Hindustani, and made a respectful salaam when he was informed in several European languages, as well as in Chinese, that you were unable to catch the drift of his observations.

A. H. Smith
China in Convulsion, 1901

HOME AWAY FROM HOME

The Emperor's Hall of Fasting was used as the head-quarters of the British army in this part of the city, and every day was partly filled with many cart-loads of loot—silks, furs, silver and jade ornaments, embroidered clothing, and the like. This was daily forwarded to the British Legation. . . . The personal apartments of the Emperor in the rear served as the bedrooms of the officers, who looked mildly surprised when the circumstance was communicated to them at their dinner, and merely gave an inquiring glance, as much as to say, 'Well, what of it, don't you know?'

A. H. Smith
China in Convulsion, 1901

COSTLY SACRIFICE

The sacrifice which the emperor of China spreads before the altar is very costly. The sacrificial animals amount annually to 240 cows, 439 sheep and goats, 339 pigs, 405 stags, and 449 hares. Divers soups and dishes are also prepared and presented to the idols, and gold and silver paper is burned before them in great abundance. It has been calculated, indeed, that the institutions for the service of the one true God in other countries cost a far less sum than the emperor of China pays for idolatry. The gold and silver paper consumed in wanton waste before his idols alone, costs a hundred times more, Mr. Gutzlaff says, than all the money expended for Bibles, tracts, and missionary societies! This is a humbling consideration for the Christian world.

Religious Tract Society
The People of China, c.1855

PREREQUISITES

It is required of the Chinese hierophants that they be free from any recent legal crime, and not in mourning for the dead. For the first order of sacrifices they are required to prepare themselves by ablutions, a change of garments, a vow, and a fast of three days. During this time they must occupy a clean chamber, and abstain —1. from judging criminals; 2. from being present at a feast; 3. from listening to music; 4. from cohabitation with women; 5. from intercourse with the sick; 6. from mourning for the dead; 7. from wine; 8. from eating onions or garlic.

John Francis Davis
The Chinese, 1836

SMALL MINDS

In the Chinese City there is little of interest beyond the shops and streets, as the great inclosures of the Temple of Heaven and the Temple of Agriculture are fast shut, and one sees what one may through an opera-glass as one walks the city wall. No foreigner has ever assisted at the services at the Temple of Heaven, and few have entered its inclosures. For some years after 1860, entry to the lovely park by the south wall was easily gained, but after certain vandal acts the entry of visitors was prohibited. Every foreigner became possessed then to gain entry, and bribery, trickery, and every other device were resorted to to penetrate the forbidden realm. Full illustrations and full explanations of all the temple precincts and ceremonies are given in the standard works on China, which sufficiently gratify a normal curiosity or any legitimate interest, and the majority of these zealous investigators schemed to enter the park of the Temple of Heaven to gratify a love of adventure and that last ambition of small minds, 'to say they have been there.'

E. R. Scidmore
China: The Long-Lived Empire, 1900

A PASSION FOR SPACE

Those incomparable builders, with their passion for space and their deep sense of the value of the things of nature, thought nothing of walling in a park three miles round to hold one temple, used for ceremonial only twice a year, and set about it the trees of the forest to add to the beauty of worship.

Ann Bridge
The Ginger Griffin, 1934

134

OREGON PINE

The Temple of Heaven, that is, the great walled compound with all of its edifices, was built five centuries ago by Yung Loh, one of the early Ming emperors; it was restored by Ch'ien Lung, of the Manchu dynasty. In 1889 the Happy Year Hall—that particular building to which foreigners have given the name Temple of Heaven—was struck by lightning and burned to the ground. This bolt was a direct act of Heaven, so my rickshaw boy told me, because an impious, but now famous, centipede crawled up the walls to the golden peak. My boy seemed to know every detail of the path which that profane insect followed. When it was desired to rebuild the temple, and the Manchus were determined to copy in detail the building which had been destroyed, it was found that China's forests were bereft of timbers which could uphold the heavy tiled roof. After much argument with themselves, the necromancers of the court finally decided that pine logs from the forests of Oregon would constitute proper *feng-shui*. This decision very happily corresponded with the best engineering advice, and the New World furnished the pillars which you now see.

Lucian S. Kirtland
Finding the Worthwhile in the Orient, 1926

BARE UNDER THE SKY

The most striking thing about these buildings is their extreme simplicity, a simplicity reflecting the old uncomplicated monotheistic worship of *Shang Ti*, 'The One Above the Earth,' which goes back four thousand years. The mind cannot resist a tribute of astonished admiration to the austere and pure conception which gave to Earth's greatest altar no roof but the sky, surrounded it with the three hundred and sixty pillars of the terrestrial degrees, and approached it by the triple gates of the Four Winds of Heaven. No flimsy trappings or ritual furniture disturbed the purity of the marble circle, no priests intervened—bare under the sky, it awaited the feet of the Son of Heaven as, alone, he climbed the steps at dawn to make atonement for the sins of his people. . . . Now it lies desolate. The great tiled brazier where the bull-calf of pure colour was consumed as a burnt-offering is cold from year's end to year's end: the bronze baskets for burning the rolls of tribute silk—most civilised and innocent of sacrifices—are rusty and empty. Tiles drip off like water, slowly and continually, from the perished cement of walls and roofs; foreigners picnic and boil tea-kettles everywhere: some Americans once gave a dance on the Altar itself—a vulgar outrage which did at last rouse the Chinese to close the Temple for a time. For the most part, however, beyond erecting a booth for the sale of tickets at the entrance-gate, the heirs of so much beauty do little for its preservation. It belongs to the unworthy past, which the new officialdom of the Republic would willingly forget—a benighted past, unlit by electric light: a slow past, unhastened by the telegraph and the internal combustion engine. But Nature, more tender than mankind, has come quietly in to cover the slow ruin of man's handiwork. Big soft primulas, like auriculas, conceal the brilliant fragments of coloured glaze at the foot of the walls, and droop over the half-empty moat which surrounds the Hall of Abstinence, where the Emperor fasted through the night before the sacrifice: anemones, of a more imperial purple than those which the Berkshire villagers believe to spring only from the short turf of their downs where once the blood of Danes was spilt, grow in great tufts among the pale dead grass beyond the causeway; and in spring the groves of junipers are carpeted all through with great drifts of a wild crucifera, a foot or more high, in every tone of mauve and lilac and white, so that the fragrant shade is lightened from below with a glow.

Ann Bridge
The Ginger Griffin, 1934

ROYAL COMMISSION

Opposite to the Temple of Heaven, and on our right, is the Temple or Altar of the Earth, where the emperors of China repair according to traditional custom on the first day of spring to inaugurate the happy season by ploughing the first furrow. The little boy who now wields the sceptres of the khans must be too young to hold a plough, and I suppose he does it by commission, if indeed he is not too degenerate to do it at all.

Alexander Michie
The Siberian Overland Route, 1864

UPGRADING

The headquarters of the American troops during the military occupation of Peking were in the Temple of Agriculture, a spacious series of enclosures in the southern part of the Chinese city. One of the main halls was employed as a hospital, and another as a supply depôt for the commissariat, displaying long rows of hams, cases of tobacco, boxes of army beans, and barrels of beef. . . .

The officers for whose headquarters the main halls were used had no sooner taken possession, than they began to have holes cut in the venerable walls and large plate-glass windows inserted, a proceeding which must have appeared to the shades of the divinities worshipped as an additional profanation and humiliation.

A. H. Smith
China in Convulsion, 1901

COLOUR-CODED

At the great festival which celebrates spring the Emperor also officiates as Pontifex Maximus, or high-priest. This time it is at the temple of the god of agriculture, where at the close of a religious service he ploughs, or pretends to plough, a little bit with a plough which is painted yellow. Imperial representatives do the same in the provinces with red ploughs.

Revd E. G. Hardy
John Chinaman at Home, 1905

AGRICULTURAL PURSUITS

The Seën-nung-tan is erected in honour of the inventor of agriculture; but the spirit of the heavens and the earth, and the planet of Jupiter, have all their respective altars. Sacrifices are offered before them to the five sacred mountains, the five predominant mountains, and the five common mountains; their meaning we leave the reader to guess, nor can we discover what they have to do with agriculture.

Revd Charles Gutzlaff
China Opened, 1838

CHAPTER 8

DAILY LIFE

*Chinamen of high standing will often send their birds for
a drive or even for a short railway journey in order that they
may see the world.*

R. V. C. BODLEY
Indiscreet Travels East, 1934

Foreigners have remarked with wonder upon the day-to-day life of the citizens of Peking from the time there were first foreigners there to remark upon it. They have observed the variety of ways in which people have earned their living, and the limits on orthodox employment (Peking has always had a substantial oversupply of labour) that led to the formation of unusual professional associations: guilds of thieves, of beggars, even of theatrical cheerleaders.

Daily life was observed the more easily because it was lived in the street. In 1923 Somerset Maugham scored a theatrical coup when he opened his play, *East of Eden*, with a Peking street scene, entirely without dialogue. For Pekingers the street provided expanded living quarters, a shopfront, a stage. It was the showcase, too, for wedding and funeral processions (the two almost indistinguishable) and the progresses of great mandarins. Among the recognized professions, that of participant in processions was not least.

The one thing the street was not, it seems, was a convenient means of communication. Opinion is divided as to whether the Peking cart evolved to meet the condition of the city streets, or was itself the cause of the ruts, bumps, and general disrepair. There is, however, no disagreement among travellers right into the twentieth century about the appalling state of the roads, or the extraordinary lack of comfort of the vehicles which negotiated them.

Foreigners' experience of how people lived in the capital did not necessarily stop at observing and describing the passing scene. Just by being there, they were involved. For some, it was a fleeting experience, like the distinguished American statesman who was cast unexpectedly into the midst of a wedding procession, and believed it to be for his benefit. For others close involvement became an all-consuming objective. These were the sinologues.

The way of the sinologue has never been easy. The tendency has always been for familiarity in another culture to be achieved at the expense of credibility in one's own. 'Is there not reason to fear that by the time any outside barbarian should have reached such a pitch of comprehension of China . . .' asks Dr Arthur Smith, himself not the least of the sinologues, 'we shall be as much at a loss to know what *he* meant by what *he* said, as if he were really Chinese?'

ANT-HEAP

Peking, for its size, must be one of the most crowded cities in the world. It is like an ant-heap, and the one cry is work and work for daily bread.

Mrs Alec-Tweedie
An Adventurous Journey, 1926

SETTING THE SCENE

SCENE: *A street in Peking. Several shops are shown. Their fronts are richly decorated with carved wood painted red and profusely gilt. The counters are elaborately carved. Outside are huge signboards. The shops are open to the street and you can see the various wares they sell. One is a coffin shop, where the coolies are at work on a coffin: other coffins, ready for sale, are displayed; some of them are of plain deal, others are rich with black and gold. The next shop is a money-changer's. Then there is a lantern shop in which all manner of coloured lanterns are hanging. After this comes a druggist's where there are queer things in bottles and dried herbs. A small stuffed crocodile is a prominent object. Next to this is a shop where crockery is sold, large coloured jars, plates, and all manner of strange animals. In all the shops two or three Chinamen are seated. Some read newspapers through great horn spectacles; some smoke water-pipes.*

The street is crowded. Here is an itinerant cook with his two chests, in one of which is burning charcoal: he serves out bowls of rice and condiments to the passers-by who want food. There is a barber with the utensils of his trade. A coolie, seated on a stool, is having his head shaved. Chinese walk to and fro. Some are coolies and wear blue cotton in various stages of raggedness; some in black gowns and caps and black shoes are merchants and clerks. There is a beggar, gaunt and thin, with an untidy mop of bristly hair, in tatters of indescribable filthiness. He stops at one of the shops and begins a long wail. For a time no one takes any notice of him, but presently on a word from the fat shopkeeper an assistant gives him a few cash and he wanders on. Coolies, half naked, hurry by, bearing great bales on their yokes. They utter little sharp cries for people to get out of their way. Peking carts with their blue hoods rumble noisily along. Rickshaws pass rapidly in both directions, and the rickshaw boys shout for the crowd to make way. In the rickshaws are grave Chinese. Some are dressed in white ducks after the European fashion; in other rickshaws are Chinese women in long smocks and wide trousers, or Manchu ladies, with their faces painted like masks, in embroidered silks. Women of various sorts stroll about the street or enter the shops. You see them chaffering for various articles.

A water-carrier passes along with a creaking barrow, slopping the water as he goes; and an old blind woman, a masseuse, advances slowly, striking wooden clappers to proclaim her calling. A musician stands on the curb and plays a tuneless melody on a one-stringed fiddle. From the distance comes the muffled sound of gongs. There is a babel of sound caused by the talking of all these people, by the cries of coolies, the gong, the clappers, and the fiddle. From burning joss-sticks in the shops in front of the household god comes a savour of incense.

A couple of Mongols ride across on shaggy ponies; they wear high boots and Astrakhan caps. Then a string of camels sways slowly down the street. They carry great burdens of skins from the deserts of Mongolia. They are accompanied by wild-looking fellows. Two stout Chinese gentlemen are giving their pet birds an airing; the birds are attached by the leg with a string and sit on little wooden perches. The two Chinese gentlemen discuss their merits. Round about them small boys play. They run hither and thither pursuing one another amid the crowd.

END OF SCENE I

W. Somerset Maugham
East of Suez, 1923

142

BIRDS OF A FEATHER

One of the most amusing sights in Peking is to see men walking about the streets or public gardens, or sometimes sitting in tea-houses, carrying birds in cages. These men are not, as might be supposed, bird fanciers displaying their wares, but the owners of the birds, or, more frequently, servants of the owners taking their pets for an airing. Chinamen of high standing will often send their birds for a drive or even for a short railway journey in order that they may see the world. There was an occasion when a British Minister's servant in Peking demanded higher wages on the grounds that in his position he could not take his master's noble canaries to a common park or tea-house where they might overhear inferior birds singing.

R. V. C. Boldey
Indiscreet Travels East, 1934

SCHOOL OF HARD KNOCKS

As in other countries the theatrical profession is a hard and strenuous one, and though a few gain fame and fortune, there are many failures, while the great majority have to be content with a bare living.

The training is conducted in private schools which are connected with one or other of the theatres. Young boys, as a rule of the very poorest families, are offered to the principals and, if accepted, a contract is signed by the parents giving up their rights for a period of years.

The surrender, until the expiration of the term, usually 2 or 3 years, is absolute, and one of the clauses in the agreement used to read as follows: *Ta Ssu Pu Kwan* (打死不管), 'there will be no interference even though (he is) beaten to death.' Since the establishment of the Republic however this clause has been deleted.

R. W. Swallow
Sidelights on Peking Life, 1927

DUAL PURPOSE

An actor's eyes should be very large and outstanding, and in order to bring this about they put a horsehair band, called a *wang tsi* (網子) round their heads, and then tie very tightly round it a long piece of black gauze, which has been soaked in water. The *wang tsi* also helps them to keep on their hats.

R. W. Swallow
Sidelights on Peking Life, 1927

DRAMATIC LICENCE

An actor assures one that he comes from Peking even if he were born elsewhere, just as, in the not too distant past, all hats came from Paris, or at least so the labels said.

George Kin Leung
Mei Lan-Fang, Foremost Actor of China,
1929

DANCING MICE . . .

Next day, secretary Lange and I rode through the streets. . . . As we passed, we observed a juggler diverting a crowd. On our coming near he played several tricks with great dexterity. He took an handful of small pence . . . and laid them on a table. He then thrust them into his nostril, one by one, with his finger; and this he continued to perform, till the whole was exhausted. After this, he suspended an iron chain, of round links, about four feet long. He then took a mouse out of a box, and made it dance upon the table, quite loose. Then the mouse, at his order, went in at one link of the chain, and out at another, till it ascended to the top; from whence it came down again, the contrary way, without missing so much as one single ring.

John Bell
A Journey from St Petersburg to Pekin
1719–1722, 1763

144

. . . AND SINGING FROGS

Wang Tzu-sun told me that when he was at the capital he saw a man in the street who gave the following performance: He had a wooden box, divided by partitions into twelve holes, in each of which was a frog; and whenever he tapped any one of these frogs on the head with a tiny wand, the frog so touched would immediately begin to sing. Some one gave him a piece of silver, and then he tapped the frogs all round, just as if he was striking a gong; whereupon they all sang together, with their *Do, Ré, Mi, Fa,* in perfect time and harmony.

Herbert A. Giles
Strange Stories from a Chinese Studio, 1908

ENSURING RESPECT

I was often to hear the expression 'yang-kuei,' literally 'sea-devil' or 'pirate,' first applied, no doubt with sufficient justification, to those foreigners from the West who once infested, along with the Chinese pirates, the coast of China.

As a student in Peking, I had learned to be ever on the alert for these ominous words. My fellow students and others long resident in the country duly instructed me that the only way to deal with this insulting nuisance and ensure respect was at once to single out the culprit from the crowd, seize him and hit him hard over the head.

Col. A. W. S. Wingate
A Cavalier in China, 1940

UNEXPECTED RECOGNITION

On the arrival of the distinguished American statesman Mr. Seward in Peking, an amusing incident occurred. Out of deference for his age and infirmities, it had been arranged to carry him in a mule-litter; but the rest of his suite, and also the other foreigners and Chinese accompanying the procession, rode, *more Pekinese*, on ponies, mules, or donkeys—chiefly donkeys: the general effect of uniformed United States officers riding on donkeys was as absurd as that of a native marriage procession. Suddenly, in approaching their Legation, and rounding a bend in the broad Peking street, the eager eyes of the visitors encountered a gorgeous and unwonted spectacle: smart flags and banners; shrill flutes and clanging cymbals; bearers of trousseaux, pots, pans, wardrobes; a gay, closed chair (containing the bride); and then more finery.

'Look!—look!' said some of the local *malins*, anxious that the newly arrived American guests should miss no opportunity of gaining a glimpse into genuine Peking life; 'a mandarin marriage procession!'

The marriage people, on their part, were specially delighted with the negro attendant (on his donkey), who never left Mr. Seward's side; the wedding procession even stopped, all eyes gleaming with interest and pleasure, and gave the coloured man a hearty cheer. The unsophisticated Americans somehow got the notion into their heads that this 'mandarin procession' was a formal welcome to their distinguished statesman sent direct from the Government of China; hitherto so hold-offish, so determined to ignore European merit. So old Mr. Seward rose in his litter, bowing right and left appreciatively at this righteous, but at the same time unexpected recognition of the disinterested policy of the United States, which he seems to have mistaken for a State welcome into the capital, such as the Czars of Muscovy used to grant to foreign envoys.

E. H. Parker
John Chinaman and a Few Others, 1901

REVERENCE FOR CHARACTERS

The Society for the Reverence of Paper Bearing Chinese Characters seems also to require a little explanation. . . . In China, more than anywhere else, knowledge is power—and a knowledge of reading and writing is double power. Hence, even scraps of paper bearing Chinese ideographs are considered to be objects of reverence be they a torn up draft copy of an important document or a printed wrapper for the basest kind of merchandise. To demonstrate such reverence is a gesture of respect to the God of Literature who will shower blessings on such people as a reward, perhaps arranging the possibility of permitting the family of the devotee in question to carry on as a 'reading' family or making a 'reading' family of a 'non-reading' family, and so forth. Paid labourers in the society's employ may be seen from time to time on the streets carrying a big bag made of yellow cloth, bearing their dogmatic motto in Chinese characters, picking up scraps of character-bearing paper and when a sufficient quantity has been gathered, burning them in a bonfire—the most honourable manner of destroying anything.

H. Y. Lowe
The Adventures of Wu, 1940

ACADEMIC PROGRESS

In this university there is a *chaem*, who commands over all the heads of the colleges, and is called by a title of eminent dignity, *xileyxitapou*, that is to say, lord of all the nobles. This *chaem*, for that he is more honourable and of an higher quality than all the rest, keeps as great a court as any *tuton*; for he hath ordinarily a guard of three hundred Mogors, four-and-twenty ushers that go with silver maces before him, and six-and-thirty women, which mounted on white ambling nags, trapped with silk and silver, ride playing on certain very harmonious instruments of music, and singing to the tune thereof, make a pleasing consort after their manner. There are also led before him twenty very handsome spare horses, without any other furniture than their cloths of silver tinsel, and with headstalls full of little silver bells, every horse being waited on by six halberdiers and four footmen very well apparelled. Before all this train goes four hundred *huppes*, with a number of great long chains, which, trailing on the ground, make such a dreadful rattling and noise as does not a little terrify all that are within hearing. Then next to them marches twelve men on horseback called *peretandas*, each of them carrying an umbrella of carnation satin, and other twelve that follow them with banners of white damask, deeply indented, and edged about with golden fringe. Now after all this pomp comes the *chaem* sitting in a triumphant chariot, attended by threescore *conchalys, chumbims,* and *monteos,* such as amongst us are the chancellors, judges, and counsellors of the courts of justice, and these go all on foot, carrying upon their shoulders scimitars rightly garnished with gold. Last of all follow lesser officers, that are like unto our registers, examiners, auditors, clerks, attorneys, and solicitors, all likewise on foot, and crying out unto the people with a loud voice for to retire themselves into their houses, and clear the streets, so as there may be nothing to hinder or trouble the passage of this magnificence.

Fernand Mendez Pinto
The Voyages and Adventures of Fernand
Mendez Pinto, 1614

UNEXPECTED

China is one of the most democratic countries in the world. I have seen the great Li Hung Chang stepping into the Yamen over the bodies of the coolies, who refused to move and who chaffed him as he passed. I have seen a whole Council huddle up their fans and disperse like startled poultry, because a coolie put his head in at the door and exhorted the old gentlemen to be quick, because it was going to rain, and the coolies were going home.

It is the rule of the road in China that all passengers must give way to carriers of burdens, and it was enforced without respect of persons. Being carried in a sedan, with four bearers and four coolies running alongside, I was horrified to perceive the head coolie incontinently knock down an old mandarin who was in the way. The poor old gentleman rolled over and over, Red Button [badge of office] and all; and when he arose, his gorgeous silks all befouled with mud, the coolie spat in his face. China is full of the unexpected.

Admiral Lord Charles Beresford
Memoirs, 1914

SLEIGHING ON THE CANAL

Quite early in winter the thermometer goes down to zero, the canal freezes about half way to the bottom, and the proprietors of *pai-tzu*, which are sleighs as big as carts, do a brisk business pulling pleasure-seekers round the city. The sleigh-men belong to the coolie class and are, I suspect, ricksha-coolies at other seasons of the year. There is certainly a strong family resemblance between their ambitions at the end of a ride and the ambitions of an average ricksha-coolie, and both should be listened to with reserve.

Gilbert Collins
Extreme Oriental Mixture, 1926

ELOQUENCE

Profanity is eloquent in Peking. It has always seemed a grave reflection on the Japanese character, that their language, with the exception of the word 'fool'—and 'countryfied fool' is extremely strong—should contain no opportunities for invective. I was satisfied, however, in Peking.

Peter Quennell
*A Superficial Journey Through Tokyo and
Peking*, 1932

DING-A-LING

The song hit of a recent minstrel show in Peking was entitled 'The Street Calls of Peking'. A young man born and brought up in China gave the various calls arranged in a musical chorus and as he gave them the various tradesmen in costume appeared to illustrate them—the man with fried cakes, the barber, the scissors grinder, the shoe cobbler, the seller of toys and sweets, the peddler of hardboiled eggs or melons or other fruits. If we should hear one of those musical calls in the middle of Fifth Avenue or the Strand,

I am sure it would at once send our thoughts back to beloved old Peking.

Mrs Burgess in 'Peking Caravan' has a charming jingle for children of these street calls, to be recited with appropriate gestures:

> The scissors-grinder goes clank-clank,
>   The barber goes p-ling!
> The oil-man's wood goes clack-clack-clack,
>   Chu-war-di, ding-a-ling.
> The dofu-seller yells his wares,
>   The cloth-man beats his drum,
> The candy-vender rings his bell—
>   Oh, how the streets do hum!

Marian Rider Robinson
Chinese Chapters from the Book of Stanley
Club, 1935

LUXURY AND RAGS

This morning I happened to meet a great funeral procession. The sky was grey and a sharp wind tormented the fringe of the parasol-canopies. On each side, the procession was bordered by a string of men walking in single file, dressed in closely-clinging green shirts which were stencilled with Chinese characters in rust-colour. They had felt hats like flat plates with a ragged plume sticking up in the middle, and carried red staffs tipped with gilded Buddhist emblems. There was also a number of large paper dolls, representing servants and concubines, which were to be burnt, by way of dispatching them to the dead man, and certainly they looked only fit to be cast into flames as quickly as possible in order to rid the world of their foolish smiles and complete inanity of aspect. Then there were children carrying platters of gilded paper squares, which took their place in this illusory apparatus as the riches destined for the dead; other children were carrying bunches of artificial flowers, whose tender colours seemed to be overwhelmed by the menace of the sky. A man in linen breeches with bare legs and feet walked at regular intervals in the ranks striking a gong, to regulate the pace of the procession. He wore a scarlet shirt and cap like those which were once worn by our convicts. When he stopped beating the gong the procession came to a standstill, the children began to laugh and joke among themselves and to furl the parasols with some difficulty, as if they had been sails, and as this was taking place you saw the phœnixes painted on the parasols being folded down on huge, bursting, wine-coloured bull-finches, like birds of prey swooping upon their victims. Some members of the procession fell to scratching themselves, others lighted cigarettes. Some of the lowest rabble in Pekin take part in these processions and nothing is done to give them a presentable appearance. That sense of the fitness of things peculiar to the *bourgeoisie* of Europe is entirely lacking in Asia; there on the contrary you find more pomp than decency and a mixture of elaboration and negligence, of luxury and rags, which, when you have acquired the taste for it, has its own splendour.

Abel Bonnard
(trans. Veronica Lucas)
In China, 1926

FEATHERBEDDING

There exists at Pekin a phalanstery which surpasses in eccentricity all that the fertile imagination of Fourier could have conceived. It is called Ki-mao-fan, that is, 'House of the Hens' Feathers.' By dint of carrying out the laws of progress, the Chinese have found means to furnish to the poorest of the community a warm feather-bed, for the small consideration of one fifth of a farthing per night. This marvellous establishment is simply composed of one great hall, and the floor of this great hall is covered over its whole extent by one vast thick layer of feathers. Mendicants and vagabonds who have no other domicile come to pass the night in this immense dormitory. Men, women, and children, old and young, all without exception, are admitted. Communism prevails in the full force and rigour of the expression. Every one settles himself and makes his nest as well as he can for the night in this ocean of feathers; when day dawns he must quit the premises, and an officer of the company stands at the door to receive the rent of one sapeck each for the night's lodging. In deference no doubt to the principle of equality, half-places are not allowed, and a child must pay the same as a grown person.

On the first establishment of this eminently philanthropic and moral institution, the managers of it used to furnish each of the guests with a covering, but it was found necessary to modify this regulation, for the communist company got into the habit of carrying off their coverlets to sell them, or to supply an additional garment during the rigorous cold of winter. The shareholders saw that this would never do, and they should be ruined, yet to give no covering at all would have been too cruel, and scarcely decent. It was necessary therefore to find some method of reconciling the interests of the establishment with the comfort of the guests, and the way in which the problem was solved was this.

An immense felt coverlet, of such gigantic dimensions as to cover the whole dormitory, was made, and in the day time suspended to the ceiling like a great canopy. When every body had gone to bed, that is to say, had laid down upon the feathers, the counterpane was let down by pulleys, the precaution having been previously taken to make a number of holes in it for the sleepers to put their heads through, in order to escape the danger of suffocation. As soon as it is daylight, the phalansterian coverlet is hoisted up again, after a signal has been made on the tam-tam to awaken those who are asleep, and invite them to draw their heads back into the feathers in order not to be caught by the neck and hoisted into the air with the coverlet. This immense swarm of beggars is then seen crawling about in the sea of dirty feathers and inserting themselves again into their miserable rags, preparatory to gathering into groups and dispersing about the various quarters of the town to seek by lawful or unlawful means their scanty subsistence.

Abbé Huc
The Chinese Empire, 1855

KING OF THE BEGGARS

Among those who partake of the refreshments [at a marriage or funeral] will probably be one or two individuals known as *Hwa Tsu T'ou* (花子頭). They are representatives of the beggars, and if they are well received and given a sum of money on their departure, no trouble need be expected from their fraternity. Should, however, they fail to get what they expect, the doorway will be encumbered with pitiable human objects, who will make themselves as objectionable as possible. Formerly their presence in a house was denoted by hanging two black whips over the doorway, but this custom has been discontinued. They were in fact what is popularly known as Kings of the Beggars, but since the establishment of the modern police force their power has greatly diminished.

R. W. Swallow
Sidelights on Peking Life, 1927

THEATRE SPORTS

Another frequent diversion [at the theatre] is provided by the activities of the towel-distributors, who enjoy a great vogue. They are servants of the management, and two in number; the master towel-distributor establishes a home station at the side of the auditorium and furnishes it with a bucket of hot wet towels, while his journeyman moves about amongst the crowd. The method of distribution is as follows. Master-distributor picks a towel out of the bucket and hurls it to his journeyman, who may be anything up to thirty yards away; the latter catches the flying, spray-scattering utensil and hands it to a heated playgoer, who mops his brow with it and hands it back; towel then makes a rapid return flight, is neatly caught and dropped into a bucket for dirties. Sometimes, if trade is brisk, an outgoing clean towel will pass an incoming used one on the wing, but never will the two collide, and never in history has one of these towel-distributors been known to miss a catch; their dexterity is as wonderful as the speed at which they distribute.

Gilbert Collins
Extreme Oriental Mixture, 1926

DEMOCRACY IN ACTION

Babel [of rickshas after a theatrical performance], a hopeless scrimmage around the doors, shouts and clashing spokes and furious curses. Chinese policemen, brandishing leather straps, hit right and left to clear the way. No nonsense in Peking about human equality; though it may be doubted whether the liability to be beaten, and the opportunity to beat oneself if one gets a chance, is not in essence more subtly democratic—since it hints that the mere possession of a strap is ultimately the only real and lasting difference—than the suaver methods which are employed in Western countries.

Peter Quennell
A Short Journey Through Tokyo and Peking,
1932

THE RULES OF VISITING

We find in ancient courts, and even in some of the present day, that the very soul of the higher spheres in life, is the strict observance of the rules of etiquette. This principle is realized at Peking to its full extent. The ceremonial appears nowhere to such advantage as in visits. Lest there should be any confusion of ranks and stations, the rules of visiting are minutely defined. There are regulations for kings having an interview with dukes, for princes of the blood with the Mongol nobility, for mandarins in visiting each other. Now it is a most important matter, whether a man stands before the gate for one or two hours, or a few minutes; whether the card he sends in is one or two cubits long, and whether he bows six or nine times in ascending the hall. By these regulations, propriety and decorum are kept up. Without knowing the parties, a man well versed in the code of rites, might determine their rank by observing their politeness in an interview. To such perfection have the Chinese brought matters. They shame the court of Lewis XIV and the most accomplished nobility in Europe.

Revd Charles Gutzlaff
China Opened, 1838

FREE LOVE

The number of public women who prostitute themselves for money, reckoning those in the new city as well as those in the suburbs of the old, is twenty-five thousand. To each hundred and to each thousand of these there are superintending officers appointed, who are under the orders of a captain-general. The motive for placing them under such command is this: when ambassadors arrive charged with any business in which the interests of the Great Khan are concerned, it is customary to maintain them at His Majesty's expense, and in order that they may be treated in the most honourable manner, the captain is ordered to furnish nightly to each individual of the embassy one of these courtezans, who is likewise to be changed every night. As this service is considered in the light of a tribute they owe to the sovereign, they do not receive any remuneration.

Marco Polo
The Travels of Marco Polo
(Romroff edition), c.1300

WHERE ARE YOUR TROUSERS?

It is customary in Shantung, when any one is sick, for the womenfolk to engage an old sorceress or medium, who strums on a tambourine and performs certain mysterious antics. This custom obtains even more in the capital, where young ladies of the best families frequently organise such *séances* among themselves. On a table in the hall they spread out a profusion of wine and meat, and burn huge candles which make the place as light as day. Then the sorceress, shortening her skirts, stands on one leg and performs the *shang-yang*, while two of the others support her, one on each side. All this time she is chattering unintelligible sentences, something between a song and a prayer, the words being confused but uttered in a sort of tune; while the hall resounds with the thunder of drums, enough to stun a person, with which her vaticinations are mixed up and lost. By-and-by her head begins to droop, and her eyes to look aslant; and but for her two supporters she would inevitably fall to the ground. Suddenly she stretches forth her neck and bounds several feet into the air, upon which the other women regard her in terror, saying, 'The spirits have come to eat;' and immediately all the candles are blown out and everything is in total darkness. Thus they remain for about a quarter of an hour, afraid to speak a word, which in any case would not be heard through the din, until at length the sorceress calls out the personal name of the head of the family and some others; whereupon they immediately relight the candles and hurry up to ask if the reply of the spirits is favourable or otherwise. They then see that every scrap of the food and every drop of the wine has disappeared. Meanwhile, they watch the old woman's expression, whereby they can tell if the spirits are well disposed; and each one asks her some question, to which she as promptly replies. Should there be any unbelievers among the party, the spirits are at once aware of their presence; and the old sorceress, pointing her finger at such a one, cries out, 'Disrespectful mocker! where are your trousers?' upon which the mocker alluded to looks down, and lo! her trousers are gone—gone to the top of a tree in the court-yard, where they will subsequently be found.

Herbert A. Giles
Strange Stories from A Chinese Studio, 1908

HOPPING LIKE GEESE

Manchu women and girls, especially, are firm believers in spiritualism. On the slightest provocation they consult their medium, who comes into the room gorgeously dressed, and riding on an imitation horse or tiger. In her hand she holds a long spear, with which she mounts the couch and postures in an extraordinary manner, the animal she rides snorting or roaring fiercely all the time. Some call her Kuan Ti, others Chang Fei, and others, again, Chou Kung, from her terribly martial aspect, which strikes fear into all beholders. And should any daring fellow try to peep in while the *séance* is going on, out of the window darts the spear, transfixes his hat, and draws it off his head into the room, while women and girls, young and old, hop round one after the other like geese, on one leg, without seeming to get the least fatigued.

Herbert A. Giles
Strange Stories from A Chinese Studio, 1908

GAMBLING

The Great Kaan hath prohibited all gambling and sharping, things more prevalent there than in any other part of the world. In doing

this, he said: 'I have conquered you by force of arms, and all that
you have is mine; if, therefore, you gamble away your property, it
is in fact my property that you are gambling away.' Not that he
took anything from them however.

Marco Polo
(trans. Col. Sir Henry Yule)
The Book of Ser Marco Polo the Venetian . . . ,
c.1300

HIGH STAKES

The Chinese are passionately addicted to gambling, and the
endless variety of games of chance in common use among
them does credit to their ingenuity and invention.

The respectable merchant, who devotes the hours of
daylight assiduously to his business, sparing no labour in
adjusting the most trifling items of account, will win or lose
thousands of dollars overnight with imperturbable
complacency. Gamblers are, of course, frequently ruined by
the practice. They become desperate after a run of ill luck;
every consideration of duty and interest is sunk, and they play
for stakes which might have startled even the Russian nobles,
who used to gamble for serfs.

Alexander Michie
The Siberian Overland Route, 1864

PEKING CARTS

The Peking cart has been dwelt upon with vituperation, ridicule,
and abuse by all who have endured its jolts and poundings, but the
half cannot be told. The lines of the one conventional cart model
in common use have not been changed since Marco Polo's time,
and this primitive, archaic vehicle has solid axles with hubs like
kegs, and nail-studded wheels heavier than those of any Roman
chariot. . . .

One enters the cart head first, stepping up on a little stool, putting the knee on the shaft, crawling in on the padded floor on all fours, turning, and tucking his heels under him as he faces front. Anything less graceful or less dignified cannot be imagined, and for mighty mandarins and ministers, princes, potentates, and foreign envoys to crawl into a vehicle on all fours, and sit flat on its floor until the time comes to dismount feet foremost, dropping one foot on the tiny stool so dangerously near to the mule's heels, passes all belief.

E. A. Scidmore
China: The Long-Lived Empire, 1900

STREET CHINESE

It may be accepted as a rule that no person over thirty years of age can learn to speak Chinese correctly, as the vocal organs, after that period, appear to have lost a portion of their flexibility. Many persons under that age fail to acquire a command of the language even with the most faithful effort. Not one foreign speaker of Chinese in ten can make the ordinary Chinese cat call. Although I accomplished this feat, I failed, after seventeen years of patient effort, to produce a certain sound with which the donkey-driver urges his long-eared beast about the streets of Peking.

Chester Holcombe
The Real Chinaman, 1895

FORBIDDEN GLIMPSE

Whenever he [the Emperor Guang Xu] was about to perform annual services at any place it was duly announced in the Peking *Gazette,* and special notice was sent to each legation, in order that no foreigners should venture near the imperial procession. The route was always curtained and lined with soldiers for its whole length, every house-window closed, each door guarded, the street paved, smoothed, and strewn with fresh sand. Yet every foreigner in Peking who cared to had seen an imperial procession and enjoyed a good look at Kwangsu, the Son of Heaven, borne along in an open chair, or rather canopied platform, by eighteen or twenty bearers. There were always bannermen and house-owners to be bribed, and once the Chien-men tower guards were surprised and bought up by an energetic Englishman bent on seeing the Emperor and his train proceeding by torchlight to the New Year ceremonies at the Temple of Heaven. All described the dragon countenance of Kwangsu as a pale and sickly one, the glance timid rather than terrifying, and the lonely figure in its simple dark robes extinguished by the blaze of color, the sheen of tinsel and gold, in the uniforms of his suite. Even his chair-bearers wore bright-red and yellow satin tunics close-belted at the waist, and strings of attendants in long yellow satin gowns with rainbow borders in wave patterns dazzled the peeping eye. One tourist, looking through a curtain-slit at the imperial cortège, reported that the gorgeous robes of the Emperor's train were as shabby and greasy, as dirty and threadbare, as the worst that the peddlers ever offer for sale.

E. A. Scidmore
China: The Long-Lived Empire, 1900

BETWEEN THE LINES

Nowhere is the habit of what, in classical language, is styled 'pointing at a deer and calling it a horse' carried to a higher pitch, and conducted on a more generous scale [than in the journal of official record, the Peking *Gazette*] . . . When a whole column of the 'leading journal' of China is taken up with a description of the various aches and pains of some aged mandarin who hungers and thirsts to retire from His Majesty's service, what does it all mean? When his urgent prayer to be relieved is refused, and he is told to go back to his post at once, what does that mean? What do the long memorials reporting as to matters of fact really connote? . . .

Firmly are we persuaded that the individual who can peruse a copy of the Peking *Gazette* and, while reading each document, can form an approximately correct notion as to what is really behind it, knows more of China than can be learned from all the works on this Empire that ever were written. But is there not reason to fear that by the time any outside barbarian shall have reached such a pitch of comprehension of China as this implies, we shall be as much at a loss to know what *he* meant by what *he* said, as if he were really Chinese?

A. H. Smith
Chinese Characteristics, 1894

LOOKED UPON AS MAD

The student interpreter sent out to Peking by H. M. Government, with a view to acquiring a knowledge of the language, is apt to laugh when older men solemnly warn him against the insidiousness of the study on which he is embarking. There can be little doubt that when once a man has got keen on the language he counts no more as a practical man of affairs. The sinologue is rightly looked upon as mad until he proves his sanity.

'A Resident of Peking'
China As It Really Is, 1912

DEALING WITH GHOSTS

Not only does the Peking mind, even the most free-thinking, abound with portents, omens and magics, but many ghosts haunt it, together with will-o'-the-wisps and fairies. These ghosts are more harmful than ours, for they are perpetually, in order to gain their own freedom, luring and driving men to their death, or even, with true simplicity of plan, killing strangers by the shock of their materialisation. Continually the drowned thus rise on dark nights to misguide the feet of human beings and lead them into the water: while evil spirits exist who build up round men invisible rooms, thus walling them up alive, and others who urge them to hang themselves, actually holding the rope in position for their victims (one of these lives in a garden in the Legation Quarter!), or Demon Barbers come and shave off a man's hair while he is asleep, so that it never will grow again. Idols in temples can be possessed, and so can living people; these last often by dead relatives, who impose upon them their ways of speaking and tricks of manner. Of fairies, the fox-fairy is the most usual, and, though by nature intensely mischievous, aids mortals more often than he injures them. (The Fox Tower was formerly badly haunted by these fox-fairies, and one is said to live, too, in the Temple of Heaven, but he is an exception to his tribe, epicene and malignant. He appears either as a beautiful woman or good-looking man, and friendship with him entails death at no very distant period.) Snake, badger and hedgehog, though not as influential in the spirit world as the fox, are also to be mistrusted on psychical grounds: their powers, as opposed to the often helpful activities of the fox, are those of the poltergeist, throwing stones and rattling doors and windows: and victims must remember that the professional exorcizer who can deal with a fox may be powerless with a hedgehog, and so it is important first to identify precisely the species. Finally there is an innocuous but unpleasant ghost, a black patch, without arms, legs or head, who likes to wander about at night. . . . Against these ghosts and evil influences there are many remedies, such as biting the tip of the middle finger and smearing the intruders with the blood from it, or rubbing your hair very violently: while a mirror over your door will defeat spirits that want to enter it, then thrown awry in their orientation. A lion on the roof cornice is also said to be of some use.

Osbert Sitwell
Escape With Me!, 1939

162

CHAPTER 9

SHOPPING

There were glass flowers of all kinds and colours to put into bowls of water or to hold candles, and we bought cocktail sticks and lots of the little glass animals you put into finger-bowls.

EILLEEN WALKER
A Naval Wife Goes East, 1936

*I*n the thirteenth century, according to John de Cora, the shopping in Peking was better than in Paris or Rome. Peking was then capital of the wealthiest country in the world, a storing-house for tribute, and the last stop on the silk route from Europe. It had become famed as a repository for all that was costly and rare.

When foreigners arrived in numbers at the end of the nineteenth century, they shopped voraciously for the costly and rare, and for quite a lot else besides. 'Curios' were snapped up and carried off to bring a touch of the exotic to drawing rooms in Europe and America.

In the unsettled circumstances of the time, moreover, pieces of genuine worth (if uncertain provenance) were often to be had. They had been looted, or sold off by families fallen on hard times. Eliza Scidmore describes collectors waiting impatiently for the time when the next upheaval might bring fresh stocks onto the market. Two years after she wrote came the Boxer uprising.

Liulichang has for long been the main street for buying antiques and works of art. Other areas were traditionally associated with other commodities—the Street of Lanterns outside Qian Men, the tea shops about the four pailous (memorial arches) in the Tartar City, the Mongol horse market at present-day Tiananmen, and so on.

Western shoppers have, by and large, never been terribly well informed about the goods on offer. Enthusistic (and wealthy) friends of the American diplomat Leslie Einstein, himself apparently a discriminating purchaser, perplexed him with their eagerness to buy at face value the dubiously authentic works of long-dead Chinese artists. That many such purchases subsequently found their way into major Western collections is a confusion that largely remains to be resolved.

CAPITAL INFLOW

You find in this country a greater variety of merchandize than in the territories of Rome or of Paris. They have great store of gold and silver and of precious stones. For when any merchants from foreign parts come thither to trade, they leave there their gold and silver and precious stones, and they carry away the products of the country; spices, silk, cloths of silk and cloths of gold, of which they find great quantities for sale here.

John de Cora
The Book of the Estate of the Great Caan . . ., c.1330

ESSENTIAL

At Peking, curio-hunting is as essential an item for the sightseer as a trip to the Forbidden City or the Summer Palace.

Francis de Croisset
(trans. Paul Selver)
The Wounded Dragon, 1937

SUPPLY AND DEMAND

From every street rise the sounds of gongs and drums being beaten in a thousand different ways (each with its own significance to the initiated), of flutes and pipes and multifarious cries, the wooden clack of rattles, the jingle of bells, the hum of the tuning-fork, the clink of metal on metal. These indicate the presence of the ubiquitous street-vendors who supply Peking housewives with necessities and luxuries, the whole day long and right through the night, at their very doorsteps: and though the instrument, tuning-fork or drum, may be shared by a score of occupations, the effect of its playing differs as much as the trades it represents. There are, too, auditory tokens of that opposite kind of itinerant dealer, who wishes to buy; the parchment drum of the ambitious seeker for jade and jewels, who taps out a special rhythm as he wails his wants, or, humbler and more easily gratified, the unaccompanied growl of 'I will give money for foreign bottles, I also buy scrap iron and broken glass'. But the cries of the vendors were, of course—for supply always seems to me to outstrip demand—much more plentiful and heterogeneous than those of the purchasers.

Osbert Sitwell
Escape With Me!, 1939

THE VALUE OF WHITE

By profession my friend was a judge of the newly established Supreme Court, the duties of which did not seem to be particularly arduous. I knew him principally as a judge of porcelain, and I remain grateful to him for having trained my eye to a better understanding of the Chinese appreciation of colour, which is far more delicate than our own. Once he urged me to purchase a small cup, which owing to a slight flaw was unsuitable for his collection but would be useful, he insisted, in order to educate me to a proper understanding of white. He compared its hue to the complexion of a girl of twelve and then contrasted this with the shade of a neighbouring vase which was like that of a woman of forty; and after he had pointed out these differences, the value of white possessed a new significance to me.

Lewis Einstein
A Diplomat Looks Back, 1968

COIN OF THE REALM

The 17th, I sent to inform the captain of the Chinese guard, that I intended to take a turn through the city; who immediately gave orders for a soldier to attend me. When we passed through the gate, the clerk marked our names in his book, and dashed them out at our return. I went into several shops, where were sold different kinds of merchandise; particularly those of the goldsmiths, whose business it is to exchange gold for silver, or silver for gold. In these shops are found vast quantities of those valuable metals, cast into bars of different sizes, and piled up one upon another; which are sold only by weight, as there is no current coin in this country; except one small round piece of brass, with a square hole in the middle, through which may be run a string, for the convenience of carrying them to market. This coin, called *joss* by the Chinese, is about the value of one tenth of a penny sterling; and is extremely useful among the common people. With one of them, a man can buy a dish of hot tea, a pipe of tobacco, or a dram of brandy, in the streets; and a beggar may dine for three of them.

John Bell
A Journey from St Petersburg to Pekin
1719–1722, 1763

FUN OF THE FAIR

Peking, 7 March 1866

I don't recollect whether I ever mentioned to you the Liu Li Chang, a street of booksellers and curiosity shops, and one of my favourite lounges here. . . . A very amusing fair is held there. It is perfectly thronged with people, and a very gay scene. Toys and artificial flowers are the best things sold; some of the former are capital. Lifelike models of insects, tiny beasts and birds, tops, kites of all shapes, and above all some little figures of European soldiers and sailors—caricatures of the late war—that were irresistibly comic. . . .

A peep-show represented views taken in China and Europe, of which the exhibitor was as ignorant as his audience: he described St. Paul's Cathedral and the Bay of Naples as places of repute in the Lew Chew Islands; and I really should be

ashamed to tell you what was painted on the reverse of the view of St. Paul's.

A. B. Freeman-Mitford
The Attaché at Peking, 1866 pub. 1900

MADE IN JAPAN

There is a factory of cloisonné enamels near the Liu-li-chang, which produces large pieces after the best old designs; and as Chinese taste and artistic invention seem alike dead in this decade, it is best that they tread the conventional way. They cannot repeat the softest colors of the old Ming enamels, but the Japanese deceive Peking connoisseurs as easily with their artistic forgeries of old enamels as with their counterfeits of old porcelains, and of both such importations the Liu-li-chang holds full supply.

E. A. Scidmore
China: The Long-Lived Empire, 1900

CHINESE LANTERNS

The shops of Lantern Street outside the Ch'ien Mên, however, still have a glittering exhibition which draws the happy holiday crowd and serves as an advertisement to attract purchasers. The varieties displayed are infinite—all shapes, materials, decorations, sizes and prices, and all alight in the open shops. Wall-lanterns to put on either side of the front door are offered in pairs. Others are sold in sets, eight or sixteen, intended to be hung together and thus form a complete picture; 'Guest-lanterns'—large white silk moons decorated with the purchaser's name and lucky bats—intended to light visitors across a courtyard to the reception hall, stand ready on bamboo tripods. Cheap paper lanterns cunningly made to copy living creatures hang from the ceiling; fantastic crabs with moving claws, dragon-flies with flapping wings, birds with swaying necks. Glass or gauze panels painted with historic scenes, mounted in carved wood frames, are displayed in great variety. Inside the shops there are many special lanterns for special purposes. Of such are those in the shape of little boys, intended for presents to childless families; 'heavenly lanterns' to be hoisted on a high pole in the courtyard and decorated with fir branches; round toy-lanterns made to roll on the ground like a fire-ball, lanterns set on wheels, red paper lamps pricked with tiny pin-holes to form a lucky character, like 'happiness' or 'prosperity.' '*Tso ma têng*' or horse-racing lanterns which consist of two or more wire frames, one within the other, 'arranged on the principle of the smoke-jack so that a current of air sets them revolving;' and, finally, cross-word-puzzle lanterns with riddles pasted on their sides intended to hang outside a scholar's home for the amusement of his literary friends.

Juliet Bredon and
Igor Mitrophanow
The Moon Year, 1927

COOL WATER

Peking streets echo with the song of the ragged peddler:

'Soothing syrups cooled with ice,
Try them once, you'll take them twice,
A copper a glass to forget the heat,
And the taste is sweet, the taste is sw-e-e-t.'

Customers gather round the stall sipping these water-ices flavoured with 'driving-away-heat ingredients'—dried orange-peel, magnolia-rind, cardamon and hibiscus—from cracked glasses, and stirring them with spoons no thicker than tin foil. In bygone days, when the Emperor watched over his people with fatherly solicitude, jars of cool water for free distribution were placed near police stations with the inscription: 'The Imperial mercy is all-embracing.' Rich and charitable folk continued the custom for a while, but their generosity was sometimes ill repaid, if we may believe the cynical saying: 'Some give the ice water, others steal the drinking spoons.'

Juliet Bredon and
Igor Mitrophanow
The Moon Year, 1927

THE ICEMAN COMETH

We met with one very pleasant thing in the Imperial City, which is abundance of Ice, an infinite quantity is consum'd, and yet it is not worth above half a Farthing a Pound. The manner of using it is not the same as among us, but they take a piece as clean and transparent as the very Chrystal, which is put into a earthen-ware Bason, and over it they pour some fair Water, so by degrees it dissolves, and the Water is so very cold there is no drinking of it. This Drink is wholesom in that Country, and very convenient because of the vast Heat. They have not got the way in China of making the Ice Cisterns as we do in Europe, but it is very pleasant to see Cart-loads of Ice at every Corner of a Street, and Men going about to offer it as you go by.

Domingo Navarrete
*The Travels and Controversies of Friar
Domingo Navarrete*, 1676

SOMETHING FOR EVERYONE

The ten temple markets are practically one moving market, open at each temple on special days of the month, usually every ten or fifteen days and for not more than two days at a time except when the temple has some special festival. As the temples do not ordinarily have their markets on the same day the dealers go from one market to another and are busy practically every day of the month. Connected with these temple markets there are always entertainers, story-tellers, boxers, magicians, singers and sometimes lecturers of the Board of Education.

Sidney D. Gamble
Peking: A Social Survey, 1921

TOFFEE APPLES

Dear to the children is the crab-apple man with the great broom on his shoulder, every straw stick strung with little red apples preserved in honey. His recipe came originally from the Mongols who wear these fruits, preserved in this way, strung on strings around their necks, and often take a bite from their necklace as they ride or bargain. It was in fact the Mongols who developed the sweet tooth of Asia, carrying their love of sugared dainties with them in their conquests and passing it on to the Turks, the Persians and all the peoples of the Orient, so that by their sweets one may still trace the path of the once-powerful Khans.

Juliet Bredon
Peking, 1922

POCKMARKED WANG

In one neighbourhood on the so-called Brass Street in Peking there are about seven or eight cutlery shops, crowded solidly together shoulder to shoulder, all displaying signs of *Wang Ma Tze* (王麻子), or 'The Shop of Wang the Pockmarked', for it was once noticed by the critical buying public that one man with such markings on his face and going by the name of Wang sold the best pairs of scissors in town. To keep themselves 'in the money', these shops unanimously adopted the same name and to avoid friction with a view to harmony and co-existence, each of them has affixed a word before the name and side by side stand the shops of *Wang Ma Tze*, and *Lao* (老) (Old) *Wang Ma Tze, Chen* (真) (Genuine) *Wang Ma Tze, Chen Cheng* (真正) (Genuine and Straight) *Wang Ma Tze*, and *Chen Cheng Lao* (真正老) (Genuine Straight and Old) *Wang Ma Tze*, and so on and so forth and Mr. Customer is the only one ever puzzled by these names.

H. Y. Lowe
The Adventures of Wu, 1940

THE TABLES TURNED

As in Japan, so in China the halcyon days of curio-hunting are past. No longer is it common for a foreign connoisseur to drop into a shop and pick up something of great value for a mere song; it is much commoner for a tourist to blunder into a shop and pick up something of no value at all for a handsome price.

Gilbert Collins
Extreme Oriental Mixture, 1925

MUSEUM PIECES

After the Chinese Revolution, almost incredible stores of raw jade came into the hands of the Peking dealers, the loot of Imperial treasure houses in the Forbidden City, where some of it had been kept for unknown periods. Only in recent years, however, with the rise in price of Chinese antiquities, did it become worth the while of the Chinese dealers to bring to the working of these jades the scholarly study and highly paid workmanship which they demanded. Then, the foreign fashion in Chinese art having swung from the seventeenth and eighteenth centuries toward more remote periods, there began to appear in 'Jade Street' an astonishing profusion of Han jade—the right stone, the right colour, the right designs. The dealers said that to meet the demand they had sent agents into the interior, who had returned with what they smilingly assured the buyer to be the select pilferings from tombs of the most respectable antiquity. In point of fact, it is worked in Peking, from Han and other ancient designs, diamond drills being used to emulate the superb polish of the ancient craftsmen. I suppose that all of the skilled buyers, even the honest ones, have tumbled to it by this time; but I doubt not that before they did a number of pieces were acquired by the best-regulated museums.

Owen Lattimore
The Desert Road to Turkestan, 1928

WILLING BUYERS

Our hotels are filled with globe-trotters and the travelling salesmen of half-a-dozen S'hai and T'tsin stores, and the ginger jars in which Chyloong used to pack chowchow ginger and other preserves are being sold as curios—blue and white—for Tls. 400! One strawberry vase, six inches high, has just been bought by Holcombe (ex-missionary, ex-chargé, future U.S. Minister, and now curio-dealer) for Tls. 1500, it is going to America and will probably fetch Tls. 10,000 there from pockets so filled with money that their masters are glad to have an excuse for attempting to enjoy the novel sensation of depletion!

Sir Robert Hart
Letter to J. D. Campbell, 5 October
1890

SOUVENIRS

There are, besides, a number of smaller articles which to the visitor will prove very interesting as souvenirs, such as:—

Sets of chopsticks,
Box of dominoes,
Coolie purses,
Coolie water pipe,
Genteel water pipe,
Ladies' shoes, ordinary,
Abacus counting board,
Peking snuff bottles,
Brass padlocks,
Packs of playing cards,

Genteel purses,
White metal pipe,
Enamelled water pipe,
Embroidered sachets,
Shoes, small footed,
Enamelled buttons, in sets,
Painted fish bowls,
Sets of mandarin buttons,
Embroidered spectacle
cases.

Thomas Cook & Co
Peking and the Overland Route, 1922

GOLDEN OPPORTUNITY

I suppose the truly gullible can buy more appalling rubbish in Peking than anywhere else in the world.

Ronald Farquerson
Confessions of a China Hand, 1950

RUN TO GROUND

I was glad to find at Peking my friend Charles L. Freer, who had got over his interest in the Nabbatean forgeries which brought him to Constantinople. He was then in quest of a picture by Li Lung Mien, who had been Prime Minister in the Sung dynasty but had left the Emperor's service in order to become a painter. Authentic specimens of a talent which flourished nearly a thousand years ago are rarer than Giorgiones, and although many works have been claimed for his brush few undisputed examples of his art exist except among the treasures of the Emperor of Japan. Freer however felt convinced that he was on the track of one in Peking. The picture was not for sale nor was he allowed even to see it; but the knowledge of its existence excited his pursuit, and when he asked for a suggestion of how it could be obtained the intermediary advised him to return in twelve months, as the family might then be in need of money.

After the year had elapsed Freer arrived once more in Peking and related to me with immense pride that he had been able to purchase not one, but seven of this artist's masterpieces, which most unexpectedly had come to light in the interval!

Leslie Einstein
A Diplomat Looks Back, 1968

CONSUMER RESISTANCE

Monday, 6th January [1913]—Bettina has been marketing in the Chinese town. She brought back two Japanese plates and a basket for Tricksy. She says that she saw a leper leaning up against the carcase of a calf that hung outside a butcher's shop. For the rest of her stay in China she is resolved to remain a vegetarian. I suggested that she had better not visit the vegetable market, or there will be nothing left for her to eat.

Daniele Varè
Laughing Diplomat, 1938

BEFORE THE CRASH

The Liu-li-chang, the booksellers' street, used to be the Peking delight and treasure-house. There scholars and dilettanti still prowl to buy the immortal classics in ten thousand volumes, rubbings of old inscriptions, scroll pictures, painted books, and the conventional ornaments and necessaries for the writing-table; but the curio-shops, where jade and porcelain, lacquer and bronze, used to embarrass the visitor's choice, have suffered a serious falling off, and thus robbed Peking of its greatest delights and temptations. Each war, with its vicissitudes among the great families, flooded the market with treasures galore; but between such crises one searches long, and he needs to be on the alert for the imitations that abound. All the dragons there now have five claws, all the hawthorns have the double ring of Kanghsi or the seal of Chenghua. There are treasures yet cherished in Peking, so great was the activity of artists and artisans in the centuries just gone, when ten thousands of pieces of porcelain were sent annually to the Peking palace for gifts; but the owners of such art objects can afford to keep them until some great political convulsion, the fall of the dynasty, a foreign war with another sack of the palaces, brings them into the market. Every amateur is eagerly waiting for some such crash, and dozens avow themselves ready to take flight to Peking from the ends of the earth.

E. A. Scidmore
China: The Long-Lived Empire, 1900

AGRICULTURAL AND PASTORAL

At Pekin also, I attended a very large horse fair. The stables and courtyards of the inns near the market, were crowded with horses of every description to be found in the empire. The sellers were most obliging, giving persons who were desirous of purchasing steeds every facility for riding them on trial, along the adjacent thoroughfare. At this fair I purchased a horse, which candour compels me to confess was not at all remarkable either for proportions or speed, I also visited the sheep and pig market at Pekin. The sheep were not confined to pens, but were bound together by ropes in lots of five or six, and tethered to posts. Each pig was rendered completely *hors de combat*, by being bound by the legs, and lay upon the ground with a doleful expression of utter helplessness.

J. H. Gray
China: A History of the Laws, Manners and
Customs of the People, 1878

DOUBLEDEALING

Scarcely less effective in their dress, because, though less elaborate and splendid, their clothes are more wild and tattered, we may meet a group of Mongolian clansmen—their faces precisely those wrongly attributed by Europeans to the Chinese in their entirety. These have come to sell droves of ponies—that absurdly resemble those T'ang pottery horses so many of which have found their way from tombs to London drawing-rooms—and having sold them, to spend the resultant money, and also a sum, previously saved up for several years for this purpose, in Peking. (Always they carry their money straight to Jade Street, to buy jewellery, their only form of investment, and the shopkeepers, informed beforehand by underground channels of the day of their arrival, invariably, in order to do good business, prepare and adopt the same stratagem, with reason confident that it will never be discovered. Aware that

176

these clownish tribesmen possess a magpie-like impulsion toward the theft of any brightly glittering objects upon which they can lay their hands, the cunning Chinese goldsmith will leave within easy reach a few scintillating baubles of no value, and pretend not to notice when they disappear, for he knows that, once they have been allowed to pocket them, the strangers, in their ignorance, and in their secret delight at having already got something for nothing, will be willing to pay the most exorbitant price for the articles they buy in the ordinary way of business.)

Osbert Sitwell
Escape With Me!, 1939

GOD'S GOOD THINGS

In this city there are sixscore piazzas or public places, in each of the which is a fair kept every month. Now during the two months' time that we were at liberty in this city, we saw eleven or twelve of these fairs, where were an infinite company of people, both on horseback and on foot, that out of boxes hanging about their necks sold all things that well-near can be made, as the haberdashers of small wares do amongst us, besides the ordinary shops of rich merchants, which were ranged very orderly in the particular streets, where was to be seen a world of silk stuffs, tinsels, cloth of gold, linen and cotton cloth, sables, ermines, musk, aloes, fine porcelain, gold and silver plate, pearl, seed pearl, gold in powder, and ingots and such other things of value, whereat we nine Portugals were exceedingly astonished. But if I should speak in particular of all the other commodities that were to be sold there, as of iron, steel, lead, copper, tin, latten, coral, cornelian, crystal, quicksilver, vermilion, ivory, cloves, nutmegs, mace, ginger, tamarinds, cinnamon, pepper, cardamom, borax, honey, wax, sanders, sugar, conserves, acates, fruit, meal, rice, flesh, venison, fish, pulse, and herbs; there was such abundance of them, as it is scarce possible to express it in words.

The Chinese also assured us that this city hath a hundred and threescore butchers' shambles, and in each of them a hundred

177

stalls, full of all kinds of flesh that the earth produceth for that these people feed on all, as veal, mutton, pork, goat, the flesh of horses, buffaloes, rhinoceroses, tigers, lions, dogs, mules, asses, otters, chamois, badgers, and finally of all other beasts whatsoever. Furthermore, besides the weights which are particularly in every shambles, there is not a gate in the city that hath not its scales, wherein the meat is weighed again, for to see if they have their due weight that have bought it, to the end that by this means the people may not be deceived. Besides those ordinary shambles there is not scarce a street but hath five or six butchers' shops in it, where the choicest meat is sold; there are withal many taverns, where excellent fare is always to be had, and cellars full of gammons of bacon, dried tongues, powdered geese, and other savoury viands, for to relish one's drink, all in so great abundance, that it would be very superfluous to say more of it; but what I speak is to show how liberally God hath imparted to these miserable blinded wretches the good things which He hath created on the earth, to the end that His holy name may therefore be blessed for evermore.

Fernand Mendez Pinto
The Voyages and Adventures of Fernand
Mendez Pinto, 1614

FINE JUDGEMENT

The heat is not so overpowering this evening; let us go out and visit the art-dealers, in search of *curios* as they call them here. The most important of these curiosity-shops occupy a whole quarter to themselves. The dealers will greet us with bows and smiles, and then they are accustomed to leave their visitors to betray the nature and level of their tastes by the choice that they make. If they think you worth the trouble they will carefully unpack their rarest objects, and are quite equal to showing you real and false antiquities with exactly the same expression on their faces.

And yet, however impassive they may force themselves to appear, they are as inquisitive as children. Should you arrive in one of these shops carrying a purchase that you have already made, they will not rest until they have stealthily discovered what it is, and I think there is more chance of your making a bargain if they perceive that you have just been buying something elsewhere. Suppose that you lay the parcel down and walk away, they will creep up to it, and gently lift a corner of the paper wrapped round it and if you turn suddenly round they will just manage to find time to change the expression of their faces from puerile curiosity to the usual impenetrability. When you ask them the price of anything they are artless enough to hesitate a moment. They are evidently appraising the foreigner's resources, the depths of his ignorance; they are communing with their perceptions to decide how much the foreigner will stand in the way of being 'rooked.' They might be compared to a sportsman selecting the cartridge which is to bring the game down. At last they decide; they fire: the price is named!

Abel Bonnard
(trans. Veronica Lucas)
In China, 1926

GENUINE FAKE

The point is that in China there is no such thing as a 'fake,' or rather, the word 'fake' does not imply the disparagement which we Westerners associate with it. In China a 'fake' is a rearrangement, almost an improvement. It involves the idea of achieving a higher degree of beauty, of reaching closer to perfection. When an art worker adds three hoofs to a camel which was made ten centuries ago and now has only one leg; if he adds a head to a Rann warrior who has been beheaded or an arm to a Kwanin krang-si, he does not do so to defraud anyone. By restoring the missing parts of a curio, he is paying it the respectful tribute of his honest admiration. This is no 'fake'; it is an act of worship.

Francis de Croisset
(trans. Paul Selver)
The Wounded Dragon, 1937

THE FOUR PAILOWS

One thumps and jolts his way northward a mile and more, either by
shady streets of old Manchu residences, or along the main street
running from the Hata-men's arch, the latter a broad, busy
thoroughfare, lined with shops with gaudy fronts and gables, and
double-lined with booths, mat- and canvas-covered stalls. Carts
traverse a raised causeway—a dike between two awful ditches
of open sewers or cesspools—and the traffic is so great, and blockades
are so frequent, that one is in constant terror of being backed into
these foul ditches and pools of horror by a locked wheel, a balking
mule, or a crumbling bank's edge. Where a broad, lateral street
crosses at right angles each approach is spanned by a grand pailow,
these commemorative wooden arches in Peking being strangely
shabby and rickety compared with the splendid carved granite and
marble pailow of the Grand Canal and South China. At this
crossroads of commerce—the Four Pailows—the great banks, the tea,
silk-, medicine-, and confectionery-shops of the Tatar City are
gathered, and there is always a blockade of carts, chairs,
wheelbarrows, camels, mules, and donkeys, and an incredible stream
of people—Mongols from the plains, Manchu notables and common
folk, priests, spectacled Chinese,
and always the Manchu women
in their gorgeous coiffures
as brilliant features in this
fashionable shopping quarter.
The Four Pailow tea-shop has a
front so carved and gilded that
one can hardly credit its
consecration to commerce and
trade; but he buys there the same
perfumed oolong, redolent of
jasmine-buds or *Olea fragrans*, that
is served one at the superior silk-
and curio-shops, until he learns to
like it and forever associate it with
certain stone-floored interiors,
the dazzle of splendid fabrics, and
crowded displays of rich art

objects. The Four Pailow drug-store is carved and gilded out of all reason, and the confectioner's shop is as alluring without all the sugared and honeyed sweets on the counters. At the Four Pailow silk-shop one is ushered in, according to his purse and rank, to farther and farther courts, the tribute of signal esteem being isolation in a far-back, lonely, stony sepulcher or little trade temple, with two reserve alcove rooms, where braziers and hot tea are needed to thaw and cheer one between the waits for more and more baskets and armfuls of silks, satins, brocades, velvets, crapes, gauze, linen, and furs from their separate storehouses. Tailors and embroiderers ply the needle and the goose in long side-buildings, and there is a room of remnants that would set Occidental shoppers wild, while in the mirrored salesroom near the street Manchu matrons, in their flowered and gold-barred coiffures, deliberate over the stuffs for their future finery.

E. A. Scidmore
China: The Long-Lived Empire, 1900

TEMPLE FAIR

And the people of this ancient but childlike race were sauntering to and fro in crowds. Here is one, deeply serious in his futility, buying a little bird and bending to examine it with an expressionless face. Some, you see, are already walking away, cage in hand, with a cloth over the cage to save the little occupant from being scared. Here is a child who has just become possessed of a white mouse. An old man is carrying away a glass jar containing a fish he has just bought. He holds it with much circumspection, in both hands and as he recedes into the distance you can no longer see the jar of water and the red fish looks as if it were suspended in the air between his hands.

Abel Bonnard
(trans. Veronica Lucas)
In China, 1926

CHAPTER 10

FOOD AND DRINK

It really takes a lifetime for a foreigner to understand a Chinese dinner, and it takes a large part of a lifetime to eat it.

MRS ALEC-TWEEDIE
An Adventurous Journey, 1926

P eking's native food is that of Shandong. But as befits a capital, it has long housed restaurants capable of serving the regional cuisines of all China. Over its time as capital, moreover, it has seen the rise and fall of two non-Chinese dynasties, periods when the fare at court seemed alien and even barbaric to the real Pekingers. (And not just the Pekingers—the Dutchman, André Van Braam, describes an encounter with haunches of boiled meat 'of which the sight alone was enough to disgust a man with mutton for the rest of his days'.)

Both the food and the way it was served were new experiences for travellers from other countries. So was the etiquette at banquets. In Marco Polo's day 'men like giants' armed with staves were on hand to guarantee good manners. By the 1920s, direct action had been replaced by the guidance of books like Jermyn Lynn's *Social Life of the Chinese in Peking*. Lynn, a returned student from the United States, is particularly good on tipping, an indispensible part of entertaining then as now.

Latterly, foreigners, discomforted by their awkwardness in dealing with Chinese hospitality, had a ready revenge open to them in the shape of the diplomatic dinner. Western food was every bit as much a novelty to the native citizens of Peking as 'Chinese chow' was to new arrivals. Entertaining in the Western style became very fashionable, although perhaps never very popular.

REGIONAL DELICACIES

Like most capitals of the world, Peking prided itself upon the many kinds of eating houses it possessed, each having its speciality. For instance, the Cantonese could prepare a highly expensive twenty-dollar sharksfin soup, the Fukienese several varieties of tasty fish dishes, the Szechuenese and Yunnanese the hottest meat seasoned with chilies imported from their own provinces, the Shanghainese the most attractive vegetarian specialities, the Tientsinese their famous mantou in flowery form and also chiaotzu (rissoles) and the Manchurians their lovely white fish during the winter months from the River Sungari, as well as their famous dried tadpole spawn cooked with crushed chicken flesh.

Wu Lien Tuh
Plague Fighter, 1959

HOT STUFF

Most of the people of Cathay drink wine of the kind that I shall now describe. It is a liquor which they brew of rice with a quantity of excellent spice, in such fashion that it makes better drink than any other kind of wine; it is not only good, but clear and pleasing to the eye. And being very hot stuff, it makes one drunk sooner than any other wine.

Marco Polo
(trans. Col. Sir Henry Yule)
The Book of Ser Marco Polo the Venetian . . . ,
c.1300

THE BIG WINE VAT

The 'big wine vat' is so called because although the shop is equipped with a regular Chinese full-length counter where much of the trade is conducted, it is also provided with a number of big heavy vats, half sunk into the ground, leaving just so much of the height also to serve the purpose of acting as the 'legs' of tables. These vats—a number of them—are lined up against the walls, with heavy wooden covers serving as 'tops', and a number of little stools around them seat by twos and threes the customers coming in groups for their daily ritual. On these big wine jars, glazed a shiny black, are pasted squares of red paper bearing any one of a group of four charactered conventionalized phrases in praise of the precious liquors, such as *Chiu Kuo Ch'ang Ch'un* (酒國長春), 'Wine Country Always Spring', or *Wen Hsiang Hsia Ma* (聞香下馬), 'Smelling Fragrance Dismount Horse', and so forth. The shop owners apparently had some spare red paper left after making these squares, for scattered all over the walls were little stickers, reading *Mo T'an Kuo Shih* (莫談國事), meaning 'Do Not Talk Politics', and others which would translate as 'No Credit', 'Cash Only', and 'Please Do Not Open Your Honourable Mouth'!

H. Y. Lowe
The Adventures of Wu, 1940

184

ONE MAN'S MEAT . . .

The emperor's people are very worthily arrayed, and live in a rich and liberal manner. . . . They have sundry kinds of dishes made of canes, which are there very great and thick. They eat meat of all kinds of beasts, and when they will make a great feast they kill camels, and make fine dishes of the flesh after their own

fashion. They have fish in great abundance, and other things; and on these they live after their manner, as other people do after theirs.

John de Cora
The Book of the Estate of the Great Caan . . ., c.1330

LITTLE APPETITE

January 20, 1795

The outer court [of the Hall of Preserving Harmony in the Forbidden City], in which most of the guests were obliged to breakfast in the open air, was covered with thick carpets, on which were laid the cushions that each guest had taken care to make his servant bring in order that he might sit down more conveniently on the ground fronting the pavilion.

Opposite the throne was pitched a great tent of yellow cloth, in which the side-board was arranged. Then in the court before the pavilion were placed four rows of little and low tables covered with coarse linen, and so disposed that there was one between every two persons, except opposite his Excellency and me, where a separate table was placed for each of us.

This court was surrounded by persons of all ranks and all classes, not excepting stage-players and servants. The latter had the impudence to come and stand before the great Mandarins, in order to get a better view of us.

It was past eight o'clock when his Majesty came with an escort of musicians, and took his seat upon the throne. Everybody then rose, and, falling directly upon their knees, performed the salute of honour. The music continued while a table was served for the Emperor, who ate of several of the dishes set upon it. This was a signal for the guests, all whose tables were then uncovered; they approached and fell to with great avidity.

I observed that the arrangement of all the tables was the same, and that there were exactly fifty dishes on each. This must appear very surprising, perhaps even incredible to my readers, after what I have said of the smallness of these tables. But I have to add that the viands, served up in very dirty copper basons, consisted first of three rows of four dishes each, and that over this first layer or stratum were three others, amounting also to twelve dishes each. Lastly, to make the four dozen fifty, there were at the top of all two great copper basons, in which boiled legs of mutton were contained, and of which the sight alone was enough to disgust a man with mutton for the rest of his days. The other dishes consisted of farinaceous aliments, dressed in different manners, or merely boiled in the way of hasty pudding. There were also cakes much resembling the unleavened bread eaten by the Jews at their festival of the Paschal Lamb. Lastly there were sweetmeats and fruits. I took a little of the latter, feeling no temptation to taste the rest.

André-Everard Van Braam
Authentic Account of the Embassy of the
Dutch East-India Company to the Court of
China in the Years 1794 and 1795, 1797

SAVING ON LINEN

I ever heard it agreed, that the Emperor's Table was made up of Fifteen, each answering to a particular Province, and containing the Dishes and Dainties therefrom. In China they do not use Table-cloths, nor other Utensils common among us: The Tables are beautiful, many of them varnished as fine as Looking-glasses. They touch not the Meat with their Hands, but make use of little Sticks about a foot long, with which they carry it neatly to their Mouths; some are made of sweet Wood, some of Ivory, others of Glass, which are in great esteem, and were invented by the Dutch; but now the Chineses make them curiously. Great Men have them of Silver, and only the Emperor of Gold, as are the Dishes and other Vessels serv'd up to his Table, the Petty Kings are of Silver tipt with Gold. This way of eating has always been among the Chinese, the Japonese learn'd it of them. Table-cloths and Napkins, and a great deal of Lye and Sope might be sav'd in Europe, if this Fashion were introduced; we Missioners like it very well.

Domingo Navarrete
The Travels and Controversies of Friar
Domingo Navarrete, 1676

AUTRE TEMPS . . .

The cuisine of each country depends on its climate. Since I have been in France I have accustomed myself to French cookery, reputed the best of all. Whenever I return to China, and am invited to dinner by French people, I get quite upset, and often feel quite ill after dinner. Coffee irritates my stomach, and cigars make my nose bleed. Now, when I am in Europe I cannot do without my coffee and my cigar after dinner. It is not surprising, then, that Europeans cannot enjoy life in China, persisting as they do in eating only what suited them at home.

Col. Tcheng-ki-tong
(Military Attaché to the Imperial
Chinese Legation in Paris)
Bits of China, 1890

DELIGHTSOME

At this day in China the common people live in a manner altogether on roots and herbs, and to the wealthiest, horse, ass, mule, dogs, cats-flesh, is as delightsome as the rest; so Mat. Riccius the Jesuit relates, who lived many years amongst them. The Tartars eat raw meat, and most commonly horse-flesh, drink milk and blood, as the Nomads of old. They scoff at our Europeans for eating bread, which they call tops of weeds, and horse-meat, not fit for men; and yet Scaliger accounts them a sound and witty nation, living an hundred years; even in the civilest country of them they do thus, as Benedict the Jesuit observed in his travels from the great Mogor's Court by Land to Paquin, which Riccius contends to be the same with Cambalu in Cathay.

Robert Burton
The Anatomy of Melancholy, 1621

DOMESTIC CONSUMPTION

To enjoy Peking duck in a restaurant is a comparatively new practice grown out of modern tourism and the orthodox way was really to eat it in the home where it was delivered from the *lu p'u* (爐舖) or 'oven shop', which specializes in the preparation of roast ducks and roast young pigs. . . .

The enjoyment is not in the fattened meat but in the crisp golden-brown skins with a very small amount of fat attached thereto. Even a good-sized duck will have only so many square inches of skin and so a duck feast is always an expensive matter.

H. Y. Lowe
The Adventures of Wu, 1940

DRIVERS' PERKS

The guests in Peking as elsewhere pay all car fares themselves save in the case when one or two guests forget to bring some small change to pay their hired rickshaws. In this instance, the management of the restaurant will be asked to pay for them, and credit the sum to the bill of the host.

The fact remains that a host at any dinner party must pay a considerable sum of money to the drivers of his friends' cars. This is known as 'chê-fan-chien' meaning the rice money for car drivers. The system exists in Shanghai and many other parts of China but the sums are particularly large in this city. . . .

Several foreign friends of the writer have asked the question why local chauffeurs are willing to work for twenty five dollars a month for a Chinese rather than forty dollars for a foreigner. The solution lies in the system of 'chê-fan-chien.' Any Chinese who is in a position to keep an automobile, must have several dinner parties in a week if not in a day. In the case of a dinner in a disorderly house, the chauffeur will get three dollars instead of 80 cents. It is small wonder that he is unwilling to serve a foreigner who has no 'chê-fan-chien' for him.

Jermyn Chi-Hung Lynn
Social Life of the Chinese in Peking, 1928

TIPS

Customers who either refuse or neglect to pay this extra tip will certainly be given the cold shoulder by the waiters. But if you pay liberally, say twenty per cent of the whole bill, you will at once be given a rousing farewell in the form of several loud cries of 'tu-li' meaning 'much ceremony'. The two or three ushers standing at the gate of restaurants who have heard these joyous remarks, also will make very respectful bows when you are passing out.

A few hosts who have been in the habit of spending freely, pay this extra tip with pleasure. Because once you give a handsome cumshaw your name is likely to live in the memory of these grateful waiters for a long time to come. The next time you go there many smiling faces and loud cries will greet you, apart from the fact that your name will be coupled with the high-sounding title of 'ta-jen' or Your Excellency although you may never have been a government official in your life.

Jermyn Chi-Hung Lynn
Social Life of the Chinese in Peking, 1928

BRILLIANT SCENE

We dined with the Grand Duke in the evening, eating with chopsticks and two-pronged forks. . . . The room was full of the Grand Duke's retainers, brilliant as a herbaceous border, chattering and hawking and spitting on the floor.

Charles Chevenix Trench
My Mother Told Me, 1958

UNUSUAL PUNISHMENT

In all capitals, official banquets are among the minor tortures of diplomatic life. Usually they mean a stuffy atmosphere, boring neighbours, messy food, and tedious toasts. In China, where three quarters of the population can hardly feel sure of having a meal every day, state banquets were also a severe punishment because of their exaggerated length. The obligation of having to sit between two high dignitaries who spoke no foreign language, belched and clucked their food through fifty courses, since any host who offered fewer was considered parsimonious, became no more pleasurable because of the costly rarity of the dishes served. Duck's tongue and deer's tendons convey ecstatic delights to Celestial appetites which were wasted on our grosser palates. The tediousness of sitting through successions of courses was only alleviated by guests being allowed to leave the table for an indefinite time without causing any unfavourable comment. During the Peking season, a fashionable young man might even attend two or three banquets on the same evening. The briefer repasts which diplomats offered were regarded by the Chinese as proof of Western niggardliness in contrast to their own greater generosity.

Invitations for these banquets were always gracefully worded. When a host asked me to dinner he would write that 'We have cleansed the wine cups and await your instructful conversation.' Politeness demanded that a guest should arrive at a party holding out his invitation, which he would vainly attempt to return to his host on the ground that he was unworthy to receive so great an honour; a similar etiquette obliged a Chinese gentleman who passed a friend in the street to hide his face behind his fan when he had no time to stop and talk to him. A certain ostentation was displayed over many trifling details which assumed much grave importance in Celestial eyes. When a high official offered me a cup of tea, he remarked that he water with which it was made came from a fountain in Szechuan over a thousand miles away.

Lewis Einstein
A Diplomat Looks Back, 1968

TOO POLITE

The people repair to the repast in order to bow, dispute each other's places, and yield up their seats, until they are half famished, and then again refuse to eat from mere politeness.

Revd Charles Gutzlaff
China Opened, 1838

TOO MANY COOKS

Chan-tso-lin [then warlord ruler of North China] ate nothing. The host at a Chinese dinner-party often does not partake of the food he offers to his guests; an abstemiousness that is not always reassuring.

At one moment a filthy-looking scullion, who presumably was the cook, ran into the room, carrying a lighted brazier on top of which was a small cauldron containing a stew of bear's feet (a great delicacy all over the north of Asia). Brazier and cauldron were placed in the middle of the table, in the manner of a Japanese skiaki. Then Chan-tso-lin began to add various raw ingredients, which he took from small dishes on the table and added to the original stew. The cook stood by, gazing with pride at his handiwork, but apparently he resented Chan-tso-lin's interference, for he came forward again and, pushing his master unceremoniously aside, he added still more ingredients, which he put in with dirty fingers.

A Chinese noble's household is still a mediæval mixture of splendour and slovenliness, and the relationship between the gentry and their servants is both autocratic and absurdly familiar. There was something characteristic in that scene in the beautiful room, all lacquer and silk and gold: the mighty War Lord attending personally to his guest's food, and the impatient cook interfering and taking the matter into his own hands. I can still see that cook, gazing into the witches' cauldron in the middle of the table, his greasy black-satin waistcoat brushing his master's cheek.

Daniele Varè
Laughing Diplomat, 1938

MEN LIKE GIANTS

There are certain Barons specially deputed to see that foreigners, who do not know the customs of the Court, are provided with places suited to their rank; and these Barons are continually moving to and fro in the hall, looking to the wants of the guests at table, and causing the servants to supply them promptly with wine, milk, meat, or whatever they lack. At every door of the hall (or, indeed, wherever the Emperor may be) there stand a couple of big men like giants, one on each side, armed with staves. Their business is to see that no one steps upon the threshold in entering, and if this does happen, they strip the offender of his clothes, and he must pay a forfeit to have them back again; or in lieu of taking his clothes, they give him a certain number of blows. If they are foreigners ignorant of the order, then there are Barons appointed to introduce them, and explain it to them. They think, in fact, that it brings bad luck if any one touches the threshold. Howbeit, they are not expected to stick at this in going forth again, for at that time some are like to be the worse for liquor, and incapable of looking to their steps.

Marco Polo
(trans. Col. Sir Henry Yule)
The Book of Ser Marco Polo the Venetian . . . ,
c.1300

CHINESE CHOW

Someone gave a Chinese dinner-party for us in Peking, and I ate Chinese chow for the first time. When I had more or less mastered the intricacies of eating with chopsticks I enjoyed myself thoroughly, though I was still rather inclined to be a wild and messy feeder, and my chin suffered in consequence. The food is not to everybody's liking—some people cannot stand it—but I thought it good, though very rich.

Eilleen Walker
A Naval Wife in the East, 1936

PLEASURE SEEKERS

Among the pleasure-seeking people of Peking, three new kinds of dinner parties have recently come into fashion. They are the 'sheng-jih-hui' or birthday parties, 'hsiao-han-hui' or winter-killing parties and 'chi-tsai-hui' or Dutch treat parties. . . .

From the personal experience of the writer, the 'chi-tsai-huis' of college professors are usually the most lively and joyous. Not only are learned people enabled to discuss philosophy, literature, arts, politics and all other branches of human knowledge, but their appetites will be improved with their college yells, songs and jokes especially if there are a few Western returned students among them.

Jermyn Chi-Hung Lynn
Social Life of the Chinese in Peking, 1928

FORMAL ENTERTAINING

Their feasts are peculiarly troublesome to Europeans, the whole being made up of ceremonies and compliments. Their ordinary feasts require sixteen—the more solemn twenty four dishes upon each table, as well as more formalities. Sometimes there are as many tables as guests, who sit upon stools or chairs; but ordinarily two persons sit at one table, which is not covered with a cloth, but neatly japanned, at the front of which hangs a piece of silk decorated with rich needle work. Two pointed sticks of ivory or ebony, do the office of knife and fork; their meats are cut into small square pieces, and served up in bowls; their soups are excellent, but they use no spoons; so that after sipping the thin, the grosser parts of it are directed to the mouth by their chopsticks. After the first dish, wine is served in cups to each guest; but none is tasted till the entertainer has first drunk. A comedy is acted during the repast; and when the dessert is brought in, money is collected for the domestics.

Sir George Staunton
An Historical Account of the Embassy to the Emperor of China, 1797

FRENCH CUISINE

The foreign dinner-parties in the legations were in those days [the 1890s], of extraordinary length. Fifteen courses and seven different kinds of wine were the rule rather than the exception. I wonder if this was an echo from the days of the East India Company, of which William Hicky speaks in his memoirs. No menu was complete without either 'Gâteau Mille Feuille' or 'Peking Dust' (the latter being powdered chestnuts with whipped cream), the recipes of which had been handed down since the days when the French Chargé d'Affairs, M. Patenôtre, made himself famous in 1879 by bringing with him a French chef. Fame for a diplomat is thus seen not always to be dependent on skilful negotiations.

William J. Oudendyk
Ways and By-Ways in Diplomacy, 1939

NO MANNERS

Kings and lords in these parts hold als few men in their courts as they may; but the Great Caan has ilk a day in his court at his cost folk without number. But ye shall understand that meat and drink is more honestly arrayed in our country than it is there; and also in this country men sit more honestly at the meat than they do there. For all the commons of his court have their meat laid on their knees when they eat, without any cloth or towel, and for the most part they eat flesh, without bread, of all manner of beasts; and when they have eaten they wipe their hand on their skirts.

Sir John Mandeville
Mandeville's Travels, 1366

THE HIGH LIFE

Speaking of expenses, the host is left with his own choice. The same 'chiu-hsu' which costs one twenty dollars or more at Tung Hsin Lou or Chung Hsin Tang, will only cost ten dollars or so at a smaller restaurant. Politicians and society people who are fond of 'show' would spend twenty dollars in one of the aforesaid places rather than ten dollars in a place where he can be given the same enjoyment. The name of a famous restaurant is often believed to lend dignity to the host as well as to his guests. Prominent men in Peking especially the self-styled prominent ones, seldom go to a small eating-house even when they are invited.

Jermyn Chi-Hung Lynn
Social Life of the Chinese in Peking, 1928

JUDICIOUS INVESTMENT

We saw also a great many houses, which have fair buildings of a large extent, with spacious enclosures, wherein there are gardens, and very thick woods, full of any kind of game, either for hawking or hunting, that may be desired; and these houses are as it were inns, whither come continually in great number people of all ages and sexes, as to see comedies, plays, combats, bull-baitings, wrestlings, and magnificent feasts, which the *tutons, chaems, conchalys, aytaus, bracalons, chumbims, monteos, lanteas,* lords, gentlemen, captains, merchants, and other rich men, do make for to give content to their kindred and friends. These houses are bravely furnished with rich hangings, beds, chairs, and stools, as likewise with huge cupboards of plate, not only of silver, but of gold also; and the attendants that wait at the table are maids ready to be married, very beautiful, and gallantly attired; howbeit, all this is nothing in comparison of the sumptuousness and other magnificences that we saw there. Now the Chinese assured us there were some feasts that lasted ten days after the *carachina*, or Chinese manner, which in regard of the state, pomp, and charge thereof, as well in the attendance of servants and waiters, as in the costly fare of all kind of flesh, fowl, fish, and all delicacies, in music, in sports of hunting and hawking, in plays, comedies, tilts, tourneys, and in shows both of horse and foot, fighting and skirmishing together, do cost above twenty thousand taels. These inns do stand in at least a million of gold, and are maintained by certain companies of very rich merchants who in way of commerce and traffic employ their money therein, whereby it is thought they gain far more than if they should venture it to sea.

Fernand Mendez Pinto
The Voyages and Adventures of Fernand
Mendez Pinto, 1614

THE FESTIVE BOARD

The following recipes for genuine Chinese food were obtained as the result of actual observation of Chinese cooks (mostly from well

known restaurants in Peiping) engaged in the assembling and preparation of each dish . . .

As a result the conclusion was reached that rice can only be cooked in a brass kettle, fish can only be fried in an iron *ch'ien tzu* with a broken handle, mutton can only be stewed properly in a vessel made from an empty petrol can, and tea can only be prepared in a pot with the spout broken off. Dishes should only be washed with a whiskbroom, kitchen utensils should not be washed at all but wiped out, and lusty singing, merry conversation, folk songs and dances should always be engaged in when preparing anything really difficult.

Corinne Lamb
The Chinese Festive Board, 1933

FRUGAL DIET

One set of Mongols who visit Peking say their claim to be summoned to the capital rests on the fact of their being the lineal descendants of Genghis Khan, and that as such they are admitted to feast with the emperor. The feast, however, is only formal, consisting, according to their own account, of a few eatables and a large quantity of imitation viands, made of clay or some such base material, and painted to look like real food. It matters little to the guests whether the food is imitation or real, etiquette requiring them to remain motionless at the board, as if it would be presumption to eat in the presence of the emperor.

James Gilmour
Among the Mongols, 1883

LEFTOVERS

This brave high Treatment finished, the Embassadours, according to the custom of the Countrey, were to put up what they left into their Pockets to carry home. It was a very pleasant sight to see how these greazy Tartars stuffed their Pockets and Leather Drawers of their Breeches with fat Meat, that the liquor dropt from them as they went along the Streets; so greedy were they in eating and carrying away, that they were more like Peasants than Courtiers.

John Nievhoff
An Embassy from the East India Company of the United Provinces to the Grand Tartar Cham, Emperour of China, 1669

CHAPTER 11

THE WEATHER

In the latitude of Peking the thermometer ranges through about one hundred degrees Fahrenheit, which ought to afford sufficient variety of temperature to any mortal.

A. H. SMITH
Chinese Characteristics, 1899

Attitudes towards Peking's weather are, to a considerable degree, a mirror of attitudes towards Peking itself. Those who are positive towards the city are enthusiastic about the predictability of the seasons, the brilliance of the sunshine, the limpid quality of the light. Those more equivocal towards Peking tend to mention intense heat, biting cold, drought, floods, mud, and dust.

If Peking's climate lacks uniformity, it has never lacked interest. The weather is constantly to the fore in description and discussion. When J. S. McHugh (First Lieutenant, US Marines) set out to provide a conversational Mandarin primer, he shrewdly included several dialogues on the subject. 'Wherever it blew, all was dust', his students were taught to remark, a comment of unlimited validity in Peking then, and often enough now.

In Imperial times the weather, like everything else, was ultimately the Emperor's responsibility. His prayers brought the rains that assured good harvests, his transgressions risked drought or flood to the detriment of his people. Meteorology was a tricky business, when even minor sins like the appointment of second-rate officials could lead to disproportionate calamity.

Christian missionaries translated into English some Imperial invocations for relief from natural disaster in order to showcase the superstition of the Court. The Chinese did no more than note that, beyond some success with solar eclipses, the missionaries were not able themselves to impose greater discipline upon the elements.

LONGO INTERVALLO

In fact, the climate of Northern China has a greater resemblance to that of the south of England or France, than it has to that of the southern parts of the Chinese Empire; and, although hotter, used always to remind me of the beautiful summers we have in England once in every ten and twelve years.

Robert Fortune
Wanderings in China, 1847

THREEFOLD HARMONY

Contrast the weather in Boston, New York, or Chicago with that of places in the same latitude in China. It is not that China is not, as the geographies used to affirm of the United States, 'subject to extremes of heat and cold,' for in the latitude of Peking the thermometer ranges through about one hundred degrees Fahrenheit, which ought to afford sufficient variety of temperature to any mortal.

But in China these alternations of heat and cold do not follow one another with that reckless and incalculable lawlessness witnessed in the great republic, but with an even and unruffled sequence suited to an ancient and a patriarchal system. The Imperial almanac is the authorised exponent of the threefold harmony subsisting in China between heaven, earth, and man. Whether the Imperial almanac is equally trustworthy in all parts of the Emperor's broad domain we do not know, but in those regions with which we happen to be familiar the almanac is itself a signal-service. At the point marked for the 'establishment of spring,' spring appears. In several different years we have remarked that the day on which the 'establishment of autumn' fell was distinguished by a marked change in the weather, after which the blistering heats of summer returned no more. Instead of allowing the frost to make irregular and devastating irruptions in every month of the year—as is too often the case in lands where democracy rules—the Chinese calendar fixes one of its four-and-twenty 'terms' as 'frost-fall.' A few years ago this 'term' fell on the 23d of October. Up to that day no lightest frost had been seen. On the morning of that day the ground was covered with white frost, and continued to be so covered every morning thereafter. We have noted these correspondences for some years, and have seldom observed a variation of more than the usual three days of grace.

A. H. Smith
Chinese Characteristics, 1897

COLD FOR TURTLES

In the first month, in the first month—seven Shan-hsi people go out in the streets to see the lanterns.—They wear their furs outside and yet they feel cold—but look at the turtles in the river, how do they manage to live through the winter?

Guido A. Vitale (trans.)
Pekinese Rhymes, 1896

WORKING IN WINTER

Dear Campbell,

I have had no occasion to write you an A letter for a long time, and Peking winters are not the best to work in. Short days, a cold that freezes one's brains, and late parties two or three times a week suggesting procrastination and preventing fulfilment, jump one across the gulf from December to March with astonishing rapidity and little result.

Sir Robert Hart
Letter to J. D. Campbell, 12 March 1880

REMORSE

The terrible part of winter at Peking is the drought; month after month the Emperor goes to the Temple of Heaven to pray for rain or snow; month after month the god, whoever he may be, shuts his ears as fast as Ulysses' ship's crew. The cold is intense, witness the frozen river and sea; the fierce wind, tearing over the desert of Gobi, dries men up till their skins become parched, tight and powdery; their lips are chapped and the black dust, that scourge of Northern China, seems to penetrate the very marrow of their bones. Russia was not colder; but in Russia we had the brightness and the kindly snow, and the tinkling of the sleigh bells gave the winter life and gaiety. In Peking the winter was as gloomy as remorse.

Lord Redesdale
(A. B. Freeman-Mitford)
Memories, 1915

THE SAP RISING

The awakening of Spring, the day when the sap is supposed to stir from its long sleep and to feel the first throes of renewed life, is commemorated in a pretty, homely ceremony at the Palace. The radish and young shoots of lettuce, the first vegetables to receive the benefit of the rising sap, are presented on a silver salver to Her Majesty by a kneeling eunuch. She partakes of them, and then gives them to the young Empress and Ladies to taste of. When Her Majesty raises the first radish to her lips, the young Empress, Princesses, and Ladies assembled in her Throne-room, repeat the wish for Imperial happiness, synonymous with 'National prosperity.' This wish is echoed by the high attendants in the ante-chamber, and re-echoed by the eunuchs kneeling in the courts without, and still echoed and re-echoed by every inmate of the Palace, until the waves of sound reach to the outer walls. Then Her majesty makes a wish that the sap may rise in such abundance

202

as to produce a fruitful season, that all the people of the Great
Empire may enjoy peace and plenty.

Katharine A. Carl
With the Dowager Empress of China, 1906

SPRING COLLECTION

Peking beggars have a proverb: 'Now is the time to exchange
wadded robes for new yellow cotton coats', meaning garments
of sunshine. Theoretically, the days should be growing warmer.
Practically, the wretched tatterdemalions often shiver on street
corners as they repeat their cynical dictum.

Juliet Bredon and Igor Mitrophanow
The Moon Year, 1927

SCENTS

The air was full of the scent of the yellow briars round the
house, and mixed with it other scents—wood-smoke and Chinese
cooking and Chinese sanitation and donkey-dung—the intimate
penetrating Peking smell, which is like the smell of no other city
on earth. Laura smelt it with positive pleasure—its strength, in the
warm dusk, meant that spring was fully come, and the baking
splendours of a Chinese summer on the way. In the snowless winter
of cold sunshine and frost and tearing winds the smell of Peking
suffers a strange diminution, and dwindles to a mere ghost.

Ann Bridge
Peking Picnic, 1932

THE LESSER HEAT

From the middle of May onwards the temperature in Peking
mounts sharply, first to the lesser heat of June, then to the *Ta Shu*,

or Great Heat, of July, when the rain begins, ushered in by the spasmodic thunderstorms of the previous month. In June, looking out over the plain from some high point in the Western Hills, from above Pa-Ta-Ch'u or from the Emperor's Hunting Park at Hsiang-shan, the watcher sees no city, but a great wreathing of smoky white, as of a vast bonfire—the sunlit dust lifted from the unpaved streets and open spaces of the town by the hot noonday wind. At sun-down, when the wind has dropped, those who walk on the city wall to catch what movement of air there may be, what hint of coolness, find the sun-baked flagstones still warm beneath their feet; while to their nostrils mounts, more potent even than in the streets below, that peculiar stew of smells—of cess of men and animals, of charcoal fumes, of cooking with strange fats and strange condiments, of remembered dust, which is the summer atmosphere of Peking. This penetrating compound of odours, sweetish, sourish, indescribable and unforgettable, reaches even to the roof-garden of the Peking Hotel on those hot nights when the European population assembles there, to dance listlessly on the polished concrete, or to sit languid round tables set against the garish trellis of artificial roses, drinking something; while the band brays and the lights glare, till they are lowered for a waltz and he who cares may see the stars, brilliant above the few lights of the city.

Ann Bridge
The Ginger Griffin, 1934

PRUDENT

There is an old superstition in China, and especially in the neighbourhood of Peking, that it is unlucky to be out of doors while it rains. When the sky is fertilising the earth, decency and prudence forbid men to assist at the mystery.

Juliet Bredon and Igor Mitrophanow
The Moon Year, 1927

LEARNING ABOUT THE WEATHER

The weather. Yesterday the weather was bad. A great many clouds came up from the south-east. It was a cloudy day, but it did not rain. In the afternoon a wind came up and it was dusty everywhere. (Lit: 'wherever it blew, all was dust'.) Thus it was up until this morning and then it cleared (only then did it clear). The weather is very warm and everyone is very irritable. They all say it must rain. If it rains a little then it will be cool. I remember that at this time last year it rained daily without ceasing. The mud and water on the streets was excessive and travel was extremely difficult.

J. M. McHugh
Introductory Mandarin Lessons, 1931

AWFUL MUD

The three leading characteristics of Pekin are its odour, its dust in dry weather, and its mud after rain. The cleanliness introduced by the Allies did wonders towards allaying the stench; and I do not think that any place in the world, short of an alkali desert, can beat the dust of the Long Valley. But though I have seen 'dear, dirthy Dublin' in wet weather, have waded through the slush of Aldershot, and had certainly marvelled at the mire of Hsin-ho, yet never have I gazed on aught to equal the depth, the intensity, and the consistency of the awful mud of Pekin.

Capt. Gordon Casserly
The Land of the Boxers, 1903

FAMINE

In vain the Emperor prays for rain; it only comes in rare and scanty showers, and the fierce sun bakes the ground harder than ever. The country folk are in great distress, and food is at famine prices. Yet they seem happy and contented, and when we asked one of the priests here whether there was no danger of a famine riot, he answered, 'Oh, no! the people about here are too great fools to get up a disturbance.'

A. B. Freeman-Mitford
The Attaché at Peking, 1866, pub. 1900

WATCHGLASS

If we, in England, must eat, according to the proverb, a peck of dirt before we die, I feel convinced that the inhabitants of Pekin swallow at least a hundredweight before their last hour. The dust of Pekin is, next to its smells, its greatest curse. . . . There is a saying, among the Chinese, that it will worm its way into a watch-glass.

Harry de Windt
From Peking to Calais by Land, 1899

SILK, SATIN . . .

The city of Peking was once called Se-yun-tien-fu; but it received its present appellation when the emperors of China removed the government from Nanking to the north of the empire, in order to oppose the incursions of the Tartars.

It lies in a plain which stretches to the south for more than ten days' journey without interruption, whilst at no great distance towards the north it is bounded by very numerous mountains. Owing to this extensive plain on the south, and this multitude of mountains on the north, Peking is exposed to deadly heat in summer, and severe cold in winter.

The transition from one extreme to the other, however, is slow and gradual, so that the Chinese of the upper classes go on changing their clothes all the year round. In summer they wear a cotton shirt, a waistcoat of light ko-poo, linen, a loose gown of the same material, called ppow-zoo, and over this a light silk spencer, called why-ttao. When the heat begins to decrease they exchange the ko-poo for a sort of crape called shah, and this again for satin; and, as the weather gets cool, they wear the ppow-zoo lined, and the why-ttao wadded, then both these garments wadded, after which they adopt the furs of ermine, sable, and fox, in the same gradation. In the depth of winter, besides having both the ppow-zoo and why-ttao lined with foxes' skin, they wear an under waistcoat of lambs' skin, and the loose gown over it wadded; and when it snows they put on a long cloak covered over with seal-skin. In spite of all this they still shiver with cold; and Count Ismailof, the Russian ambassador, told me that he and all his suit had been obliged to add garments to those they had been accustomed to wear, as the cold was far more intense here than at Moscow.

Father Ripa
*Memoirs of Father Ripa During Thirteen
Years' Residence at the Court of
Peking . . .* , c.1730 pub. 1846

PITILESS

At Peking in July not many hours can be called bearable, and when they do occur they are immediately followed by pitiless

weather, which makes them an expensive luxury. First of all, the glaring black sky, riddled with flashes of lightning, is split open, and cloudbursts swamp the city. Then there is a respite from the storms with which the baleful sky has become overloaded. This is followed by a clotted, sweltering heat which pounces upon you like a feverish, moist, flabby animal, and the least movement becomes quite an exploit.

'Will it be as hot as this at Hsin-King?' I asked the Minister.

'Incomparably hotter,' he said.

Francis de Croisset
(trans. Paul Salver)
The Wounded Dragon, 1937

PRAYING FOR RAIN

Kneeling, a memorial is hereby presented to cause affairs to be heard. Oh, alas, imperial Heaven! were not the world afflicted by extraordinary changes, I would not dare to present extraordinary services. But this year the drought is most unusual. The summer is past, and no rain has fallen. Not only do agriculture and human beings feel the dire calamity, but also beasts and insects, herbs and trees, almost cease to live.

I, the minister of Heaven, am placed over mankind, and am responsible for keeping the world in order, and tranquillizing the people. Although it is now impossible for me to sleep or eat with composure; although I am scorched with grief, and tremble with anxiety, still after all, no genial and copious showers have been obtained. Some days ago, I fasted, and offered rich sacrifices on the altars of the gods of the land and the grain; and had to be thankful for gathering clouds and slight showers; but not enough to cause gladness. . . .

I ask myself, whether in sacrificial services, I have been disrespectful?—whether or not, pride and prodigality have had a place in my heart, springing up there unobserved?—whether from the length of time I have become remiss in attending to the affairs of government; and have been unable to attend to them with that serious diligence and strenuous effort which I ought?—whether I have uttered irreverent words, and have deserved reprehension?—whether perfect equity has been attained in conferring rewards, or inflicting punishments?

Whether, in raising mausoleums and laying out gardens, I have distressed the people and wasted property?—whether, in the appointment of officers, I have failed to obtain fit persons, and thereby rendered government vexatious to the people?—whether the oppressed have found no means of appeal?—whether the largesses conferred on the afflicted southern provinces were properly applied, or the people left to die in the ditches? . . .

Prostrate, I beg imperial Heaven to pardon my ignorance and stupidity, and to grant me renovation; for myriads of innocent people are involved by me, a single man. My sins are so numerous, it is difficult to escape from them. Summer is past, and autumn arrived; to wait longer will really be impossible. Knocking head, I pray imperial Heaven to hasten and confer gracious deliverance, a speedy and divinely beneficial rain, and to save the people's lives, and in some degree redeem my iniquities. Oh, alas! imperial Heaven! observe these things! alas! imperial Heaven, be gracious! I am inexpressibly grieved, alarmed, and frightened.

> Prayer of Emperor Dao Guang, 1832
> Quoted in Davis, *The Chinese*, 1836
> Gutzlaff, *China Opened*, 1838

A TONIC

The quality of the air—in winter dry and sparkling, the very champagne of atmospheric vintages; in spring and autumn a delicious blending of frost and sun. Life is then one continual exhilaration; the floods of light pour a tonic into the blood, the keen air braces the nerves until mere movement is a joy. After the summer heats and steamy downpours, who shall describe the first crisp blow from the north—the whispered message of autumn from the steppes? Or who forget the sweet Æolian melody of the wheeling pigeons; the almost motionless wings of the great brown hawks, poised against the blue; the sparkling, frosted hills when snow has fallen and every outline shines clear in the luminous air;

the tinkle of distant camel-bells; or, indeed, any of the hundred nothings that make up the unique and indescribable Peking atmosphere?

Archibald R. Colquhoun
Overland to China, 1900

AVOIDING TEDIOUS SALUTATIONS

Few of the Streets are paved with Bricke or Stone, so that in Winter dirt, and dust in Summer, are very offensive: and because it raineth there seldome, the ground is all crumbled into dust, and if any wind blow, it enters every Roome. To prevent which they have brought in a custom, that no man of whatsoever ranke goeth on foot or rideth without a Veile or Bonnet hanging to his brest, of that subtiltie that he may see, and yet the dust not annoy him: which also hath another commoditie that he may goe any whither unseene, so freed from innumerable tedious salutations.

Father Ricii
Quoted in *Purchas his Pilgrimes*, 1625

FLOWING LIGHT

The light is quite different now and is the harbinger of autumn. Instead of the almost glaucous stream of the summer daylight which drowns things in its depths this changed light is transparent and buoyant and brings everything into relief and prominence, and it seems as if the splendid monuments delighted in it and became more imbued with life, standing out more sharply under its influence, as a drinker springs to his feet excited by a more subtle and potent wine than that which he had been drinking. The crowd in the street looks different too. It has become heavier as the atmosphere becomes lighter. The thicker garments make it a more awkward, substantial affair altogether, and already the people look chilly. The quiet note of black silk is to be seen everywhere, and old wadded jackets and faded mantles appear just like the well-known, well-worn garments which reappear punctually every winter in our provinces, on the persons of the pious residents. . . .

One house where a shop is just opening business is hung from top to bottom with red canvas decorated with Chinese characters in gilt paper, with a mauve and yellow cornice surmounting the whole. At this season of the year, whenever there is any kind of fête the streets are hung with innumerable paper trophies in pale bright colours which stand out in sharp relief against the dull background of the old town. . . .

Then your eye travels suddenly from these fluttering trifles to the impersonal grandeur of the Imperial Palaces. The swelling roofs rise up into the clear air like permanent tents of the desert, and the sunshine glorifies the lustre of the angular tiaras of tiles. Then you fully appreciate the severe lines of the magisterial design. Like water in canals expressly prepared for it the light seems to flow more easily in the great straight main streets.

Abel Bonnard
(trans. Veronica Lucas)
In China, 1926

WEATHER FORECAST

There are in the city of Cambaluc, what with Christians, Saracens, and Cathayans, some 5000 astrologers and soothsayers, whom the Great Kaan provides with annual maintenance and clothing, just as he provides the poor of whom we have spoken, and they are in the constant exercise of their art in this city.

They have a kind of Astrolabe on which are inscribed the planetary signs, the hours and critical points of the whole year. And every year these Christian, Saracen, and Cathayan astrologers, each sect apart, investigate by means of this astrolabe the course and character of the whole year, according to the indications of each of its Moons, in order to discover by the natural course and disposition of the planets, and the other circumstances of the heavens, what shall be the nature of the weather, and what peculiarities shall be produced by each Moon of the year; as for example, under which Moon there shall be thunderstorms and tempests, under which there shall be disease, murrain, wars, disorders, and treasons, and so on according to the indications of each; but always adding that it lies with God to do less or more according to his pleasure. And they write down the results of their examination in certain little pamphlets for the year, which are called *Tacuin*, and these are sold for a groat to all who desire to know what is coming.

Marco Polo
(trans. Col. Sir Henry Yule)
The Book of Ser Marco Polo the Venetian . . . , c.1300

AUTUMNAL

By the time of the last decade (twentieth to twenty-ninth or thirtieth) of the seventh month the dates hang down in their redness and the grapes have become purple. Those who carry them about on poles slung over their shoulders, always sell them together, and when the autumn sound of their cry enters the ears, its musical note gives a suggestion of chilliness and a sad melancholy. Indeed there is no way of preventing one from feeling the emotions that go with the seasons of the year.

Tun Li Chen
(trans. Derk Bodde)
Annual Customs and Festivals in Peking,
1936

LOVELIEST OF SEASONS

Autumn in Peking is perhaps the loveliest of all the seasons. After the great heat of summer there is something divine about those brisk October mornings, crystal-cool, with a tang in the air; the days of brilliant sunshine, hot but not oppressive. The courts of houses and temples are brilliant with chrysanthemums; out in the country the willows spin fine-leaved golden patterns against the sky, shed them, still delicate in decay, upon the quiet waters of canals, upon the earth, returning now again to its beautiful uniform brown. The fields are full of stooping blue figures, lifting the harvest of peanuts and sweet potatoes, and later digging out the roots and stumps of maize and *kaoliang*—they bind them in bundles to burn them. Though the crops are not all up yet, the area of rides spreads every day; the leaves of the ginkgos are as primrose-yellow as their tiny golden apples which fell a month before; sometimes there is mist before sunrise. The last of the convoys of solid-wheeled, blue-hooded carts come creaking into Peking along the narrow sandy tracks from the north and west, before the Gobi Road closes for the winter. And upon all these scenes and activities the sun, glorious and splendid, shines all day long, pouring out over the beautiful and busy earth a flood of light of a quality and brilliance beyond European imagining. The great continent of Asia, the greatest land-mass in the world, is cooling down after the terrific heating of the summer—but how slowly and temperately, with what a matchless serenity of atmosphere and light and colour. Here, undisturbed by the turbulence of cyclonic currents, by the intrusion of oceanic winds or moisture, the seasons pass in majesty, still, glorious and slow, with the large royalty of movement of a planet in stellar space.

Ann Bridge
The Ginger Griffin, 1934

DAZZLING

I am sure there is a quality in the atmosphere of the north, sharp, clear, and dry, that helps to emphasize line and colour. I know that in the early evening when the sun had just set, bowling in a rickshaw through Peking, the air flowing with grateful coolness through one's hair, one felt the eyes dazzled and belief stretched almost beyond capacity.

Innes Jackson
China Only Yesterday, 1938

NAKED AND ASHAMED

Peking 25th October 1865

We are working gradually into winter. In another fortnight the trees will all be bare, and Peking, throwing off the green clothes which it puts on in summer, in order to delude stray visitors into the idea that it is a pretty place, will stand naked, dirty, and ashamed.

A. B. Freeman-Mitford
The Attaché at Peking, 1865, pub. 1900

WRETCHED

The natives are already swaddled up in furs and wadding, and commend me to a cold Chinaman for looking wretched.

A. B. Freeman-Mitford
The Attaché at Peking, 1865, pub. 1900

ICY TUB

Winter in Northern China is extremely severe, and Tientsin, the port of Peking, is yearly closed to navigation for six or eight weeks through the sea and river being frozen. The thermometer frequently falls below zero, but owing to a bright atmosphere the cold is not felt so much as might to expected. At night the stars blink and blaze with intense brilliancy, and the still, frosty air seems almost to ring with a metallic voice. Beggars and homeless wanderers are nightly frozen by the dozen, and the whole land lies powerless in the grip of King Frost.

My bedroom I could keep fairly warm by means of a large American stove heated up till it was white, but in the mornings, on passing into my bathroom, which boasted a brick floor and paper windows, I found the temperature almost coinciding with that of the open air, albeit a small stove roared in the corner, while steam from the hot water in a wooden bath was so thick as to make the daylight dim. Ablutions were a hurried function, ending in precipitate retreat to the warmth of the bedroom. The small stove would burn itself out, the steam would congeal and disappear, and the bath water, unless removed, would be quickly frozen.

As winter wore on the sides of my bath-tub became coated with ice, which increased with every splash until there was a thickness of three or four inches, for it would have injured the bath to keep breaking it off, so that, ultimately, I took my morning tub in a nest of ice, only the bottom of which was completely thawed by the daily supply of hot water.

Oliver G. Ready
Life and Sport in China, 1903

MIRRORING THE SUN

And always the sun of Northern China hangs in a cloudless winter sky, an infinitude of glittering gold, clothing in the same radiant light ancient beauty and modern ugliness, temples and palaces, barracks and banks. But it likes shining on the temples and palaces best. For these meet and magnify and multiply it in the translucent mirror of glazed roofs, of majolica *pailows*, cinnabar pillars, in the dazzling white of marble stairs, courtyards, terraces.

A. E. Grantham
Pencil Speakings from Peking, 1918

SEASONAL EXCURSIONS

Both sections [of the Forbidden City] I have visited many times, under snow and wind and spring calm and great heat, and the particular quality of beauty which each part manifests leads me to choose a different kind of weather by which to see it. First, for the frosty beauty of the great courts and the dark sumptuousness of the State Apartments, I should select a typical Peking winter day of bright, yellow-fleeced sun in a blue heaven, of an intensely animating cold (which makes the crowds in the fair we have left talk and laugh more than ever, though, as well, it causes their teeth to chatter); but, for the appreciation of the residential quarters, and the facets and adjuncts of the Chinese life they represent, gay as the drawing of a flower or a bird upon a Chinese paper, we must have a spring day, a morning from that brief season, enduring only a fortnight, that falls, very regularly, about a month later than the Feast of Excited Insects, and is all too short, since, in it, after a winter when every twig and piece of earth looked hard and dead as iron, the year suddenly leaps into life, and the lilac and shrubs and fruit-trees rush within the space of a few days into intoxicating flower and scent.

Osbert Sitwell
Escape With Me!, 1939

CHAPTER 12

THE ENVIRONS

All the plain breathed an air of elegance and tranquillity; bandits could roam in the hills which bordered it or floods ravage the plains below it, but it seemed impossible that any sort of catastrophe could touch it.

GRAHAM PECK
Through China's Wall, 1945

Until they were torn down, the walls of the Tartar and the Chinese cities defined the extent of China's capital. Inside the walls was the city of Peking; outside were the suburbs, and beyond that the countryside.

Within the frame of the hills which mark the limits of the North China plain, the countryside over time turned into a civilized adjunct to the town. During the lifetime of the citizens of Peking, the surrounding plain with its temples and pleasances provided a retreat from the capital's heat and busyness. In death, it provided a site for the well-located tomb that would assure tranquillity in the hereafter. The different elements came together into a whole that was organic, so that to the artist's eye of Graham Peck, 'the whole landscape gave the effect of a tastefully furnished room'.

Peking's environs were a recreation ground for local people and foreigners alike. The race course, the golf course, and the zoo (with its 'unhappy elephant') lay close without the city walls. Six hundred years after the Great Khan was carried out hunting in a chamber of beaten gold, the foreign community was conducting paper chases in the same locality, and enterprising locals poaching game in the Imperial Preserves.

The monastic ideals of tranquillity and contemplation often led to temples being established some distance outside the city. In the case of some, such as the lamist Yellow Temple, common prudence on the part of the authorities may also have been a factor. If one had to find somewhere to put up the lamas, one could at least make sure they were safely outside the city walls.

The temples in the Western Hills, places of pilgrimage for Peking's devout, became the object of pilgrimages of a different kind after 1860. A. B. Freeman-Mitford, posted to the British Legation between 1865 and 1866, records the beginning of a long-standing custom among foreigners of taking temples for the summer months in order to escape Peking's heat. To travel to the Western Hills during that season in the early part of this century was to encounter a microcosm of Peking's foreign society, most of whom had fled there to get away from one another.

FINE FURNISHINGS

Until the city overwhelmed me and made such activity seem superfluous, I frequently went outside the walls to walk or bicycle through the near-by countryside, usually towards the hills in the west. I rode along willow-bordered canals, through glistening brown fields and into dusty, sun-baked villages where the dogs barked and children fled at sight of a white face, but when I thought I was getting beyond Peking's urbane and favoured sphere I was deluding myself. Obtruding on every rural scene were the sophisticated little villas and tombs of the wealthy Pekinese, also jewelled pagodas and dagobas and carved marble turtles which dated from the days when half the plain was walled and decorated to make a Summer Palace for the Emperor. Moreover, the high blue hills which bounded the plain on the west and north—the undulating body of the subterranean dragon-seemed to form the outermost of Peking's walls and make this sheltered countryside almost a part of the city. All the plain breathed an air of elegance and tranquillity; bandits could roam in the hills which bordered it or floods ravage the plains below it, but it seemed impossible that any sort of catastrophe could touch it.

Perhaps there never has been another locality so perfectly constructed for man's pleasure. Originally endowed with a balanced proportion of mountains and flat lands, it had, through the many centuries when it was the capital of the Eastern world, been continually groomed and improved by the addition of whatever it naturally lacked. Artificial lakes and hills had been contrived in suitable places and the whole scene had been architecturally upholstered with countless temples, pavilions, and ornamented archways. Even the massive line of the Western Hills had been humanized and brought into scale by a pagoda strategically placed on one of them; to an extraordinary extent this whole landscape gave the effect of a tastefully furnished room.

Graham Peck
Through China's Wall, 1945

DELIGHTFUL TOMBS

The plain between these hills and the town is very beautiful. It is thickly studded with farmsteads, knolls of trees, and tombs, which are always the prettiest spots in China, for as a balance against the dirt and squalor in which they pass their lives, the Chinese choose the most romantic and delightful places for their final habitations.

A. B. Freeman-Mitford
The Attaché at Peking, 1866, pub. 1900

COUNTRY LIFE

Fifteen miles out of Peking all the indecencies and filthiness which are its characteristics disappear entirely.

A. B. Freeman-Mitford
The Attaché at Peking, 1866, pub. 1900

WOMEN ENOUGH

The 21st, the conductor came to congratulate the ambassador on his arrival at the borders; and acquainted him, that, the horses and camels being ready, he might proceed when he pleased. I cannot omit an inconsiderable circumstance, that happened at this place, as it strongly represents the caution and prudence of the Chinese. Our conductor, having seen some women walking in the fields, asked the ambassador, who they were? and whither they were going? He was told, they belonged to the retinue, and were going along with it to China.

He replied, they had women enough in Pekin already; and, as there never had been an European woman in China, he could not be answerable for introducing the first.

John Bell
A Journey from St Petersburg to Pekin
1719–1722, pub. 1763

FAITH AND WORKS

From the hot plains of India they came, from the frozen steppes of Mongolia, from the mountains of Tibet. To accommodate Tibetan lamas and Mongolian nobles, Khang Si, the great Manchu Emperor, constructed the Yellow Temple, a mile or two outside the northern walls of Peking. Chien Lung the Magnificent added the wonderful marble stupa, as a memorial to a Grand Lama who died here in 1779.

Now, from memorial and temple, from the whole complex of what must have been imposing buildings designed and fit for living Buddhas and other distinguished guests, from the very idea of such lavish hospitality on the one hand, such loyal homage on the other, the quickening impulse has passed away.

Ruin and decay are in complete possession, the accusing signs of wanton external violence painfully evident, but more marked still, and so much deadlier in their effect, the signs of increasing weakness from within. A few repairs, if only undertaken in time, could save so much. Yet no one troubles to carry them out. With fatalistic ineptitude, the remaining monks, doubly smitten with poverty of purse and mind, watch the beautiful structure dissolving before their eyes—eyes dulled from having for the last two decades gazed on so many cataclysms, so many frightful happenings. Now the whole seems doomed: the delicate carving on the marble dagoba brutally mutilated, its steps falling asunder; the red lacquered pillars of the eastern shrine yielding; great chunks of the magnificently carved roof, with all the lustrous glitter of its tiles, crashed into weeds and brambles, helpless, hopeless, beyond repair by anything but an immense devotion. And that seems even more desolate than the temples it once erected with such splendour and in such profusion.

A. E. Grantham
Pencil Speakings From Peking, 1918

COMPARATIVE RELIGION

The religion of the lamas [at the Yellow Temple] is Buddhism of a corrupt type, and prevails in Tibet and Mongolia. Its leading tenet is the reincarnation of Buddhist divinities in the person of those who are destined to exercise spiritual or civil power—a doctrine unknown to the orthodox. As its prayers are made by machinery, turned by wind or water as well as by hand, you would hardly expect it to exert an influence for good; yet it seems to have made the Mongols less savage than the bloodthirsty followers of Genghis Khan, though it has not made them chaste, clean, or honest.

Dr W. A. P. Martin
A Cycle of Cathay, 1897

UNHAPPY ELEPHANT

Most visitors like to enter through the East Wing [of the Central Experimental Ground of Agriculture] and visit the zoo first. As soon as one has passed the second gateway he is confronted by a wooden bridge as the zoo is situated on a miniature peninsula. It is true that there are not many strange animals to be seen in this garden but all juvenile visitors are inclined to linger at the monkeys' quarters where they can buy food to feed these quaint animals. The unhappy elephant whose tooth has already been stolen by a starving guard, is also a centre of attraction for the children.

Jermyn Chi-hung Lynn
Social Life of the Chinese in Peking, 1928

IDLE PEASANTS

The moral character of the Chinese peasantry near Pekin is represented by travellers in a very unfavourable light: they are idle, and as a natural consequence, dissipated.

The Religious Tract Society
The People of China, c.1855

THE LAST RACE

After the great race tiffin [following a race meeting at the course six miles west of Peking], with speeches and toasts and cheers, when the winners in their gay satin jackets had come up to receive the prizes presented in graceful little speeches by different ladies, there came the mad breakneck, steeplechase, free-to-all, great race of the day, through fields, over ruts and ditches, across lots, anyhow—the foreigners' race home from the races before the city gates should close. Those who were in the saddle could of course wait for the last race of the program, long before which the grand stand was emptied. Chair-bearers could rely upon making great spurts across lots, but carts had to follow the fixed lines of ruts into the Chinese City, and then plod through the waste of sand along the walls of the Tatar City to its gates before the fatal stroke. There mules were beaten, carts bumped, and carters chirruped and repeated their *wu-wu-wu wu-u-u* and the *pr-pr-pr-rup* like Norwegian skydguts, while one bounded about in the upholstered chair and wedged more pillows beside one. Clouds of dust surrounded each cart, through which one saw dimly only the barrel glimpse ahead, nothing but the darkening waste and the endless, endless walls. With some energetic whackings, mules were made to go faster, and just when every joint seemed racked loose, mules turned in the great arch, with other carts, carters, donkeys, and camels streaming through the tunnel as the bells' slower clang and the pipes' shrill whistle proclaimed the last moments of grace. Then mules and muleteers and dust-laden passengers stopped to breathe, and caracoling knights called into cart interiors their thanksgivings at such a fortunate escape, for a survey assured us that all were safely within the walls before the gates went to with a sound not to be forgotten. Picturesque medieval customs are better read about than encountered.

E. A. Scidmore
China: The Long-Lived Empire, 1900

THE GREAT KHAN AT SPORT

And so the Emperor follows this road that I have mentioned, leading along in the vicinity of the Ocean Sea (which is within two days' journey of his capital city Cambaluc), and as he goes there is many a fine sight to be seen, and plenty of the very best entertainment in hawking; in fact, there is no sport in the world to equal it!

The Emperor himself is carried upon four elephants in a fine chamber made of timber, lined inside with plates of beaten gold, and outside with lion's skins (for he always travels in this way on his fowling expeditions, because he is troubled with gout). He always keeps beside him a dozen of his choicest gerfalcons, and is attended by several of his Barons who ride on horseback alongside. And sometimes, as they may be going along, and the Emperor from his chamber is holding discourse with the Barons, one of the latter shall exclaim: 'Sire! Look out for Cranes!' Then the Emperor instantly has the top of his chamber thrown open, and having marked the cranes he casts one of his gerfalcons, whichever he pleases; and often the quarry is struck within his view, so that he has the most exquisite sport and diversion, there as he sits in his chamber or lies on his bed; and all the Barons with him get the enjoyment of it likewise! So it is not without reason I tell you that I do not believe there ever existed in the world or ever will exist, a man with such sport and enjoyment as he has, or with such rare opportunities.

Marco Polo
(trans. Col. Sir Henry Yule)
The Book of Ser Marco Polo the Venetian . . . ,
c.1300

STRAITENED CIRCUMSTANCES

On account of the narrowness of the passes in some parts of the country where the Great Khan follows the chase, he is borne upon two elephants only, or sometimes a single one.

Marco Polo
(trans. Col. Sir Henry Yule)
The Book of Ser Marco Polo the Venetian . . . ,
c.1300

NATURE'S CHILD

Jehol is near the Celestial Capital. To reach it takes no more than two days. It is a wide expanse of lonely country. The choice of this district cannot encroach upon my duties. In harmony with the natural contours of the country, I have built pavilions in the pine groves, thereby enhancing the natural beauties of the hills. I have made water flow past the summer-houses as if leading the mountain mists out of the valleys. To create such beauty is beyond the power of human skill. It is the gift of nature itself, and causes no expense of carving beams or painting columns.

With my love for the sublime peace of the forests and springs, I can calmly watch the creatures, the waterfowl playing on the blue water, not fleeing at the approach of men; the deer going in herds in the evening light; the eagle circling in the sky or the fish leaping out of the water, one high and one low, according to the laws of nature; and I can also enjoy the purple distances, or gaze at the vault of heaven which sometimes seems near and sometimes far above me.

Whether I am wandering about enjoying the view, or resting, my mind is always upon the harvest. Neither day nor night do I forget the lessons of history. For the encouragement of cultivation I pray constantly for full baskets; for the sake of good harvests I rejoice at the blessed rain which falls at an auspicious time. That, in general words, is a picture of my life in the Summer Palace in Jehol.

When I find pleasure in orchids, I love uprightness; when I see the pines and bamboos, I think of virtue; when I stand beside limpid brooks, I value honesty; when I see weeds I despise dishonesty. That is what is meant by the proverb 'the ancients get their ideas from objects'. It must ever be remembered that all an Emperor has comes from the people. Not to love is not to understand this. Therefore I have written this that I may remember it day and night, and remain always upright and reverent.

Edict of Emperor Kang Xi, c.1713
Quoted in Hedin, *Jehol*, 1933

AN EMPEROR'S PLEASURE

I saw him [Emperor Kang Xi] several times about the gardens, but never on foot. He was always carried in a sedan-chair, surrounded by a crowd of concubines, all walking and smiling. Sometimes he sat upon a high seat, in the form of a throne, with a number of eunuchs standing around him; and, watching a favourable moment, he suddenly threw among his ladies, grouped before him on carpets of felt, artificial snakes, toads, and other loathsome animals, in order to enjoy the pleasure of seeing them scamper away with their crippled feet. At other times he sent some of his ladies to gather filberts and other fruits upon a neighbouring hill, and pretending to be craving for some, he urged on the poor lame creatures with noisy exclamations until some of them fell to the ground, when he indulged in a loud and hearty laugh.

Father Ripa
Memoirs of Father Ripa During Thirteen
Years' Residence at the Court of Peking,
c.1730 pub. 1846

FROZEN STIFF

Game is so abundant, especially at the Capital, that every year during the three winter months you see at different places, intended for despatch thither, besides great piles of every sort of wildfowl, lines of four-footed game of a gunshot or two in length: the animals being all frozen and standing on their feet. Among other species you see three sundry kinds of bears. . . . and great abundance of other animals, as stags and deer of different sorts, boars, elks, hares, rabbits, squirrels, wild-cats, rats, geese, ducks, very fine-jungle fowl, &c. &c., and all so cheap that I never could have believed it.

Gabriel de Magaillans
A New Description of China . . . , 1688

JADE CUPS

From the winter solstice onward, when stretches of water are once more frozen, such places as the Lake of Ten Temples, the city moat, and the Second Sluice (on the canal running from Peking to T'ung Chou) all have their 'ice beds', which when pulled by one man, are exceedingly rapid in movement. They are about five feet long, three feet broad, and are made of wood. They have iron runners on the bottom, and can seat three or four people. To ride in one after the snow has cleared away and when the sun is warm, is like moving within a cup of jade, and is a joyful thing indeed.

Tun Li Chen (trans. Derk Bodde)
Annual Customs and Festivals in Peking,
1936

ROAD MAINTENANCE

Outside of Tungchow we crossed the splendid carved marble bridge where the Chinese army made its last stand in 1860—

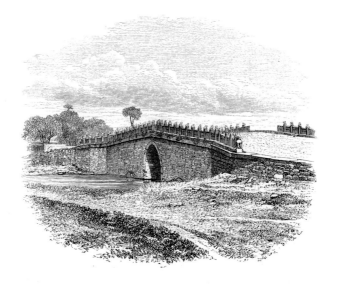

Pa-li-kao, the 'Eight Li Bridge,' which won for General Montauban the title of Count Palikao. Then all day there succeeded such ruts and gullies and muddy ditches, such jolting, thumping, and bumping, as decided one that Peking was dearly seen at the price of one such ride in a lifetime. The actual or recognized, the traditional, conventional road, a mere cut or ditch worn deep in the clay of the plain, was a floundering, bottomless mud trough all the way, and we drove around it, never in it, zigzagging at right angles all over the Peking plain. In every field and millet-patch some man lay in wait to ostentatiously throw a spoonful of dirt in the rut or the ditch he had himself made, and then extend his hand for coin. . . . In every rainy season for uncounted years the same tricks have been resorted to on the Peking plain, the people digging holes to break donkeys' legs, and tossing handfuls of dirt in as a cart approaches. A good macadamized road would rob the country people of their chief income and would be promptly cross-gullied for their benefit.

E. A. Scidmore
China: The Long-Lived Empire, 1900

LEST WE FORGET

[Travelling from Peking towards Tientsin after the relief of the legations in 1900] I saw a number of French soldiers on a bridge over the canal. An excited superior officer rode ahead of them and drove them back. Then he rode over the bridge and down to the other side, where about a thousand more French soldiers, who were on their way to Pekin, had been spread in a line, presenting arms, and facing a cornfield, the stalks of which were several feet higher than their heads and screened from their sight anything that there might be to be seen.

I halted to see what was taking place. The superior officer, after ordering the bugles to play various high notes—the military significance of which I do not know—and after clearing his voice in all the recognised ways, thundered an oration to his men— whom he called '*compagnons d'armes*'—on the historical battle which had been gloriously won at this bridge by the French troops in 1860.

There was a good deal in the speech about '*Vos frères ainés qui sur ce pont gagnèrent une victoire glorieuse*' ('Your elder brothers who scored a glorious victory at this bridge'), each *r* rolled as if it had been twenty; but all at once another officer, with a map spread open, galloped to his superior with this astounding news: '*Mais sapristi! mon Colonel, mais ce n'est pas ce pont ci!*' ('By Jove, Colonel, this is not the right bridge.')

Henry Savage Landor
China and the Allies, 1903

BEEN THERE

North China is well, indeed over supplied with temples, and we must have 'done' them all. Looking through mother's diaries I can see no comment on the Temple of the Pool of the Black Dragon, but a laconic and derogatory '*Been . . . seen.*'

Charles Chevenix Trench
My Mother Told Me, 1958

DIPLOMATIC PRIVILEGE

Pi Yün Ssu [Biyun Si], 7th July 1865

The hills west of Peking are the Switzerland of Northern China. They are not very high nor extraordinarily beautiful, but there are some very pretty gorges and valleys, richly wooded, and at any rate the air is fresh and pure. Every gorge has a perfect nest of temples, built by the pious emperors of the Ming dynasty and the earlier Tartars, for which good deeds the *Corps diplomatique* at Peking cannot be too grateful.

Our temple is called 'Pi Yün Ssu,' 'the temple of the azure clouds,' a romantic name, and certainly the place is worthy of it. It is built on terraces ascending the hill to a length of about half a mile, and on every terrace is a shrine, each more beautiful (if that is the proper word to apply to the grotesque buildings of this country) than the last; black and white marble statues and vases, bronze dragons, alto-relievos and basso-relievos representing kings and warriors, gods and goddesses, and fabulous monsters, all of rare workmanship— inscriptions graven on marble and stone, and bronze or gilt upon wood, meet one at every step; and the whole is set in a nest of rock-work, fountains, woods, and gardens.

Our habitation consists of several little houses on one side of the temple; we dine in an open pavilion, surrounded by a pond and artificial rockery, with ferns and mosses in profusion; high trees shade it from the sun, and close by us a cold fountain pours out of the rock into the pond, in which we can ice our wine to perfection.

A. B. Freeman-Mitford
The Attaché at Peking, 1865, pub. 1900

INCONSIDERATE TREATMENT

One building alone [at the Biyun Si] contains Buddha and his five hundred Lo-hans, or saints of the third class, larger than life . . . then whole courtyards are surrounded by buildings, in which heaven and hell are represented by hundreds upon hundreds of wooden dolls. The Buddhist heaven is a very queer place according to this view of it, where the height of happiness seems to consist in riding a tiger or griffin, or some equally uncomfortable mount; but hell is really too grotesque, especially the ladies' department, where the unfortunate women who have sinned in this world are to be seen experiencing what is, to say the very least of it, very inconsiderate treatment at the hands of a number of lavender-kid-glove-coloured fiends. In the gentlemen's department a favourite punishment is for sinners to have their heads cut off, and be compelled to walk about with them under their arms like a crush hat at a ball.

A. B. Freeman-Mitford
The Attaché at Peking, 1865, pub. 1900

TEMPLE OF THE LORD

I have friends among Peking residents who rent temples for their 'Summer Camp,' and unbelievably charming places they are. The priests retain the altar buildings so that daily prayers may ascend to the Gentle Buddha. Some of these temples are deep in the hills, others are near the winding road you are following. One of these, the Wo Fo Ssu, has been rented by the American Y. M. C. A., and it is one of the very oldest and most interesting. At the same hour that Western voices are raised in the singing of Gospel hymns, you may hear the priests chanting their *sutras* in the great hall of the Sleeping Buddha.

Lucian S. Kirtland
Finding the Worthwhile in the Orient, 1935

PLANT COLLECTING

We requisitioned the saddle-pads off the donkeys for seats and sat down to tea, having first set the donkey-boys to hunt up and dig certain beautiful golden and crimson and white lilies and irises and orchids we had seen starting out of the grassy hillside [within the Imperial Hunting Park]. We promised our retinue two copper cents per root. It seemed a safe guarantee, but turned out to be a rash one and had to be repudiated. Hardly had we cut into the second currant cake when up staggered the headman of the tribe and two elders under enough rare and choice vegetable matter to start a second Kew Gardens.

Gilbert Collins
Extreme Oriental Mixture, 1926

TRICK CYCLISTS

The various games and shows of the temple societies are comparable to the variety performances or perhaps to foreign vaudeville, the only difference being that each society has its own specialty which the name of the society clearly indicates. There are the Bamboo Flagpole Balancers, Fancy Cymbals. Fancy Kettledrums, Treasure Chests. Lions, Road Openers (players of the 'fork', a warring weapon), and Five Tiger Rod, Weight Lifters, Stilted Dancers (otherwise known as Singers of Rice-planting Songs) and some others. The modern addition to them are the Fancy Bicycle Riders.

H. Y. Lowe
The Adventures of Wu, 1940

TO BE A PILGRIM

In our court of four small houses surrounding a quadrangle [at Tanzhe Si, during the autumn pilgrimage], there were sixty pilgrims. We four foreigners found one house cramping, but there were twenty in each of the other houses, and the numerous other courts of the huge monastery were as crowded. Our pilgrims were 'The Society of the Sea Lantern', merchants and their wives from Peking. They showed us with pride the offering they had brought, a model of a temple gateway, concocted of pink, majenta and orange chenille, fit to gain the attention of the most somnolent of gods.

Our first night of more or less communal living was enlivened by a gambling game, which engaged the attention of most of the sixty. It waxed noisier until, past midnight, it came to a climax with claims of cheating. The wives joined the fray and all sixty tried to drown each other in words; but a shrill, shrewish voice won the war, for she was last, loudest and longest. However, they had consciences, these pilgrims, for their leader apologized to us, next day, for keeping us awake. That night they repented in earnest by singing hymns, the gist of which was. 'We are good men; we do not smoke, we do not drink, we do not gamble.'

Mary Augusta Mullikin
*Chinese Chapters from the Book of
Stanley Club*, 1935

RISE AND SHINE

We arrived at one small town [between Peking and Chengde] after dark, in a drizzling rain, and were glad to find shelter in a tiny temple, which having no front wall, stood wide open to its one small court-yard. We waked, at daylight, to find this court full as it could hold with onlookers patiently and quietly waiting to see the foreigners get out of bed.

Mary Augusta Mullikin
Chinese Chapters from the Book of
Stanley Club, 1935

GIVING ENGLAND A CHANCE

We [Henry Cockburn's family, when he retired to England after long service in China] rented four or five different houses in four years. Each of them was discovered, after a few months, to have some intolerable defect. Secretly, as he admitted to me later, my father had come to the conclusion that it would really be more satisfactory to buy a house in the hills west of Peking, but he wanted to give England every chance.

Claude Cockburn
I, Claude, 1956

BLUE TIE

As an old man Sir Robert [Hart] had many peculiarities; he had his very old-fashioned hats specially copied for him in London, and he always wore a narrow blue-ribbon tie because once, long ago, while staying in a temple in the Western Hills, he nearly grasped a small snake in mistake for his black tie. After that he never went out to the hills.

William J. Oudendyk
Ways and By-Ways in Diplomacy, 1939

BLACK TIE

Sir John Jordan rented a temple in the Western Hills, at Pa-ta-chu, and went there off and on during the summer months, to get out of the heat and the smells of Peking. I forget the name of his temple, but it was high up on the hill-side and one climbed to it by a path, which zigzagged alongside a mountain stream, among stunted pines and oaks and maples.

I rented a temple farther down, and Sir John and I used to meet on the stone-flagged path. It was he who pointed out to me a Chinese poem sculptured on a smooth rounded rock that the stream flowed over. We could read the characters through the running water. I said to Sir John that it reminded me of the verse in which Keats spoke of himself (though not in the same sense):

> My name is writ in water.

And we stood there discussing whether it was Shelley or somebody else who had added, after Keats' death:

> And every drop a tear.

That same evening they brought me from Peking a telegram, with a piece of news that at the time appeared to be important. I thought I would show it to Sir John. It was then about half-past seven, but still light. I started off up the path and, when I reached Sir John's temple, I walked in unannounced. He was dining in one of the courtyards. And though he was all alone, on a hot summer evening in a Chinese temple, he was correctly dressed in a dinner-jacket with a black tie.

There is something typical of the English character in that scene: the background of lacquered columns and curved roofs; the warm air scented with lotus (there were some lotus ponds near by); the Chinese servants, in their blue cotton coats and red satin waistcoats, moving about to serve the white-haired gentleman who dined in the open, at a little table with a fine table-cloth and glass and silver. He was dressed for dinner—because one *does* dress for dinner when one is a British Minister, even alone in far-off temples in the hills.

Daniele Varè
Laughing Diplomat, 1938

CHAPTER 13

THE OLD SUMMER PALACE

*The actual disposition of the ground, the little, low artificial hills,
the streams, the remains of bridges, all exhale an atmosphere that
only lingers in places that have been superlatively beautiful.*

OSBERT SITWELL
Escape With Me!, 1938

On the plain west of Peking the Qing Dynasty Emperor Kang Xi built the Yuan Ming Yuan, 'the Garden of Perfect Brightness'. It was extended and embellished by his descendants. Following the destruction of the magnificent complex, foreigners came to call the site the Old Summer Palace, to distinguish it from the New Summer Palace, a partial recreation undertaken by the Dowager Empress Ci Xi.

Kang Xi's son, the Emperor Yong Cheng, adopted the Yuan Ming Yuan as his principal residence. He and his successor, the great Qian Long, spared no effort or expense to create there the most beautiful and luxurious pleasance ingenuity could devise. Not just Chinese ingenuity—they enlisted the help of Jesuit priests, among them the talented artists Attiret and Castiglione, to create palaces after the European style. Since rococo was the style then in vogue, the European palaces made a striking contribution to the already ornate whole.

The gardens of the Yuan Ming Yuan have some claim to be considered the high point of Chinese garden architecture, but arbiters of taste in Europe were not sure it was quite the thing, especially for their own countries. They found opportunities to express their reservations, often for some reason in verse. The critics must have been alarmed by the threatened apostasy of on-the-spot observers such as Jean-Denis Attiret, who confided to the superiors of his order in France that 'my taste, since I have been in China, has become a little Chinese'.

The British joint commander of the Anglo-French Force of 1860, Lord Elgin, ordered the destruction of the Yuan Ming Yuan in reprisal for the ill-treatment and death of captives held by the Chinese (his French colleague wanted to sack the Forbidden City instead). For the looting and vandalism that followed, the English blamed the French and the French blamed the English, and both blamed the Cantonese, who had been recruited to accompany the expedition as baggage carriers.

So vast were the pleasure grounds that an onslaught limited to two days left much intact or little damaged. What the invaders had started, however, time and neglect completed. For the Qing Court, the Garden of Perfect Brightness had lost its perfection. The Imperial Household did not return, and what had been its pleasure ground became a place for the curious to muse upon the transience of human ambition, and its architectural expression.

COMPLETE HUMAN
HAPPINESS

The ruins of the Summer Palace, about ten miles from Peking, are very beautiful in the sadness of their desolation. One seems to be brought here face to face with the wreck of an empire. The builders of this palace seem to have been imbued with something of the spirit of those who in the middle ages raised in Europe such noble monuments of their devotion and piety. The whole soul of a man must have been in the work; no part was neglected, no money, time, or labour spared; infinite care was bestowed on every detail—and, notwithstanding the desolations and ruin, there still seems to breathe over all the spirit of a master mind. Roaming about the palaces now overgrown with weeds, or looking out on that still lake whose mirror-like surface must have reflected so many and such curious sights, one cannot help feeling that the architect must have had a faith in something, even if it were only in the possibility of complete human happiness.

Captain William Gill
The River of Golden Sand, 1883

KO-POO-PEE

The Emperor's country residence, called Chan-choon-yuen, which signifies 'eternal spring,' was built by Kang-hy himself for his recreation. It is situated in a plain, and surrounded by other mansions, all of which are enclosed within walls, and inhabited by his sons and the nobility. The entrances to this palace and its grounds are always guarded by Tartar soldiers, who allow none to pass but the eunuchs, and those to whom permission has been granted, in which case their names are written down upon tablets. On arriving at the gate, those who are not known are asked Ko-poo-pee, signifying, what is your name? and if the name they give is inserted upon the tablets, they are permitted to enter. After going through a kind of open hall, another gate is

reached, where some eunuchs write upon a large white board the names of those who go in, and efface them with a damp cloth when they come out. In this manner they know whether any stranger stops in the palace after a certain hour in the evening, when no one is permitted to remain but eunuchs. The same precaution is taken in the imperial palaces at Peking and Je-hol, in consequence of the excessive jealousy with which the Emperor's ladies are guarded.

This, as well as the other country residences which I have seen in China, is in a taste quite different from the European; for whereas we seek to exclude nature by art, levelling hills, drying up lakes, felling trees, bringing paths into a straight line, constructing fountains at a great expense, and raising flowers in rows, the Chinese on the contrary, by means of art, endeavour to imitate nature. Thus in these gardens there are labyrinths of artificial hills, intersected with numerous paths and roads, some straight, and others undulating; some in the plain and the valley, others carried over bridges and to the summit of the hills by means of rustic work of stones and shells. The lakes are interspersed with islets upon which small pleasure-houses are constructed, and which are reached by means of boats or bridges. To these houses, when fatigued with fishing, the Emperor retires accompanied by his ladies. The woods contain hares, deer, and game in great numbers, and a certain animal resembling the deer, which produces musk. Some of the open spaces are sown with grain and vegetables, and are interspersed with plots of fruit trees and flowers. Wherever a convenient situation offers, lies a house of recreation, or a dwelling for the eunuchs. There is also the seraglio, with a large open space in front, in which once a month a fair is held for the entertainment of the ladies; all the dealers being the eunuchs themselves, who thus dispose of articles of the most valuable and exquisite description.

Father Ripa
Memoirs of Father Ripa During Thirteen
Years' Residence at the Court of Peking . . . ,
c.1730 pub. 1846

SPEECHLESS

The Emperor further ordered that Don Pedrini should come and lodge in the house of Tton-kew-kew, for the purpose of tuning the cymbals and spinets, which his Majesty had in great numbers in all his palaces [at the Yuan Ming Yuan]. When it was stated that Pedrini did not understand the language, he replied that was of no consequence, as cymbals were tuned with the hands, and not with the tongue.

Father Ripa
Memoirs of Father Ripa . . . ,
c.1730 pub. 1846

THE EMPEROR'S KEW

Where China's London boasts her verdant Kew,
A fair Elysium, from her walls in view. . . .
Kien-Long the great, the valiant and the wise
Sweet slumber sought, but slumber shunn'd his eyes:
He frown'd, and spoke: the lords in waiting round,
Knocked their broad foreheads nine times on the ground . . .

Anon.
Kien Long. An Chinese Imperial Eclogue,
translated from a curious Oriental
MS . . . , 1775

RELAXING THE HEART

Every Emperor and ruler, when he has returned from audience and has finished his public duties, must have a garden where he may stroll and look about and relax his heart. If he has a suitable place to do this, it will refresh his mind and regulate his emotions, but if not, he will become engrossed in sensual pleasures and lose his will-power. If thoughts of palaces, costumes, strange performances, curiosities and other attractions completely occupy his thoughts, his interest in meeting officials, receiving criticisms, and diligence in government will gradually fade away. Would not such a condition be too dreadful for words?

Edict of Emperor Qian Long
Quoted in Danby:
The Garden of Perfect Brightness, 1950

FESTIVAL OF LIGHT

Several historic lantern festivals are described in the old records. Among the most extravagant is a fête ordered at Nanking by a certain Ming Emperor. Ten thousand lamps were set afloat on the lake, and the effect was so beautiful that Buddha came down from Heaven to see it. Ch'ien Lung gave a similar party in the gardens of his summer palace near Peking, where every pavilion—and there were several hundred—was outlined with lanterns, every canal afloat with little lighted boats, every tree hung with flaming fruits, and the miles of marble balustrades decorated with tiny stars of light glowing in their painted silk cups.

Juliet Bredon and
Igor Mitrophanow
The Moon Year, 1927

CHINOISERIE

Of late, 'tis true, quite sick of Rome, and Greece,
We fetch our models from the wise Chinese:
European artists are too cool, and chaste,
For Mand'rin only is the man of taste;
Whose bolder genius, fondly wild to see
His grove a forest, and his pond a sea,
Breaks out—and, whimsically great, designs,
Without the shackles of rules, or lines:
Form'd on his plan, our farms and seats begin
To match the boasted villas of Pekin.
On every hill a spire-crown'd temple swells,
Hung round with serpents, and a fringe of bells:
Junks and balons along our waters sail,
With each a guilded cockboat at his tail;
Our choice exotics to the breeze exhale,
Within th'inclosure of a zigzag rail;
In Tartar huts our cows and horses lie,
Our hogs are fatted in an Indian stye.
On ev'ry shelf a Joss divinely stares,
Nymphs laid on Chintzes sprawl upon our chairs;
While o'er our cabinets Confucius nods,
'Midst Porcelain elephants and China gods.

Revd James Cawthorn
Of Taste: An Essay, 1771

BEYOND WORDS

This place is truly an Imperial residence; the park is said to be
eighteen miles round, and laid out in all the taste, variety, and
magnificence which distinguish the rural scenery of Chinese
gardening. There is no one very extensive contiguous building but
several hundreds of pavilions scattered through the grounds
and all connected together by close arbors, by passages apparently
cut through stupendous rocks, or by fairyland galleries, emerging

or receding in the perspective, and so contrived as to conceal the real design of communication and yet contribute to the general purpose and effect intended to arise from the whole. The various beauties of the spot, its lakes and rivers, together with its superb edifices, which I saw (and yet I saw but a very small part), so strongly impressed my mind at this moment that I feel incapable of describing them.

Lord Macartney
Journal, 23 August 1793

IMPERIAL ARCADE

Ch'ien Lung was no ascetic kill-joy. To the east of the Lake of Happiness, at the Summer Palace of Yüan Ming-yüan, in a garden called the 'Park of Universal Joy,' he was fond of giving theatrical entertainments to his Court. At the New Year he used to have booths erected along the main road of the garden and there organised a market fair for the amusement of the Court. There were curio and porcelain stores, embroidery shops, dealers in silks, as well as restaurants, wine-taverns and tea-houses. Even pedlars and hawkers were allowed to come and ply their trade. The shops were managed by eunuchs, and the jade and other articles were supplied from the large establishments in Peking, under arrangements made by the Supervisor of the Octroi, who selected what goods should be sent. High officials and their wives were admitted to this fair, and allowed to make purchases or to order food or tea at the restaurants, just as they pleased. Everything was done exactly as at a real market fair: waiters and shop attendants were brought from the chief restaurants in the city, care being taken to select only those of good appearance and clear pronunciation. As His Majesty passed down the line of booths, the waiters would shout out their menus for the day, the hawkers would cry their goods, and the clerks would be busy calling out the figures which they were entering on the day-books. The bustle and animation of this scene used to delight the Emperor. The fair continued daily till the end of the 1st Moon, when the booths were taken down. This pleasant custom was also abandoned by Chia

Ch'ing, whose temperament was morose and opposed to all forms
of gaiety.

E. Backhouse and J. O. P. Bland
Annals and Memoirs of the Court of Peking,
1914

THE SMALL-FOOTED MAID

In Yüan-ming-yüan, all gaily arrayed
In malachite kirtles and slippers of jade,
'Neath the wide-spreading tea-tree, fair damsels are seen
All singing to Joss on the soft candareen.

But fairer by far was the small-footed maid
Who sat by my side in the sandal-wood shade,
A-sipping the vintage of sparkling Lychee,
And warbling the songs of the poet Maskee.

Oh fair are the flowers in her tresses that glow,
The sweet-scented cumshaw, the blue pummelow,
And dearest I thought her of maids in Pekin,
As from the pagoda she bade me chin-chin.

One eve, in the twilight, to sing she began,
As I touched the light notes of a jewelled sampan,
While her own jetty finger-nails, taper and long,
Swept softly the chords of a tremulous gong.

She sang how 'a princess of fair Pechelee
Was carried away by the cruel Sycee,
And married by force to that tyrant accursed,
That Portuguese caitiff, Pyjamah the First.

'Though her eyes were more bright than the yaconin's glow,
And whiter than bucksheesh her bosom of snow,
Yet alas for the maid! she is captive, and now
Lies caged in thy fortress, detested Macao!

'But she muffled her face with her sohotzu's fold,
And the jailor she bribed with a tao-t'ai of gold,
And away she is fled from the traitor's harem,
Tho' the punkahs may flash and the compradores gleam.'

Thus she ceased;—and a bumper of opium we took,
And we smoked the ginseng from a coral chebouque,
And we daintily supped upon birds' nests and snails,
And catties, and maces, and piculs, and taels.

Then we slew a joss-pigeon in honour of Fo,
And in praise of Fêng-shui we made a kotow;
And soon the most beautiful girl in Pekin
Fell asleep in the arms of her own mandarin.

E. C. Baber
Quoted in Giles: *A Glossary of Reference*,
1878

BECOMING CHINESE

I confess, without pretending to decide on the preference, that the style of building in this country pleases me greatly, and my taste, since I have been in China, has become a little Chinese. . . .

In the pleasances there reigns almost everywhere a graceful disorder, an anti-symmetry is desired almost everywhere. Everything is based on this principle. It is a natural, rustic countryside they wish represented, a solitude, not a well-ordered palace conforming to all the rules of symmetry and harmony; and I have not seen one of these little palaces, each placed at quite distance from the other in the enclosure of the Emperor's pleasance, which has any resemblance to the other. One would say that each was built according to the ideas and style of different countries; that everything is placed haphazard and spontaneously; that one portion was not made for the next. When one hears this, one would think it to be ridiculous, that it must strike the eye disagreeably; but when one sees them one thinks differently and admires the art with which the irregularity is planned. Everything is in good taste and so well-built that it is not with only a single glance that

245

all the beauty of it can be appreciated, one must examine it piece by piece; there is something here to amuse one for a long time and to satisfy all one's curiosity.

Frère Attiret
Letter, 1 November 1743

DEMORALISING WORK

Owing to the ill-treatment the prisoners experienced at the Summer Palace, the General ordered it to be destroyed, and stuck up proclamations to say why it was so ordered. We accordingly went out, and, after pillaging it, burned the whole place, destroying in a Vandal-like manner most valuable property which would not be replaced for four millions. We got upwards of £48 a-piece prize money before we went out here; and although I have not as much as many, I have done well. Imagine D—— giving sixteen shillings for a string of pearls, which he sold the next day for £500!

The people are civil, but I think the grandees hate us, as they must after what we did to the Palace. You can scarcely imagine the beauty and magnificence of the places we burnt. It made one's heart sore to burn them; in fact, these palaces were so large, and we were so pressed for time, that we could not plunder them carefully. Quantities of gold ornaments were burnt, considered as brass. It was wretchedly demoralising work for an army. Everybody was wild for plunder.

You would scarcely conceive the magnificence of this residence, or the tremendous devastation the French have committed. The throne-room was lined with ebony, carved in a marvellous way. There were huge mirrors of all shapes and kinds, clocks, watches, musical boxes with puppets on them, magnificent china of every description, heaps and heaps of silks of all colours, embroidery, and as much splendour and civilization as you would see at Windsor; carved ivory screens, coral screens, large amounts of treasure, etc. The French have smashed everything in the most wanton way. It was a scene of utter destruction which passes my description.

Capt. Charles Gordon
Letter, October 1860

NOT NEGOTIABLE

In order to exemplify the faith that foreigners place in the integrity of our officers, it is interesting to note that, after the capture of the Summer Palace, an officer of rank in the English army was seen purchasing articles from the French soldiers, and paying for them by means of cheques upon Messrs. Coutts.

Henry William Gordon
Events in the Life of Charles George Gordon,
1886

BEYOND RESTRAINT

The commission [to 'distribute the wealth' of the Palace] began its work at once, and in a calm manner. The most striking, if not most precious, objects were removed one after another. . . .

The troops watching this first phase of the looting were made up of a motley crowd, as French and British infantry, scouts, artillerymen, spahis, the Queen's dragoons, Sikhs, Arabs and Chinese coolies were freely intermingled. A rumor spread in the throng and was repeated in many tongues by all these men packed together with eyes wide open and shining, the greed aroused, their mouths dry. They were saying to one another: 'When the main loot is gone, it will be our turn to help ourselves. . . .'

I was thus given an excellent opportunity to compare the genius of the two allied nations. While the French played the game straight, and acted individually, the British proved more methodical, and from the very beginning went about the looting in an organized manner. They moved in by squads, as if on fatigue duty, carrying bags, and were commanded by noncommissioned officers who, incredible as it sounds (yet strictly true), had brought touchstones with them. Where the devil had they found them? I don't know, but I can swear that they did possess such tools normally used by jewelers, and by our commissioners at pawnbrokers' stores. . . .

The British and French, officers and soldiers, were thus mingled in the Palace, together with the Chinese and our

247

coolies, whose hatred for their northern countrymen had prompted them to storm the Taku forts on our side. . . . It would have been too much to ask our men to let this human stream, in which all races were represented, rush by without being engulfed by it. Such abnegation would have been beyond human resistance. . . .

Being a mere spectator, I deeply enjoyed this strange and unforgettable vision: the swarming of men of all types and colors, the over-crowding of representatives of all human races on a heap of spoils, hurrahing in all tongues of the world, hurrying about, bumping into one another, stumbling, falling down and getting up again, swearing and shouting, all the while carrying their loot away as fast as they could. It all looked like a giant ant hill half-crushed under the foot of a passer-by, with its panic-stricken black workers fleeing in every direction carrying a grain, a larva, an egg, or a straw between their mandibles. Some soldiers had buried their heads in the red-lacquered chests of the Empress, others were half-hidden among heaps of embroidered fabrics and silkware, still others were filling their pockets, shirts and kepis with rubies, sapphires, pearls, and pieces of crystal. . . . Others were leaving the grounds with armfuls of clocks and watches. Sappers had brought their axes and were smashing the furniture in order to collect the jewels which were set in the wood. One of them, looking very earnest, kept striking a lovely Louis XV clock in order to get its dial showing the hours with figures in crystal, which he believed to be diamonds.

Compte d'Herisson
(trans. Martin Kieffer)
Journal d'un interprète en Chine, 1886

APPEARANCE AND REALITY

General Montauban led us to the Palace, solemnly protesting all the while that he had strictly prohibited his troops from entering within the walls, as he was determined that no looting should take place before the British came up. . . .

The great part of the curiosities lay about the rooms, and we proceeded to examine them as we would the curiosities of a museum, when to our astonishment, the French officers commenced to *arracher* everything they took a fancy to. Gold watches and small valuables were whipped up by these gentlemen with amazing velocity. . . .

After allowing his people to load themselves as fast as they could for about ten minutes, the General insisted upon them all following him out, and kept on repeating that looting was strictly prohibited, and he would not allow it, although his officers were doing it without reserve before his own eyes.

Robert Swinhoe
Narrative of the North China Campaign,
1861

HARE AND HOUNDS

We were ushered through a number of courtyards, where there was nothing to be seen but ruined and charred walls, and the ghosts of departed pine-trees, and along a pretty covered walk to a pavilion by the lake where we were to breakfast. It was a lovely spot. The lake is a mass of lotus plants now in full flower; there are quantities of little islands covered with trees and buildings. A number of boats with naked fishermen in them gave a touch of wildness and barbarity to the scene, and further added to our amusement; for one of the men, in the hopes of finding Heaven knows what small loot among the masses of rubbish where there is not so much as a tile left whole, had come on shore and was lying hidden among the ruins; whom when the guardians perceived, they set up such a game of hare and hounds, and such a throwing of stones and bad language, as reminded me of Eton days when a boy from another house was found in my dame's without being able to give a good account of himself.

A. B. Freeman-Mitford
The Attaché at Peking, 1866, pub. 1900

MARKET FORCES

Cloisonné enamel, by the bye, went out of fashion at the end of the last century, and the Chinese ceased to make it; but when, after the sacking of the Summer Palace, the specimens looted there and sent home fetched such wonderful prices in London and Paris, they routed out the drawers in which their forbears had carefully locked their recipes—for a Chinaman never destroys anything— and soon the market will be flooded with new work.

A. B. Freeman-Mitford
The Attaché at Peking, 1866, pub. 1900

STRANDED

A few columns and scraps of archway still remain, heavily laden with somewhat gross and showy ornament. Melancholy is the impression they make today. No sea-beast, washed up on an alien shore or left to languish in a dismal aquarium tank, ever looked so helplessly out of its element as these ruins in the desolate Chinese plain.

Peter Quennell
A Superficial Journey Through Tokyo and Peking, 1938

PLACE OF ENCHANTMENT

Soon little more will be left of temples and altars, of pagodas and monasteries, than of Yüan-Ming-Yüan, the Old Summer Palace, which formerly stood outside the grounds of the present Summer Palace built by the Empress Dowager. There, until the Anglo-French armies burnt it in 1860, and looted its treasures in order to take mementoes home to York and Lille and Roubaix and Surbiton, existed an edifice that, with its grounds, ranked as one of the marvels of the world. This was the opposite to *chinoiserie,*

an oriental variation on Western themes. A unique episode in the history of taste, it was ordered by the Emperor K'ang Hsi, and carried out by Chinese architects and workmen under the superintendence of the Jesuit Fathers. Of palaces and pavilions, of formal and landscape gardens, nothing remains now but a dust-heap, in which the small children of neighbouring farmers play, throwing large stones at the few plumed helmets and trophies that remain, and battering at the balusters of a marble bridge—as I saw them doing during my first visit to the site—for the sheer joy of the thing, with a ram they had made of wood. Even the Europeans, who were so curiously responsible both for its creation and destruction, never think it worth while to drive there to see what is left, and, if asked about it, reply vaguely that it was 'not at all Chinese' and 'rather odd'—for they only admire the earliest and most primitive works, Stonehenges in bronze and pottery as opposed to Trianons. And yet, a visit is most rewarding, though scarcely a stone is upright or on the surface, for every piece of ornament, broken column or mask, has a quality, original, strange and exquisite. The actual disposition of the ground, the little, low artificial hills, the streams, the remains of bridges, all exhale an atmosphere that only lingers in places that have been superlatively beautiful. Long after the site is forgotten, and the last fragments of stone or marble have sunk into the ground, future generations will wonder at the enchantment that emanates from this small stretch of varied country, with its pleasantly flowing streams.

Osbert Sitwell
Escape With Me!, 1938

CHAPTER 14

THE NEW SUMMER PALACE

She [Dowager Empress Ci Xi] may have caused China to lose the war against Japan, but she preserved for it that perfect little jewel the Summer Palace, worth infinitely more than those sadly overrated things, naval victories.

A. E. GRANTHAM
Pencil Speakings from Peking, 1918

A djoining, although not part of, the site of the Yuan Ming Yuan, is the park the Emperor Qian Long devised as a gift for his mother on her sixtieth birthday. The Dowager Empress Ci Xi had it rebuilt towards the end of the nineteenth century, and named it the Yi He Yuan (the Garden where Peace is Cultivated). To most foreigners, however, it is the New Summer Palace, or just the Summer Palace.

Ci Xi settled for the Yi He Yuan only after failing to secure funding for a grandiose scheme to restore the Yuan Ming Yuan. She diverted funds intended for the Chinese navy in order to carry out the work, and reputedly built the marble boat still to be seen on the shore of Kun Ming Lake as a nod towards the unwilling benefactor.

Ci Xi built the Summer Palace as a retirement home (although she did not long stay retired, and in fact subsequently put the palace to good use as a place of confinement for the Guang Xu Emperor, whom she deposed in order herself to resume charge). More resilient than her predecessors, she had the palace rebuilt after it had been vandalised by foreign troops at the time of the Boxer uprising, and spent much of her time there right up to her death in 1908.

Two of those who attended upon the Dowager Empress at the Summer Palace wrote later about their life there. One was 'Princess' Der Ling, the daughter of a Manchu noble, who had accompanied him on a diplomatic posting to Paris, and there acquired a familiarity with Western etiquette, as well as fluency in English. Der Ling, her mother and her sister facilitated Ci Xi's contacts with the foreign visitors she cultivated in her later years.

The second chronicler was an American artist, Katharine Carl, whom the Dowager Empress commissioned in 1903 to paint her portrait. While carrying out the commission, Miss Carl lived with her subject. Her occasionally breathless account of life in the imperial household is the most immediate description any foreigner has achieved of day-to-day court life. If court life comes across as somewhat banal, we should not assume that the fault is all Miss Carl's.

NO TIME FOR RELAXATION

EDICT BY THE EMPRESS-DOWAGER

From the time when I first lowered the curtain and attended to State affairs, I have been filled day and night with fear and awe, as though I were travelling along the edge of a chasm. Although the Empire is now fairly peaceful, this is no time for leisurely relaxation or for any diminution of strenuous endeavour. I am conscious of the fact that the former sainted Emperors of our dynasty laid upon Their Successors the necessity of devoting Themselves to the duties of government and to relieving the sufferings of the people. All parks and gardens created by our sainted Predecessors were intended to provide facilities for martial exercises, and not for purposes of sumptuous display and the pleasures of the chase, as was the case with the parks established by the sovereigns of earlier dynasties.

I am, however, aware that the Emperor's desire to restore the palace in the West springs from his laudable concern for my welfare, and for that reason I cannot bear to meet his well-meaning petition with a blunt refusal.

Moreover, the costs of construction have all been provided for out of the surplus funds accumulated as a result of rigid economies in the past. The funds under the control of the Board of Revenue will not be touched, and no harm will be done to the national finances.

Nevertheless there are current rumours which show that all the facts of the case are not fully understood, and the audacious suggestion has even been made that the proposed works include the gradual rebuilding of the Yüan-ming Yüan. This is a gross error, which has filled me with consternation. . . .

I do not know how many there are who are capable of reverently following the counsels of our Imperial Predecessors and transmitting Their glorious traditions. It is particularly necessary to adapt our actions to the times in which we live and to confine our attention to essentials. That the desires of my heart are not directed towards idle relaxation will assuredly be recognised throughout the land.

The Emperor has now reached manhood. He will henceforth devote himself with all diligence to his administrative duties and learn how to combine self-control with love of the people. He must not let his filial devotion lead him for my sake into lavish expenditure on idle luxuries.

Furthermore I enjoin all servants of the State, great and small, in the capital and in the provinces, to be loyal, diligent and strenuous, and to beware of wasting their substance on frivolity and extravagance. Let them act in accordance with the highest principles and not disappoint the deepest longings and aspirations of my heart.

> Edict of the Dowager
> Empress Ci Xi, 1888
> Quoted in Johnston, *Twilight in the*
> *Forbidden City*, 1934

WORKERS OF THE WORLD

More than twenty large firms have taken over contracts for finishing the Eho Palace gardens, which have been built by the Emperor as a place of recreation for the Empress-Dowager, after her retirement from managing the arduous affairs of State. Her Majesty prefers to visit and stay in them during the summer, and the time appointed to have the gardens in a complete state for her reception is very near. More than ten thousand workmen have been engaged to hasten the work. Of these, three thousand or more are carvers, who have caused much trouble while working in other portions of the Imperial Palace ere this. Knowing that the date for completing the gardens was near at hand, they struck for higher wages, and in this demand all the carpenters joined. They were receiving individually three meals and about eightpence per diem. They demanded half a crown a day. On their employers refusing to comply with this exorbitant request, a signal gun, previously agreed upon, was fired, and thousands of workmen, carvers, carpenters, and masons began to make threatening demonstrations. The officials on guard, finding the police unable to cope with the multitude, especially as the carpenters were armed with axes, quickly sounded the alarm, calling on the rifle brigade, Yuen-ming-yuen guards, and cavalry for assistance. These came with all speed and surrounded the strikers. The officials and the

head firms now began to negotiate, and all parties were satisfied
with an increase of 8*d.* a day for each man.

Shenpao (Chinese newspaper)
Quoted in Little, *Intimate China*, 1899

ABSURD

Lady Harriet stopped again, before the Marble Boat this time, in
disapproving astonishment.

'That is really quite ugly, don't you think?' she said, gazing at it
through her lorgnette. 'And so absurd! It isn't marble, and it isn't
a boat! Do you know, I wonder at an intelligent woman like the
Empress Dowager wishing to build this ridiculous place, and being
so absurdly pleased with it.'

Ann Bridge
Four-Part Setting, 1939

JUST REDEEMED

The Chinese can hardly go wrong in architecture, and their
buildings rarely lapse from taste; but the Summer Palace does so
lapse, and is only redeemed by the presence of hill and water and
the gentle grace of trees from sheer absurdity.

Ann Bridge
Four-Part Setting, 1939

A HIGHER GOOD

Mere children were raised to the Dragon Throne in order that her
[Ci Xi's] own power and that of her clan should be indefinitely
prolonged. Large sums destined for strengthening the navy, and
badly needed for that purpose, by all manner of indirections found

their way into her hands, and were gaily spent on beautifying her Summer Palace.

However, on this latter point, seeing the incalculable amount of evil wrought by battleships, the huge cost of their construction, the shortness and sinister ugliness of their life compared to the perennial beauty of the summer retreat of an attractive woman, can one blame her so much? Is she not rather deserving of praise?

She may have caused China to lose the war against Japan, but she preserved for it that perfect little jewel the Summer Palace, worth infinitely more than those sadly overrated things, naval victories.

A. E. Grantham
Pencil Speakings from Peking, 1918

THE HUNCHBACK BRIDGE

On the hunchback bridge—one step is higher than the other—under the bridge the leaves of the lantern grass float on the water—the goldfish run after the silverfish and bite their tails—and the toads with big bellies—cry kurkuà kurkuà.

Trans. Guido A. Vitale
Pekinese Rhymes, 1896

NO GRANDEUR

Tourists generally are all raving about the Summer Palace, and it is quite a place to spend a happy day in, if it were but for the pure air by the lakeside among the hills. . . . But the Summer Palace is not ancient, and I saw no masterpieces there, except the bronze ox, a bronze pavilion and the marble bridges. There is no austere grandeur of approach. It is a sort of glorified Rosherville.

Mrs Archibald Little
Round About My Peking Garden, 1905

DRESSING ROOM ON LEGS

The head eunuch came, knelt down on the marble floor and announced that Her Majesty's chair was ready and she asked us to go with her to the Audience Hall, distant about two minutes' walk, where she was going to receive the heads of the different Boards. It was a beautiful day and her open chair was waiting. This chair is carried by eight eunuchs all dressed in official robes, a most unusual sight. The head eunuch walked on her left side and the second eunuch on her right side, each with a steadying hand on the chair pole. Four eunuchs of the fifth rank in front and twelve eunuchs of the sixth rank walked behind. Each eunuch carried something in his hand, such as Her Majesty's clothes, shoes, handkerchiefs, combs, brushes, powder boxes, looking glasses of different sizes, perfumes, pins, black and red ink, yellow paper, cigarettes, water pipes, and the last one carried her yellow satin-covered stool. Besides this there were two amahs (old women servants) and four servant girls all carrying something. This procession was most interesting to see and made one think it a lady's dressing room on legs.

Princess Der Ling
Two Years in the Forbidden City, 1907

BIG JOKE

Every morning, as usual, we waited on Her Majesty and reported anything of interest which had occurred during the previous day. Then we all preceded Her Majesty to the theatre, where we awaited her arrival standing in the courtyard. On Her Majesty appearing, we would all kneel down until she had passed into the building opposite the stage, kneeling in rows—first the Emperor, behind him the Young Princess, next the Secondary wife, then the Princesses and Court ladies, and last of all the visitors. The first two days everything went off all right, but on the third morning the Emperor, from whom we received the signal, suddenly turned and said: 'Her Majesty is coming.' Down we all went on our knees, the Emperor alone remaining standing and laughing at us. Of course there was no sign of Her Majesty and everybody joined in the laugh. He was never so happy as when he could work off a joke like this.

Princess Der Ling
Two Years in the Forbidden City, 1907

LIKE IT OR NOT

Down at the water level many strange and some beautiful things are to be seen. It is fascinating to stand in the eternal breeze and look out over the lake and watch silvery carp leap up between the gigantic waving lotus-fronds. There are 'Korean dogs' of rich cast bronze upon pedestals of no less magnificent sculptured marble; a *pailou*, or commemorative arch, which borders on barbaric splendour and seems hardly to belong to the same world as the hundreds of dingy *pailous* in Peking City; and the marble boat which every tourist must see, whether he is interested in marble boats or not.

Gilbert Collins
Extreme Oriental Mixture, 1926

CUSHIONS ON THE FLOOR . . .

In front of the Throne dais [in the Audience Hall], during the hours of Audience, there are five cushions placed on the floor for the members of the Grand Council to kneel upon when they are memorializing Their Majesties. The Prime Minister's cushion is nearest the Throne. A cushion to kneel upon is a privilege only granted members of the Grand Council. Any other official, when making communications to Their Majesties, must kneel upon the bare marble floor, and must kneel beyond the space occupied by these five cushions. He is thus placed at a disadvantage. The distance at which he is from Their Majesties may prevent his hearing some of their words, especially the Emperor's, whose voice is very low and without any carrying quality. The official may overcome this difficulty and shorten the distance by paying the eunuch who conducts him to the Audience Hall, to remove some of the cushions, so that he may kneel nearer the dais. The Prime Minister's and Grand Secretary's cushions may on no condition be removed, but the other three are subject to the will of the introducing eunuch. If this latter be sufficiently paid, and there is a fixed price for each cushion, he will remove the three of the lower members of the Cabinet.

When the official who has been granted an Audience is conducted to the Audience Hall by the eunuch appointed for the purpose, the latter throws open the great doors, falls upon his knees at the threshold, and announces the name and position of the official, gives the hour and minute of his arrival at the Palace, and, before he rises, he has deftly removed the cushions for which he has received the required sum. After his name has been announced, the official enters and kneels as near the dais as is consistent with his rank and the sum paid the eunuch.

Katharine A. Carl
With the Empress Dowager of China, 1906

. . . AND ON THE KNEES

The officials who are obliged to go often to Audiences resort to an amusing subterfuge to protect their knees from the marble floor. They strap heavily wadded cushions around their knees before they go in, and they can thus kneel in comfort.

Katharine. A Carl
With the Empress Dowager of China, 1906

NO REGRET

It was obvious, as one entered the great pavilions, that the Empress Dowager's personal taste in bric-à-brac must have coincided, to an extraordinary degree, with that of the least enlightened English tourists. Screens with grisly inlay of mother-of-pearl, vases of monstrous shape and hue, frightful bronzes, worthless pictures and tortured lacquer work made an ensemble which would have disgraced a Victorian drawing-room. Blackwood chairs framed slabs of streaky marble. There were many clocks, one in the form of a lighthouse. A row of gilt seats, upholstered in yellow satin, evoked the gas-lit routs of the Second Empire.

We left the Summer Palace without regret.

Peter Quennell
A Superficial Journey Through Tokyo and Peking, 1933

FEMININITY

It is not as a work of art that the Summer Palace should be judged at all, only as a bit of life, of feminine life, as the most delightful piece of femininity that ever translated itself into bricks and mortar.

A. E. Grantham
Pencil Speakings from Peking, 1918

HER MAJESTY'S BARGE

Her Majesty's own barge lay at the foot of the marble steps and numbers of other barges and boats lay around, forming quite a little fleet. She descended the steps and entered the barge. The young Empress, Princesses, and Ladies followed. Her Majesty sat in the yellow, throne-like chair in the middle of the raised platform of the barge.

Several of the high eunuchs stood at the back of the Empress Dowager's chair with her extra wraps, bonbons, cigarettes, water-pipes, etc. There were two rowers on the barge who stood with their long oars to guide it, for it was attached by great yellow ropes to two boats, manned by twenty-four rowers each, and was towed along by them. Only the eunuchs of the highest rank, Her Majesty's personal attendants, went on the barge with her, and the two boatmen simply guided it. All the Palace boatmen stand to their oars, for they cannot sit in the presence of Her Majesty, even though not upon the Imperial barge.

A number of flat boats followed the Imperial barge with the army of eunuchs that go to make up the train of Their Majesties when they move about the Palace or grounds. One boat carried portable stoves and all the necessary arrangements for making tea.

Katharine A. Carl
With the Empress Dowager of China, 1906

SIMPLE PLEASURES

I put my head out of the window [of the Imperial barge] and noticed the Young Empress and several other Court ladies were in the other boat. They waved to me, and I waved back. Her Majesty [Ci Xi] laughed and said to me: 'I give you this apple to throw to them.' While saying this she took one from the big plates that stood upon the center table. I tried very hard, but the apple did not reach the other boat, but went to the bottom of the lake. Her Majesty laughed and told me to try again, but I failed. Finally, she took one and threw it herself. It went straight to the other boat and hit one of the ladies' head. We all laughed quite heartily.

Princess Der Ling
Two Years in the Forbidden City, 1907

PAID EMPLOYMENT

In the back of the [Great Audience] hall were three pianos, two upright and a new Grand piano, which had but lately arrived at the Palace. Her Majesty wished us to try the Grand piano, and one of Lady Yu-Keng's daughters, who had studied music in Paris, played a few airs. Her Majesty thought the piano a curious sort of instrument, but lacking in volume and tone for so large an instrument. She asked me to play also, and then said she would like to see how the foreigners danced, and suggested my playing some dance music. The Misses Yu-Keng waltzed, and she thought it very amusing to watch them. She could not, however, understand how ladies and gentlemen could enjoy dancing together, nor what pleasure they found in it. She said the Chinese pay others to dance for them, and would not think of doing so themselves for pleasure.

Katharine A. Carl
With the Empress Dowager of China, 1906

PULLING TURNIPS

One day we went out into the turnip field, and the Empress Dowager herself pulled the first turnip; then the Empress and all the Princesses pulled some, and when they found a curiously shaped one, it was given to Her Majesty. It was a strange sight to see the Great Empress Dowager, sitting there at the side of the field, on her yellow camp-stool, smiling and interested, with the turnips piled around her, and the gaily dressed Empress and Princesses in their silken gowns flitting in and out of the field, apparently enjoying, to its utmost, the simple task of pulling these prosaic vegetables. The eunuchs and attendants stood in crowds around to take the turnips when pulled. They were not allowed, however, to pull any themselves. When a small square was denuded, Her Majesty and the Ladies returned to the Palace, and an army of workmen came and pulled up the whole field.

Katharine A Carl
With the Empress Dowager of China, 1906

EMPTY SACRIFICE

The grandiloquently named Hall of Ten Thousand Ages was a rectangular, solidly constructed building with thick walls. But inside a sad scene of ruin met our eyes. Enormous fragments of shattered colossal statues choked the interior, so that one could not pass from door to door. Huge heads, trunks, and limbs lay piled in fantastic confusion. The temple had contained a number of giant images of Buddha. Some troops, on occupying the palace, had been informed that these were hollow and filled with treasures of inestimable value. The tale seemed likely; so dynamite was invoked to force them to reveal their hidden secrets. The colossal gods were hurled from their pedestals by its powerful agency; and their ruins were eagerly searched by the vandals. But it was found that the interiors of the statues, though indeed hollow, were simply modelled to correspond with the internal anatomy of a human being, all the organs being reproduced in silver or zinc. And the gods were sacrificed in vain to the greed of the spoilers.

Capt. Gordon Casserly
The Land of the Boxers, 1903

TRUE APPRECIATION

Much to our surprise, when we reached the gates of the Summer Palace, a young Chinese, dressed in foreign clothes, came up and held out his visiting card. On it was engraved the legend: *Monsieur Jean Jacques Wu.*

In those days a permit was required to visit the Summer Palace. On receiving our request for this document, the Chinese authorities had taken note of the fact that one of our party was a bishop, and they had thought it incumbent on themselves to furnish him with a personal guide. It was in this capacity that Mr. Wu now presented himself. At first his company put a damper on our good humour. But we cheered up when we discovered that, although most kind and obliging, Mr. Wu was hardly qualified to act as a guide to the Summer Palace, never having been there before. He spoke French, and his contribution to our knowledge consisted in repeating before every work of art or picturesque landscape:

'*C'est très apprécié ici!*'

Daniele Varè
The Gate of Happy Sparrows, 1937

CHAPTER 15

THE GREAT WALL
AND
MING TOMBS

There in the mist, enormous, majestic, silent, and terrible, stood the Great Wall of China.

W. SOMERSET MAUGHAM
On A Chinese Screen, 1922

Peking owes its choice as China's capital to the strategic importance of its position, commanding the three main passes into China from the north-east. That position of strength was buttressed by construction of the Great Wall, which secures each pass—Nankou, Gubeikou, and Shanhaiguan.

Marco Polo makes no mention of the Great Wall, although his famous nineteenth century editor, Sir Henry Yule, does his best to repair the deficiency. This omission caused Europe for some centuries to speculate that the Wall did not really exist. More recently, it has prompted speculation in the other direction: that Marco Polo was no more than an armchair traveller, who never himself saw the scenes he described.

As it happens, the Wall near Peking was built during the Ming Dynasty, so in its present substantial form it would not have been available for inspection in the thirteenth century, whether or not Polo was there to see it. It was, however, substantially in evidence when Lord Macartney led the British embassy to China in 1793. Journeying to and from Qian Long's summer residence at Jehol (Chengde), the envoy's party twice passed through the outer gates at Gubeikou. Their inspection confirmed to them, and through them to Europe, that the Great Wall of China did indeed exist.

From Samuel Johnson to Kafka, the Wall of China has exercised a fascination for writers in the West. For most, like Johnson, whose works and conversations are peppered with Wall references, it was a vision to be enjoyed only in the abstract. Somerset Maugham, however, viewed the construction at first hand, and captured the scene for posterity in what he considered his finest piece of descriptive prose. He read the passage out loud to Harold Acton, who pronounced it trite.

Visitors viewing the Wall at the Nankou Pass at Badaling, the nearest point to Peking, have often combined the journey with a side-trip into the valley nearby where lie the tombs of the Ming Emperors. After the massive permanence of the Wall, the neglected tombs, their decay accelerated by pilfering to embellish the burial places of the succeeding Qing Dynasty, have furnished to many an agreeable reminder of human vanity. It was left to an historian, Arnold Toynbee, to see behind the surface impermanence to the indestructability of the huge barrows which are the Ming Emperors' real memorial.

A DISTANT PROSPECT

If the weather had been finer
You could see the wall in China
If it wasn't for the houses in between.

Anon.
English children's song

TARTAR IRRUPTIONS

A new Drove of Tartars shall China subdue, which is no strange
thing if we consult the Histories of China, and successive
Inundations made by Tartarian Nations. For when the Invaders, in
process of time, have degenerated into effeminacy and softness of
the Chineses, then they themselves have suffered a new Tartarian
Conquest and Inundation. And this happened from time beyond
our Histories: for according to their Account, the famous Wall of
China, built against the irruptions of the Tartars, was begun a
hundred years before the Incarnation.

Sir Thomas Browne
Prophecy Concerning the Future State of
Several Nations, c.1658

OBSERVATION POINT

To study the history of Egypt one should place himself on the top
of the pyramids. To study the history of China there is no point of
observation so favorable as the summit of the Great Wall.

W. A. P. Martin
A Cycle of Cathay, 1900

FIERCE AND IGNORANT

We have now gratified our minds with an exact view of the greatest work of man, except the wall of China. Of the wall it is very easy to assign the motives. It secured a wealthy and timorous nation from the incursion of Barbarians, whose unskilfulness in arts made it easier for them to supply their wants by rapine than by industry, and who from time to time poured in upon the habitations of peaceful commerce, as vultures descend upon domestick fowl. Their celerity and fierceness made the wall necessary, and their ignorance made it efficacious.

Samuel Johnson
Rasselas, 1759

WOLVES AND LAMBS

We only know the story from the Cain side, where the Chinese pose as innocent and needing defence; it would be interesting to hear what the Abels thought of it—how the Mongols regarded the 'White Wall,' as they called it, a barrier to cut them off from the water for their flocks, and if they complained, a barrier whence would issue an army to cut them down, and slander them afterwards. The wolf first quarrels with the lamb, then eats him, then tells the world that the lamb was attacking him. The Wall divided the wolves from the lambs, but which was on which side is a question.

William Geil
The Great Wall of China, 1909

THE PYRAMIDS COMPARED

After beholding China's wonder of the world, I would hesitate to cross the street to see Egypt's Pyramids.

William Geil
The Great Wall of China, 1909

UNSUSTAINABLE
DEVELOPMENT

There are frequent towers, 100 sazhens one from the other. The Wall is built in this way: at the foundation, cut stone of huge dimensions, undressed granite, and above that, brick. The height is four sazhens, the breadth is two sazhens. In some places, among

the mountains it has fallen down. The Chinese, speaking of it, boast that when it was built there remained no stone in the mountains, no sand in the desert, in the rivers no water, in the forest no trees.

Spathary
(17th century Russian traveller)
Quoted in Baddeley, *Russia, Mongolia and China*, 1919

INDISTINCT NOTICE

It has often been cast in Marco's teeth that he makes no mention of the great wall of China, and that is true; whilst the apologies made for the omission have always seemed to me unsatisfactory.

. . . Yet I think if we read 'between the lines,' we shall see reason to believe that the Wall *was* in Polo's mind at this point of the dictation, whatever may have been his motive for withholding distincter notice of it. I cannot conceive why he should say: 'Here is what we call the country of Gog and Magog,' except as intimating 'Here we are *beside the* GREAT WALL known as the Rampart of Gog and Magog.'

Col. Henry Yule
Note to *The Book of Ser Marco Polo the Venetian* . . . , ed. 1871

LANDFALL

Next day we proceeded, and about noon we could perceive the famous wall, running along the tops of the mountains, towards the north-east. One of our people cried out Land, as if we had been all this while at sea.

John Bell
A Journey from St Petersburg to Pekin 1719–1722, 1763

A PERFORMANCE OF REAL USE

This wall was begun and completely finished in the space of five years; every sixth man in China being obliged to work himself, or find another in his stead. It is reported, the labourers stood so close, for many miles distance, as to hand the materials from one to another. This I am the more inclined to believe, as the rugged rocks would prevent all use of carriages; nor could clay, for making bricks or cement, of any kind, be found among them.

The building of this wall, however, was not the only burden the Chinese supported, on this occasion. They were also obliged to keep a numerous army in the field, to guard the passes of the mountains, and secure the labourers from being interrupted by their watchful enemies the Tartars, who, all the while, were not idle spectators.

I am of opinion, that no nation in the world was able for such an undertaking, except the Chinese. For, though some other kingdom might have furnished a sufficient number of workmen, for such an enterprise, none but the ingenious, sober, and parsimonious Chinese could have preserved order amidst such multitudes, or patiently submitted to the hardships attending such a labour. This surprising piece of work, if not the greatest, may justly be reckoned among the wonders of the world. And the Emperor, who planned and completed it, deserves fame, as much superior to his who built the famous Egyptian pyramids, as a performance of real use excels a work of vanity.

John Bell
A Journey from St Petersburg to Pekin
1719–1722, 1763

JOHNSON SERIOUS

I said I really believed I should go and see the wall of China had I not children, of whom it was my duty to take care. 'Sir, (said he,) by doing so, you would do what would be of importance in raising your children to eminence. There would be a lustre reflected on them from your spirit and curiosity. They would be at all times regarded as the children of a man who had gone to view the wall of China. I am serious, Sir.'

James Boswell
Life of Johnson, 1791

SERVING AT THE WALL

The Army the Emperor of China kept to guard his Wall, consisted of a Million of Men, others say a Million and a half. As in Spain we send Criminals to Oran and to the Galleys, so here they are sentenced to serve at the Wall. This Punishment was also allotted for Sodomy; but if all that are guilty of this Vice were to pay that Penalty, I reckon that China would be unpeopled, and the Wall over-garison'd.

Domingo Navarrete
The Travels and Controversies of Friar
Domingo Navarrete, 1676

BARBARIANS AT THE GATE

We reached the North Gate [of the Wall at Shanhaiguan] just in time to climb it, take one glance round, and scramble down again. For the first moment my eye was drawn towards the great Manchurian plain—the region of outer darkness, across which our train had been travelling towards the Wall all night. Then my eye as caught again, and this time held fascinated, by those white festoons high up along the mountain side. Was it just a ribbon, or was it something alive: one of those fabulous titanic 'worms' of Teutonic mythology that were supposed to guard buried treasure? What but a live thing could manage to cling to those almost perpendicular slopes? My fantasy was abruptly cut short by the necessity of re-boarding the train.

So here we were, barbarians all, on the point of crossing the threshold of civilization. 'What would your family say? Have you left your conscience behind?' It was just a benevolent Quaker fellow-passenger looking down at me from the door of the *wagon lits* coach and reproaching me for buying raw fruit from a Chinese vendor on the platform. But for one instant of bewilderment, as her mild adjuration struck my ears, I fancied that I must be some missing link in that endless chain of barbarian invaders—Khitan and Kin and Manchu—who had crossed this formidable threshold at their peril and had been inexorably demoralised by a civilization too subtle and sophisticated for them to master.

Arnold Toynbee
*A Journey to China or Things Which Are
Seen,* 1931

OUTLANDISH NATURE

A few weeks later I once more found myself standing on a gate in the Wall—this time high up among the mountains, at the summit of the Nankow Pass. Those ribbon-like festoons, or dragon-like coils, which I had seen from far away, and far below, at Shan-Hai-Kwan, were now writhing close around me. My eye followed them over ridge and ravine; my feet followed my eye; and I veritably believe that the Wall would have drawn me on—up one gigantic flight of steps and down another and up the next again, and round this corner and then round that—until I might have dropped from exhaustion in the wilderness, if the muleteer had not soberly reminded me that I had a four hours' walk down the pass to accomplish before dark.

No photograph or picture that I have ever seen gives any adequate impression of the way in which the Wall strides across these mountains. For these are not mountains of the form with which we are familiar in our world. So unfamiliar to our eyes are those sugar-loaf peaks and serrated hog's-backs and ridges running in all directions at once, like a choppy sea, that when we find them faithfully portrayed in Chinese landscape-painting, we assume that they are creations of the same fantastic imagination that conceived the dragon and the kylyn. And if any Western eye did become convinced of their reality, the one thing certain is that the owner of that eye would never dream of attempting to set his impress upon so outlandish a piece of Nature.

Arnold Toynbee
A Journey to China or Things Which are
Seen, 1931

MONUMENTAL

It is to my mind a most suggestive monument of wasted human energy.

Lady Susan Townley
My Chinese Notebook, 1904

FROM THE AIR

'Did you see the Great Wall in China?'
'I flew over it in an aeroplane.'
'Interesting?'
'As interesting as a wall can be.'

George Bernard Shaw to
Hesketh Pearson
Bernard Shaw: His Life and Personality,
1961

EXTRATERRITORIALITY

From Ku-pei-k'ou [an exit point through the Wall] are eleven miles to Liou-king-fong, which ends this day's journey. A little incident has happened at this place which strongly marks the jealousy that subsists between the Chinese and the Tartars. A Tartar servant of the lowest class attending at the Palace had, it seems, stolen some of the utensils furnished for our accommodation, and when taxed with the theft by Wang and Chou, answered with so much impertinence that they ordered him to be smartly bambooed on the spot. The moment he was released he broke out into the most insolent expressions, and insisted that a Chinese Mandarin had no right to bamboo a Tartar without side of the Great Wall. The punishment was, however, repeated in such a manner as to make him not only restore the stolen goods, but repent I believe, of his topographical objection to it.

Lord Macartney
Journal, 5 September 1793

SILENT AND TERRIBLE

There in the mist, enormous, majestic, silent, and terrible, stood the Great Wall of China. Solitarily, with the indifference of nature herself, it crept up the mountain side and slipped down to the depth of the valley. Menacingly, the grim watch towers, stark and foursquare, at due intervals stood at their posts. Ruthlessly, for it was built at the cost of a million lives and each one of those great grey stones has been stained with the bloody tears of the captive and the outcast, it forged its dark way through a sea of rugged mountains. Fearlessly, it went on its endless journey, league upon league to the furthermost regions of Asia, in utter solitude, mysterious like the great empire it guarded. There in the mist, enormous, majestic, silent, and terrible, stood the Great Wall of China.

W. Somerset Maugham
On A Chinese Screen, 1922

ARCHITECTURAL KNOWLEDGE

[The wall] is undoubtedly one of the most stupendous feats of engineering ever carried out, and leaves one staggered at the thought that a people whose architectural knowledge was as great as the Romans of the same period have never learnt to construct a bathroom or a sanitary drain.

R. V. C. Bodley
Indiscreet Travels East, 1934

OUTDOOR AMUSEMENTS

At the farther entrance only do we get a view of the Great Wall, properly so called, and then it is but an angle or loop of that which for 1550 miles skirts the Mongolian plateau and forms the boundary of China proper. Imposing in the boldness with which it climbs the cliffs, it grows sublime when you think of it as stretching from the sea of sand to the sea of salt. . . .

The pass, formed by a fracture in the mountain chain and widened by the erosive action of a small river, resembles some of those canyons seen on our Western railways, its grassy slopes winding with the stream and sprinkled with the snow of grazing flocks.

As we were sauntering along, our eyes fixed on this scene of quiet beauty, a well-meaning native stopped to exchange greetings, adding, as he rode away, 'There is nothing to be seen here, but go on a little farther and you may see an open-air theater and hear the song of a story-teller.'

W. A. P. Martin
A Cycle of Cathay, 1900

PERSONALLY INSCRIBED

At the upper end of the valley, masked by trees, are grouped the tombs—magnificent temple-like pavilions, tiled with imperial yellow, and supported by wooden pillars each hewn from a single giant trunk. The entrance gates and successive courtyards and terraces are on the usual plan of Buddhist temples. First among these tombs is that of the Emperor Yung Lo, who in 1426 transferred the court from Nanking, the 'southern,' to Peking, the 'northern capital.' Both the Great Wall and the 'Ming tombs' are favorite objectives of tourists, some of whom brave a roughish trip, including the prospect of two or three nights in a native inn, apparently for the questionable satisfaction of scrawling their barbarian names over the historic stones.

Archibald R. Colquhoun
Overland to China, 1900

PLEASANT RETREATS

As I came gradually nearer, the tombs nearest to me gradually revealed the red walls that surround them and the high pavilions backed by trees. The first thing to notice is the discreet elegance of their proportions. There is nothing outrageous, nothing emphatic and nothing exclusively funereal about them. They seem like pleasant country retreats.

Abel Bonnard
(trans. Veronica Lucas)
In China, 1926

BURIED

I came to the innermost court. Beyond the trees and grass a semicircle of rude stones crenellated like battlements stood out from the mountain-side where the red wall comes shoulder to shoulder with it. A high pavilion rises up on the terrace which is supported by the mountain-side and is reached by means of two lateral ramps. Under the pavilion roof is an enormous rose-coloured stele which bears the posthumous title of the Emperor, in imposing characters. That inscription suffices. Pride is so lofty here that it does not need the support of eulogy and really scorns to boast. Boasting would mean that the order of the Empire was not perfect; that it had been necessary to remedy some defect. The dust of these Emperors admits to nothing but to the fact that the Emperors reigned.

A vast tunnel into the rock under the pavilion brings you to a last barrier in the darkness of the bowels of the mountain. There is no inscription here. Smooth, dark and dumb the wall of rock commands the living man to forbear. He can go no further. Only the Emperor could go further and following the dark road of his fate the very mountain fell upon him as a veil. Never has the word *buried* had more significance. Here the dead man does not spring into space, he does not strive deliriously to reach the plane of gods. He does not depart. He returns. *He goes in.*

Abel Bonnard
(trans. Veronical Lucas)
In China, 1926

LOW IMAGES

Of the Shih-san-ling, or Thirteen Tombs of the Ming Emperors, which at unequal distances, each in its own wooded enclosure, surround a wide bay or amphitheatre in the hills, thirty miles nearly due north of Peking, I will merely observe that the famous avenue of stone animals through which one enters the valley from the south is to my mind grotesque without being impressive, the images being low, stunted, and without pedestals.

George N. Curzon
Problems of the Far East, 1896

HARVEST MOON

We rode back to Chang Ping Chou, our horses terrified at the great images, in which heaven knows what horrors they saw. It was a lovely night, and the harvest moon rose in full glory. After supper I was impelled to go back, at any rate as far as the mysterious Avenue of Statues. I felt that, like Melrose, it should be visited 'by the pale moonlight.' I am glad that I had that inspiration. When I reached the avenue the moonbeams were casting their spell upon the great, silent, motionless procession. Grim and gruesome flickers were playing upon the marble features, showing a sort of life in death; near the further end a vagabond crew—in England we should have said of gipsies—had encamped for the night, and were crouching round their fire, smoking. The flames cast dancing and uncertain lights and shadows upon the giant figures till I half felt as if they were moving. Far away in the gloom were the thirteen shrines, half hidden, nestling among the dark, pine-clad hills— altogether a weird and ghostly scene which I can never describe, but which lives with me today, after all these years.

Lord Redesdale
(A. B. Freeman-Mitford)
Memories, 1915

DRY BONES

From the top of the tower, which contains a large perpendicular slab of marble painted red, there is a beautiful view over the country, with the thirteen palaces of the dead each in its niche in the hills; it is really a scene of rare and striking beauty. Just behind the tower is an artificial mound covered with trees and verdure; this, I believe, is where the body lies—a few old bones to all this magnificence. There is a Chinese proverb which says, 'Better be a living beggar covered with sores than a dead emperor.'

A. B. Freeman-Mitford
The Attaché at Peking, 1866, pub. 1900

INDESTRUCTABLE

Yung-lo was wise in his generation when he caused his tomb to be built according to the simple tradition of the steppes. In the forefront of the tomb, the great hall and the courtyard walls were going to rack and ruin. The pavement was strewn with fragments—beautiful even in destruction—of the yellow-glazed tiles; and this snow, if it lay heavy on the eaves, would bring down more. Where the tiles had fallen from the roofs, the rafters were rotting; and when the rafters had rotted away the wooden columns beneath would gradually decay—solid tree-trunks though they were. In the end, the hall and the courtyard walls, yes, and even the mass of masonry that guarded the tunnel, would be as though they had never been. Yet, standing here on Yung-lo's barrow, I was not again overcome by that overwhelming conviction of the vanity of human wishes which I had felt, a few months earlier, when I stood among the tombs of the Muslim rulers of Sind on the ridge of Makli Hill. In all their efforts to perpetuate their pomp and state, those Muslim tomb-builders had forgotten to provide themselves with any monument that was simple enough to be proof against the ravages of Time; and so the frustration of their wishes was doomed to be complete. But the great Ming emperor, being Chinese, had appreciated the irony that lies deep in the Nature of Things. No doubt it had amused him to build that magnificent hall; but assuredly it had amused him even more to think that, in less than six centuries, hall and courts and castle and all the other pompous appurtenances with which he had masked his barrow would have gone the same way as his own mortal remains; for then at last the tomb itself—simple and huge and indestructible—would come into its own.

As I stood on the crown of the barrow, I said over to myself that poem in *The Shropshire Lad* in which the skeleton addresses the flesh and blood that are permitted to clothe it for a few moments of its own immortality. And I fancied that the spirit of Yung-lo, resting secure in the depths of that great mound, was speaking those words to the painted columns and the glittering tiles, as the touch of death was laid upon them by the falling snow.

Arnold Toynbee
*A Journey to China or Things Which Are
Seen,* 1931

CHAPTER 16

PEKING LAST

Everyone reaches Peking in tears of disappointment, and leaves it with tears of regret.

SIR OWEN O'MALLEY
The Phantom Caravan, 1954

The temptation to sum up experience in Peking is very strong, but not invariably productive. Just when one's thoughts are falling into shape, the metaphorical equivalent of the tea-laden camel that disturbed Captain William Gill's concentration is apt to come along, trailing confusion and disparate new impressions.

It is unsurprising, therefore, that no two people have drawn quite the same conclusion from their experiences. This is so even though the experience itself may be of a kind. The elements which have drawn some to the city—the people, the weather, the sounds, even the smells—are precisely the elements which have repelled others beyond hope of reconciliation.

Within the timeframe of this anthology, the last sight is of Peking in the 1930s and through to the Japanese occupation. It was a time in which the city had ceased to be the national capital, an oddly unreal interregnum when foreigners lived pleasantly and cheaply in a town without direction. Even the arrival of the Japanese was for the most part passed over with urbanity and forbearance. Osbert Sitwell chronicled the period, and Graham Peck, the American artist for whom a two-week visit stretched into more than two years.

Peking, now the politically correct Beijing, has become the capital of one more new dynasty. With modernization and enlargement, it has again changed shape. Aspects of the old remain; much has gone forever. Toynbee foresaw this page of history. He wrote of a city about to disappear, in a world which had outlived the need for a single great capital. Yet Peking has not disappeared, nor has it surrendered its distinct place among the capitals of the world. 'Peking Last' describes a stage, but not a destination.

A HOPELESS TASK

'What is Peking like?' was a question that I knew I should often be asked on my return to England, and I determined that I would, if possible, be able to answer it; but the more I saw, the more hopeless seemed the task. I took a note-book out one day to try and write down what there was to be seen, but, as I began the task, I was nearly knocked down by a camel lumbering along with a load of brick tea.

Capt. William Gill
The River of Golden Sand, 1883

FALSE SCENT

I remarked to a friend, an old resident, that nothing but a series of coloured pictures or photographs could ever give an idea of Peking as it is: 'No,' he replied; 'and even then you would not get the stinks.'

Capt. William Gill
The River of Golden Sand, 1883

A UNIQUE CIVILIZATION

In Peking so much that was excellent remained, quite apart from the palaces, pleasure-gardens, temples and imperial monuments; for the Pekingese as a whole still preserved some of the more inward qualities of the unique civilization of which they had become the last custodians. Urbanity, courtesy, a manner at once smiling and restrained; a preference for the pleasant tastes, sounds and colours that money could buy rather than for wealth itself; and an instinctive appreciation of beauty in art and nature—all these were commonly found at every level of Peking society.

Today, like so many exiles from Peking, Chinese and foreign, I wander about the world grateful for whatever happiness I find and generally cheerful enough to pass for a contented man, but always with the conviction that nowhere else shall I find a life so satisfying to senses, heart, intellect and (for those who searched diligently) spirit as Peking offered everyone who loved and understood her well.

John Blofield
City of Lingering Splendour, 1961

TWIN DELIGHTS

The first of the two moments of delight vouchsafed to every visitor to the Celestial capital is at his first sight of it. The second is when he turns his back, hoping it may be for ever, upon 'the body and soul-stinking town' (the words are Coleridge's) of Peking.

Henry Norman
The Far East, 1895

BEYOND WORDS

Some of the daily sights of the pedestrian in Peking could hardly be more than hinted at by one man to another in the disinfecting atmosphere of a smoking room.

Henry Norman
The Far East, 1895

DIRT! DUST! AND DISDAIN!

We were very sorry to be leaving Peking, and should much have liked to spend a winter there, studying it all more thoroughly. But Sir Harry Parkes, when he came back to it, said it was returning to 'Dirt! Dust! and Disdain!' and the only objection the passing traveller would be likely to make to this sentence is that it might contain a few more D's.

Mrs Archibald Little
Intimate China, 1899

POSITIVELY FRAGRANT

Even if I could make you *see* Peking, I could not make you *hear* it or *smell* it. And the sounds and the smells are just as much a part of the whole as are the sights . . . Some of the smells are malodorous, no doubt, but a vast array is aromatic and pungent if not positively fragrant.

Lucian S. Kirtland
Finding the Worthwhile in the Orient, 1926

TWO WORLDS FOR ONE

No catalogue of Peking experiences, however long, however varied, would explain why to us who have been there, even a short residence in China seems in retrospect to be such a wonderful and enriching thing. When we got home again to Bridgend, we felt we had got two worlds instead of one to live in. Short of going to the moon, we did not see how anyone in any other way could similarly enlarge their universe. I cannot rationalize this; can only suppose that the Chinese people—in spite of their shortcomings—are so old, so numerous, so self-sufficient, so complicated, so artistic, so intelligent, so experienced, so patient that the total is much more than the sum of the parts. Anyhow, the result of it was that when younger men later came down to Bridgend and asked me should they accept the offer of a Chinese appointment, I always answered: 'Of course you must accept, you will then have two worlds instead of one. I cannot quite explain this. It is like the religious experience: you cannot understand it unless you have it. It is true that all my three children nearly died, but you must not worry unduly about this; this risk, for the English, is the price of

Empire. So go; and go with a good courage and a receptive mind
and heart, and you will see when you come back that I was right.'

Sir Owen O'Malley
The Phantom Caravan, 1954

EXILE'S LAMENT

Ye Gentlemen of England who live at home in ease,
With Ramsgate for your studies and Matlock for your sneeze—
With Ryder Street's dear oysters and city's golden soups
To strengthen you and pick you up whene'er your courage
    droops—
Please think on us poor exiles doing penance for some sin
Amid the dust and stenches and dry heats of Pekin.
Who, far from love and all that's good, drag on our weary lives
And try to find some honey in these stinging Chinese hives:—
We've little to amuse us, and much to vex and rile—
Must grin before our mirrors if we long to see a smile—
'Si te nulla movet tantae pietatis imago',
'Eripe me his malis' 'et conde sepulchro!'

Sir Robert Hart
Letter to J. D. Campbell, 17 June 1883

FULL OF SOUNDS

The air was as full of sounds as of smells. Even in the quiet Legation
garden the confused noise of the city reached her, but it was a
different quality of sound from the roar of traffic in a European
city, the muffled drumming of soft feet on unpaved earth—bare
or slippered human feet, the pads of camels, the light tapping of
the small unshod feet of donkeys. In this low murmur other sounds
stood out sharply, like loud notes in soft music—the hoot of a
distant motor-horn, the ringing of tram-bells, a scream of a steam-
whistle and sounds of shunting from the railway-station just outside
the city wall. She could hear, too, innumerable cries from the

streets outside—but strange cries, with another note in the voices; now and then in the distance crackers were let off with a noise like revolver shots. There were small noises near at hand as well; a Peking crow barked now and then from over by the stables; she could hear the creak of the shadoof as the gardener hauled up water from the well, and a sort of crackling sound as his colleague rolled back the straw *lienzas* off the conservatory, now that the sun had set. The hoopees had just come back, and tripped about the lawn with their little running steps, fluting low isolated notes. Suddenly out of the sky came a faint winging of music, as from small harps overhead—she looked up and saw a flight of birds wheeling over the house. It was that loveliest of Chinese inventions, the small pipes bound to the pinion-feathers of pigeons, so that the birds cannot fly without creating this aethereal music. Who would not love and honour a race which could devise a thing like that? she thought, as she watched the birds wheeling to and fro, up and down, in the air above her.

Ann Bridge
Peking Picnic, 1932

DIRTY BUT NICE

A Russian diplomat once said to me that he considered Peking 'dirty but nice', and this description exactly coincides with my own idea.

Oliver G. Ready
Life and Sport in China, 1903

THIRTY YEARS ON

I visited Peking about thirty years ago. On my return visit last year I found it unchanged, except that it was thirty times dirtier, the smells thirty times more insufferable, and the roads thirty times the worse for wear.

Admiral Lord Charles Beresford
The Breakup of China, 1899

THE PEKING MOON

A young man from the provinces who had lived for some years in Peking returned home full of the superiority of everything in the capital. One night he was out walking with his father when they met a friend who remarked that the moon was beautiful. 'Ah,' said the young man, before his father could answer, 'you should see the moon we have in Peking; that's something like a moon!'

His father was so put out by this rudeness that he boxed his son's ears soundly. The youth burst into tears, but through his sobs he was heard to say: 'You think that a box on the ears, but that's nothing to the sort of box on the ears one would get in Peking.'

Traditional
Quoted in *The Dragon Book*, 1938

BETTER THAN SHANGHAI

Some of the Westerners liked Shanghai, liked its modernity, comforts, and racy flavor; but others loved Peking, and would, like myself, have given anything to have lived there. But it wasn't easy to do so, unless you were independent—and even then, a girl at that time could not properly have struck out alone in Peking, or indeed in most Chinese cities. In Peking there were hardly any jobs to be had—it was no place for business, having been traditionally opposed to foreign trade on any large scale. There were a few banks—but only small branches—a few firms, but again the employees were not generally left there long. It was too hard to leave Peking once you were used to it, if you had fallen in love with it—you couldn't bear the tempo of other towns after it. The quiet, the subdued magnificence, the artistic wealth—where would you find that again, in company with so few harsh modern tones?

Enid Saunders Candlin
The Breach in the Wall, 1973

DOING NOTHING NICELY

Of course the real reason for my inactivity was the same one which caused me to stay on and on—that was the extra-ordinary pleasantness of life in Peking, which moved with so graceful a languor that doing nothing nicely as an occupation seemed not at all unreal.

Graham Peck
Through China's Wall, 1945

JAPAN IN CHINA

I remember one incident in particular which seemed to sum up this whole strangely unresisted invasion. On an afternoon during the Chinese New Year I was riding down the street outside the

Legations when I saw a large and happy crowd streaming out of one of the gates of the Forbidden City. My rickshaw boy ran over towards it and I saw that at its nucleus was a troop of Chinese soldiers. Some of them blew horns and beat drums; some were on stilts; some were made up as clowns; some, dressed as women, were cavorting with exaggerated girlishness. My boy told me that every year on that day it had always been the custom for the soldiers to dress up and amuse the people.

Just at that moment, in an appropriate and perfectly-timed entrance, a long line of Japanese army trucks came rolling down the other side of the street. They were covered with mud and dust and had obviously just struggled down the mountain road from the Manchukuan border. They were manned by grim, road-worn little Japanese and under their tarpaulins bulked ominous shapes.

The Chinese soldiers went imperturbably on with their fun as the convoy rumbled past and turned in at the entrance of the Japanese Embassy. The laughing crowd hardly glanced at the trucks. They were used to them.

Graham Peck
Through China's Wall, 1945

PEKING RESURGENT

Still, Peking has been conquered before, and each time the quality in the city which made it easy to take disposed of its conquerors in the end. . . .

Now that new invaders were lodging themselves in the city, one wondered how long it would be before the Japanese commander of Peking district startled the Tokyo War Office with a report beginning—

The lotus are in bloom and yesterday for the first time a butterfly with blue wings flew into my pavilion. . . .

Graham Peck
Through China's Wall, 1945

ROSES, ROSES . . .

Apparently it was the custom of the British Legation guard to wear roses in their lapels to celebrate the anniversary of the battle of Minden, waged between French and Anglo–Hanoverian troops in Westphalia on August 1, 1759. Just before the final trouble in Peking [in 1937 when Japan occupied the city], a messenger on a bicycle had been dispatched to Fengtai where the required flowers were being grown, but, as he was delayed by fighting along his road, he was unable to return before the gates had been closed and fortified. Immediately on his appearance before the walls, the British Legation set its influence crashing against the police and after much telephoning the sandbags and barbed wire at the gate were laboriously removed and the twenty-foot bolts shot back. The great metal-studded portals swung out and the first man to enter the beleagured city cycled in, laden with roses.

Graham Peck
Through China's Wall, 1945

FAILED PLANS

I do not believe that either Emperor or Republic, or any General, was ever popular in Peking. . . .

The citizens of Peking are willing to hang out any flags required by expediency, and to render unto Caesar even the things which are not Caesar's, if he demands them. Whichever—or whoever—entered the city in triumph would be received with triumph; but it would signify nothing, except a certain characteristic enjoyment of pageantry. For the rest, people will fall in with almost any plan for their own domination, or regeneration, because they know that in the end it will fail. . . .

Even so rigid a faith as Communism, if for the sake of convenience it had temporarily to be accepted, would find itself powerless to alter the national character: on the contrary,

the national character would
very soon modify Communism
to suit itself, or even assimilate
it, as it has always assimilated
foreign conquerors.

Osbert Sitwell
Escape With Me!, 1939

JUST IN TIME

As one gazes and gazes at this extraordinary city, it gives one a certain
shock to realize that, in the literal chronological sense, Peking is not
old. The Ming city is physically younger than Wykeham's buildings
at Winchester and Oxford; even the Mongol city which it overlays is
younger than Winchester Cathedral, and how little of the Mongol
city remains—little more than that earthwork which one crosses,
without dismounting, when one rides out into the country
northwards. That earthwork, hardly six and a half centuries old,
already belongs as completely to the past as do the mounds of
Babylon. Babylon? Why, here is the explanation of how a city of this
modest physical age can make an impression of immemorial
antiquity. What impresses one in Peking is not the actual material city
that one beholds with the eye of flesh. It is the εἶδος, the archetype
laid up in Heaven, of which the city of the Mongols and the Ming is
the latest—and probably the last—incarnation. This ideal city might
proclaim, as its motto, 'Before Abraham was, I am.' Before it chose
to unfold its symmetry on this particular portion of the North China
Plain, it had unfolded it at how many points on how many of the
plains of Asia? At Loyang, no doubt, and Sian, in the times of the

T'ang and the Han; but also in Ma'mun's Baghdad, in Açoka's Pataliputra, in Nebuchadnezzar's Babylon. . . .

And I have travelled to see it only just in time—this capital of the world, this navel of 'All that is under Heaven,' which once was Babylon and now, *in extremis*, is still Peking. In the Confucian Temple, in the Hall of the Classics, in the Forbidden City, and perhaps most of all at the Temple and Altar of Heaven, I had the same overwhelming and awe-inspiring impression of seeing the last of something which was about to disappear for ever into the bottomless abyss of annihilation.

Still, I am just in time, for Peking has not foundered yet. You might suppose that she received her *coup de grâce* last year, when the Kuomintang transferred the capital of the Chinese Republic to Nanking, on the Yangtze. Yet Peking has recovered from a similar degradation at least once before. Did not the Ming likewise transfer the political capital of China from Peking to Nanking in their day, after they had succeeded in expelling those 'Northern Militarists,' the Mongols? And did not they capitulate to Peking after thirty-five years and carry to completion that magnificent work of men's hands which the Mongols had begun? It is possible (though in my humble opinion not probable) that this time also Peking will become the political capital of China again. Yet, just as the loss of her political status did not seal Peking's doom, so the recovery of that status would not avail to avert it. For Peking's destiny did not depend, and never has depended, on her being just the capital of China. The *raison d'être* of Peking is to be *caput mundi*, the capital of the world; and it is because that ancient institution has now become wholly out of date that the doom of Peking seems inexorable.

Arnold Toynbee
*A Journey to China or Things Which Are
Seen*, 1931

LOST EMPIRE

My vast and noble Capital, My Daïtu, My splendidly adorned!
And Thou my cool and delicious Summer-seat, my Shangtu-Keibung!

295

Ye also, yellow plains of Shangtu, Delight of my godlike Sires!
I suffered myself to drop into dreams—and lo! my Empire was
    gone!
Ah Thou my Daïtu, built of the nine precious substances!
Ah my Shangtu-Keibung, Union of all perfections!
Ah my Fame! Ah my Glory, as Khagan and Lord of the Earth!
When I used to awake betimes and look forth, how the breezes
    blew loaded with fragrance!
And turn which way I would all was glorious perfection of beauty!
    Alas for my illustrious name as the Sovereign of the World!
    Alas for my Daïtu, seat of Sanctity, Glorious work of the Immortal
KUBLAI!
           All, all is rent from me!

Sanang Setzen
(trans. Col Sir Henry Yule)
Lament on the passing of the Yuan
Dynasty, quoted in notes to *The Book of
Ser Marco Polo the Venetian* . . . , ed. 1871

PRIDE OF PLACE

Ah, when I think of Peking, my heart still dissolves, for the very soul of the Chinese people was there and it is no wonder that many a foreigner went to visit and stayed to live, and, now driven forth, is forever exiled. My joy was not in the cosmopolitan life of foreigners, however, although they were kind enough to me. My joy was to wander the streets alone, to linger in the palaces and the gardens, and sometimes to ride outside the city among the bare mountains and gaze at the Summer Palace, deserted and empty. My joy was to listen to the people talk, in that purest of Chinese Mandarin, the aristocrat of languages, and to watch them as they came and went, the proudest race upon the earth.

Pearl Buck
My Several Worlds, 1955

BIBLIOGRAPHY

Alec-Tweedie, Mrs (1929), *An Adventurous Journey: Russia—Siberia—China*, London: Thornton Butterworth, 2nd edition.

Allen, Revd Roland (1901), *The Siege of the Peking Legations*, London: Smith, Elder & Co.

Allom, Thomas, & Wright, G. N. (1843), *China Illustrated*, London: Fisher, Son & Co.

Arlington, L. C. & Lewisohn, William (1935), *In Search of Old Peking*, Peking: Henry Vetch.

Backhouse, E. & Bland, J. O. P. (1914), *Annals and Memoirs of the Court of Peking*, London: William Heinemann.

Bell, John (1965), *A Journey from Saint Petersburg to Pekin 1719–22*, Edinburgh: Edinburgh University Press.

Beresford, Lord Charles (1899), *The Breakup of China*, New York: Harper & Brothers.

Beresford, Lord Charles (1914), *The Memoirs of Admiral Lord Charles Beresford*, London: Methuen & Co.

Bland, J. O. P. & Backhouse, E. (1910), *China Under the Empress Dowager*, London: William Heinemann.

Bland, J. O. P. (1909), *Houseboat Days in China*, London: William Heinemann.

Blofield, John (1989), *City of Lingering Splendour*, Boston & Shaftesbury: Shambhala reprint.

Bodley, R. V. C. (1934), *Indiscreet Travels East*, London: Jarrolds.

Bonnard, Abel, (trans. Veronica Lucas) (1926), *In China*, London: George Routledge & Sons.

Boulger, D. C. (n.d.), *The Life of General Gordon*, London: Thomas Nelson & Sons.

Boxer, C. R. (ed.) (1953), *South China in the Sixteenth Century*, London: The Hakluyt Society.

Bredon, Juliet (1909), *Sir Robert Hart*, London: Hutchinson & Co.

Bredon, Juliet (1922), *Peking*, Shanghai: Kelly & Walsh, 2nd edition.

Bredon, Juliet, & Mitrophanow, Igor (1927), *The Moon Year*, Shanghai: Kelly & Walsh.

Bridge, Ann (1932), *Peking Picnic*, London: Chatto & Windus.

Bridge, Ann (1934), *The Ginger Griffin*, London: Chatto & Windus.

Bridge, Ann (1939), *Four-Part Setting*, London: Chatto & Windus.

Brown, Revd Frederick (1902), *From Tientsin to Peking with the Allied Forces*, London: Charles H. Kelly.

Buck, Pearl S. (1955), *My Several Worlds*, London: Methuen & Co Ltd.

Burton, Robert (1927), *The Anatomy of Melancholy*, New York: Tudor Publishing Co.

Candlin, Enid Saunders (1973), *The Breach in the Wall—A Memoir of Old China*, London: Cassell & Co.

Carl, Katharine A. (1906), *With The Empress Dowager of China*, London: Eveleigh Nash, 2nd edition.

Casserly, Capt. Gordon (1903), *The Land of the Boxers*, London: Longmans, Green & Co.

Ch'ien Chung-shu (Dec. 1940), *China in the English Literature of the Seventeenth Century*, Quarterly Bulletin of Chinese Bibliography I(4).

Ch'ien Chung-shu (June–Dec. 1941), *China in the English Literature of the Eighteenth Century*, Quarterly Bulletin of Chinese Bibliography II(1–4).

Cockburn, Claude (1956), *I, Claude*, London: Penguin.

Collins, Gilbert (1925), *Extreme Oriental Mixture*, London: Methuen & Co.

Collis, Maurice (1956), *The Great Within*, London: Faber & Faber, 5th impression.

Colquhoun, Archibald R. (1900), *Overland to China*, London: Harper & Brothers.

Corner, Miss (n.d.), *The History of China & India, Pictorial and Descriptive*, London: Dean & Co.

Cranmer-Byng, J. L. (ed.) (1962), *An Embassy to China: Being the journal kept by Lord Macartney during his embassy . . .*, London: Longman.

Cummins, J. S. (ed.) (1960), *The Travels and Controversies of Friar Domingo Navarrete*, Cambridge: The Hakluyt Society.

Curzon, George N. (1896), *Problems of the Far East*, Westminster: Archibald Constable & Co.

Danby, Hope (1950), *The Garden of Perfect Brightness*, London: Williams and Norgate.

Davis, John Francis (1836), *The Chinese*, London: Charles Knight & Co.

De Croisset, Francis, (trans. Paul Selver) (1937), *The Wounded Dragon*, London: Geoffrey Bles.

Der Ling, Princess (1907), *Two Years in the Forbidden City*, London: T. Fisher Unwin Ltd.

Doolittle, Revd Justus (1868), *Social Life of the Chinese*, London: Sampson Low, Son, and Marston.

Douglas, R. K. (1901), *Society in China*, London: Ward, Lock & Co.

Edwards, E. D. (ed.) (1938), *The Dragon Book*, London: William Hodge.

Einstein, Lewis (1968), *A Diplomat Looks Back*, New Haven: Yale University Press.

Fairbank, John King, et al (ed.) (1975), *The I. G. In Peking: Letters of Robert Hart, Chinese Maritime Customs, 1868–1907*, Cambridge: The Belknap Press,

Farquherson, Ronald (1950), *Confessions of A China Hand*, London: Hodder & Stoughton.

Fei Shi (1924), *Guide to Peking*, Peking: The Tientsin Press, 2nd edition.

Fleming, Peter (1934), *One's Company*, London: Jonathan Cape.

Fortune, Robert (1847), *Wanderings in China*, London: John Murray, 2nd edition.

Freeman-Mitford, A. B. (1900), *The Attaché at Peking*, London: McMillan & Co.

Gamble, Sidney D. (1921), *Peking: A Social Survey*, New York: George H. Doran & Co.

Geil, William Edgar (1909), *The Great Wall of China*, New York: Sturgis and Walton Company.

Giles, Herbert A. (1908), *Strange Stories from a Chinese Studio*, London: T. Werner Laurie.

Giles, Herbert A. (1974), *A Glossary of Reference on Subjects Connected with the Far East*, London: Curzon Press Reprint.

Gill, Captain William (1883), *The River of Golden Sand*, London: John Murray.

Gilmour, James (1883), *Among the Mongols*, London: The Religious Tract Society, 2nd edition.

Gordon, Henry William (1886), *Events in the Life of Charles George Gordon*, London: Kagan Paul, Trench & Co, 2nd edition.

Grantham, A. E. (1918), *Pencil Speakings from Peking*, London: George Allen & Unwin.

Gray, J. H. (1972), *China: A History of the Laws, Manners and Customs of the People*, Dublin: IUP Reprint.

Gutzlaff, Revd Charles (1838), *China Opened*, London: Smith, Elder & Co.

Hardy, Revd E. J. (1905), *John Chinaman at Home*, London: T. Fisher Unwin Ltd.

Hedin, Sven (1993), *Jehol: City of Emperors*, New York: E. P. Dutton & Co.

Holcombe, Chester (1895), *The Real Chinaman*, London: Hodder & Staughton.

Hooker, Mary (1910), *Behind the Scenes in Peking*, London: John Murray.

Hornby, Sir Edmund (1929), *Sir Edmund Hornby—An Autobiography*, London: Constable & Co, 2nd edition.

Huc, M. (1851), *Travels in Tartary, Thibet and China*, London: National Illustrated Library.

Huc, M. (1855), *The Chinese Empire*, London: Longman, Brown, Green & Longmans.

Jackson, Innes (1938), *China Only Yesterday*, London: Faber & Faber Ltd.

Johnston, Reginald F. (1934), *Twilight in the Forbidden City*, London: Victor Gollancz.

Kiernan, E. V. G. (1939), *British Diplomacy in China 1880–1885*, Cambridge: Cambridge University Press.

Kirtland, Lucian S. (n.d.), *Finding The Worthwhile In The Orient*, London: George G. Harrop Ltd.

Komroff, Manuel (ed.) (1928), *The Travels of Marco Polo*, London: Jonathan Cape.

Lamb, Corrinne (1935), *The Chinese Festive Board*, Shanghai: Henri Vetch. Reprinted by Oxford University Press, 1986.

Lane-Poole, Stanley (1901), *Sir Harry Parkes in China*, London: Methuen & Co.

Lattimore, Owen & Eleanor (1973), *Silks, Spices and Empire*, London: Universal-Tandem.

Lattimore, Owen (1928), *The Desert Road to Turkestan*, London: Methuen & Co.

Letts, Malcolm (ed.) (1953), *Mandeville's Travels*, London: The Hakluyt Society.

Leung, George Kin (1929), *Mei Lan-Fang, Foremost Actor of China*, Shanghai: The Commercial Press.

Ley, C. D. (ed.) (1947), *Portugese Voyages 1498–1665*, London: J. M. Dent & Sons.

Little, Mrs Archibald, (1899), *Intimate China*, London: Hutchinson & Co.

Little, Mrs Archibald (1905), *Round About My Peking Garden*, London: T. Fisher Unwin.

Lowe, H. Y. (1983), *The Adventures of Wu*, Princeton: Princeton University Press reprint.

Lynn, Jermyn Chi-Hung (1928), *Social Life of the Chinese in Peking*, Tientsin: China Booksellers Ltd.

Martin, W. A. P. (1900), *A Cycle of Cathay, or China, South and North*, Edinburgh & London: Oliphant Anderson & Ferrier, 2nd edition.

Maugham, W. Somerset (1952), *The Collected Plays*, London: William Heinemann.

Maugham, W. Somerset (1935), *On A Chinese Screen*, London: William Heinemann, 2nd edition.

Maxim, Sir Hiram Stevens (ed.) (1913), *Li Hung Chang's Scrap-book*, London: Watts & Co.

McHugh, J. M. (1931), *Introductory Mandarin Lessons*, Shanghai: Kelly & Walsh.

Medhurst, W. H. (1857), *China: Its State and Prospects*, London: John Snow.

Mennie, Donald (1920), *The Pageant of Peking*, Shanghai: A. S. Watson & Co.

Michie, Alexander (1864), *The Siberian Overland Route*, London: John Murray.

Miller, I. L. (1932), *The Chinese Girl*, Tientsin: Beijing Press.

Milne, Revd William C. (1859), *Life In China*, London: Routledge, Warvies and Routledge.

Norman, Henry (1895), *The Far East*, London: T. Fisher Unwin.

O'Malley, Sir Owen (1954), *The Phantom Caravan*, London: John Murray.
Oudendyk, William J. (1939), *Ways and By-Ways in Diplomacy*, London: Peter Davies Ltd.
Parker, E. H. (1903), *China: Past and Present*, London: Chapman & Hall.
Parker, E. H. (1901), *John Chinaman and a Few Others*, London: John Murray.
Pearl, Cyril (1967), *Morrison of Peking*, Sydney: Angus & Robertson.
Peck, Graham (1945), *Through China's Wall*, London: William Collins.
Pellissier, Roger (trans. Martin Kleffer) (1967), *The Awakening of China 1793–1949*, London: Secker & Warburg.
Pindar, Peter [John Wolcot] (1792), *A Pair of Lyric Epistles to Lord Macartney and his Ship*, London: Printed for H. D. Symonds.
Putnam-Weale, B. L. (1905), *The Re-Shaping of the Far East*, London: MacMillan & Co.
Putnam-Weale, B. L. (n.d.), *Indiscreet Letters from Peking*, London: Hurst & Blackett, 10th edition.
Quennell, Peter (1932), *A Superficial Journey Through Tokyo and Peking*, London: Faber and Faber Ltd. Reprinted by Oxford University Press, 1986.
Ready, Oliver G. (1903), *Life and Sport in China*, London: Chapman & Hall Ltd.
Redesdale, Lord [A. B. Freeman-Mitford] (1915), *Memories*, London: Hutchinson & Co.
Reinsh, Paul S. (1922), *An American Diplomat in China*, London: George Allen & Unwin Ltd.
Religious Tract Society (n.d.), *The People of China*, London: The Religious Tract Society.
'A Resident of Peking' (1912), *China As It Really Is*, London: Eveleigh Nash.
Ripa, Father (trans. Fortunato Prandi) (1846), *Memoirs of Father Ripa During Thirteen Years' Residence at the Court of Peking . . .* , London: John Murray.
Robbins, Helen H. (1908), *Our First Ambassador to China*, London: John Murray.
Roberts, Francis Markley (1932), *Western Travellers to China*, Shanghai: Kelly & Walsh Ltd.
Russell, Bertrand (1922), *The Problem of China*, New York: The Century Co.
Savage-Landor, A. Henry (1901), *China And The Allies*, New York: Charles Scribner's Sons.
Scidmore, Eliza Ruhamah (1900), *China: The Long-Lived Empire*, London: Macmillan & Co.
Sergeant, Philip W. (1910), *The Great Empress Dowager of China*, London: Hutchinson & Co.
Sirr, Henry Charles (1977), *China and the Chinese*, Taipei: Southern Materials Centre reprint.

Sitwell, Osbert (1939), *Escape With Me!*, London: Macmillan & Co.

Smith, A. H. (1894), *Chinese Characteristics*, New York: Fleming H. Revell Co.

Smith, A. H. (1901), *China in Convulsion*, Edinburgh & London: Oliphaunt, Anderson & Ferrier.

Stanley Club (1935), *Chinese Chapters from the book of the Stanley Club*, Tientsin: The Stanley Club.

Staunton, Sir George (1797), *An Historical Account of the Embassy to the Emperor of China . . .* , London: John Stockdale.

Swallow, R. W. (1927), *Sidelights on Peking Life*, Peking: China Booksellers Ltd.

Sykes, Sir Percy (1936), *The Quest for Cathay*, London: A. C. Black.

Thomas Cook (1920), *Peking and the Overland Route*, Peking: Thomas Cook & Son, 4th edition.

Tong, Colonel Tcheng-Ki (1890), *Bits of China*, London: Trischier & Co.

Townley, Lady Susan (1904), *My Chinese Note Book*, London: Methuen & Co.

Toynbee, Arnold (1931), *A Journey to China or Things Which Are Seen*, London: Constable & Co.

Trench, Charles Chenevix (1958), *My Mother Told Me*, Edinburgh & London: William Blackwood & Sons.

Tun Li Ch'en (trans. Derk Bodde) (1936), *Annual Customs and Festivals in Peking*, Peking: Henry Vetch.

Varè, Daniele (1937), *The Gate of Happy Sparrows*, London: Methuen & Co.

Varè, Daniele (1938), *The Last of the Empresses*, London: John Murray, 2nd edition.

Varè, Daniele (1938), *Laughing Diplomat*, London: John Murray.

Vitale, Guido A. (1896), *Pekinese Rhymes*, Peking: Pei-T'ang Press.

Walker, Eilleen (1937), *A Naval Wife Goes East*, London: William Blackwood & Sons.

Wingate, Col. A. W. S. (1940), *A Cavalier in China*, London: Grayson & Grayson.

Woodhead, H. G. W. (1934), *A Journalist in China*, London: Hurst & Blackett.

Wu Lien Tuh (1959), *Plague Fighter*, Cambridge: W. Heffer & Sons.

Yule, Col. Sir Henry (ed.) (1871), *The Book of Ser Marco Polo the Venetian . . .* , London: John Murray.

Yule, Col. Sir Henry (1967), *Cathay and the Way Thither*, Millwood, NY: Kraus Reprint.